What Caused the Financial

WHAT CAUSED THE FINANCIAL CRISIS

Edited by

Jeffrey Friedman

PENN

University of Pennsylvania Press

Philadelphia · Oxford

Published by
University of Pennsylvania Press
Philadelphia, Pennsylvania 19104-4112
www.upenn.edu/pennpress

Printed in the United States of America
on acid-free paper
10 9 8 7 6 5 4 3 2 1

Library of Congress Cataloging-in-Publication Data

What caused the financial crisis / edited by Jeffrey Friedman.
   p. cm.
Includes bibliographical references and index.
ISBN 978-0-8122-2118-3 (hardcover : alk. paper)
   1. Financial crises—United States—History—21st century.
2. United States—Economic policy—2001—
3. Finance—United States—History—21st century.
I. Friedman, Jeffrey.
HB3722.W486   2010
330.973'0931—dc22   2010017605

Contents

Illustrations

Figures

Table

Chapter 1

Capitalism and the Crisis: Bankers, Bonuses, Ideology, and Ignorance

JEFFREY FRIEDMAN

I am privileged to introduce not only the first collection of scholarly essays devoted entirely to the question of what caused the financial crisis of 2008, but a collection that brings us much closer to a comprehensive answer.

As a proxy for the level of scholarly advance achieved in these pages, note that the claims of our distinguished contributors can, in the main, be fit into a larger mosaic with little friction between the pieces. It is true that some of our authors blame the crisis on government action while others blame it on government inaction. But the two types of claim are not mutually exclusive. Both action and inaction can be the result of government policy and, for the most part, that is how our authors treat the causes of the crisis: as policy failures, whether failures of action or of inaction. Thus, it may be said that, for the most part, our contributors agree that this was a crisis of politics, not economics.

Thus, no contributor argues that the Great Recession was just a normal business-cycle downturn or even a normal popped asset bubble: As Steven Gjerstad and Vernon L. Smith point out in Chapter 3, asset bubbles inflate and burst frequently, but worldwide near-depressions are rare. Obviously the crisis took place within "the economy," but our authors mostly agree that special, noneconomic causal factors were at work—political factors—regardless whether one names policies that backfired (as do the authors of Chapters 3, 5, 6, 7, 8, and 9) or policies that could have been imposed but were not (as do the authors of Chapters 2, 3, 4, 11, and 13).

Which brings us to the elephant in the anteroom. Granting that the financial crisis was not a typical economic fluctuation, and granting that both regulatory action and regulatory inaction may have played a role, the intellectually (and politically) important question is whether it was nonetheless a crisis that can be attributed to "capitalism." This is the question that interests people around the world who would not otherwise care what caused a given financial downturn; and it is a question that does divide our authors. Yet none of their chapters, which deal with some of the most important individual causes of the crisis, are designed, for the most part, to give a detailed answer to that larger question.

In the interest of providing such an answer, this introduction will consider the big picture to which the individual papers contribute, even at the risk of violating Daron Acemoglu's injunction in Chapter 11, echoed in a sense by Richard Posner in the Afterword, to recognize that capitalism is, of necessity, constrained (and constructed) by law. This is undeniably good counsel, but the larger issue raised by the crisis is whether, without close regulatory supervision, capitalism is prone to implode. Clearly this was a crisis of regulated capitalism, but the pressing question is whether it was the capitalism or the regulations that were primarily responsible. Contrary to Posner's implication, I believe it is possible to separate the capitalist and the regulatory contributions to the crisis, just as it is possible to advocate "more" or "less" regulation of capitalism without ignoring the fact that even "laissez faire" capitalism is, at bottom, a system of laws—that is, of regulations.

The Subprime Bubble and Housing Policy

The deflation of the subprime bubble in 2006–7 was the proximate cause of the collapse of the financial sector in 2008. So one might think that by uncovering the origins of subprime lending, the causes of the financial crisis would have thus been identified. But as we shall see, subprime lending is only the beginning of the story. Since our ultimate objective is to explain a *banking* crisis, we need to understand not only where subprime and other elements of the housing bubble originated, but how they came to be overconcentrated in the banking system. Part II will address why the bursting of the bubble brought down the financial system and, in turn, the "real" (nonfinancial) economy of most of the world. Part III will discuss whether the banks' compensation systems or their self-perception as "too big to fail" motivated bankers to take excessive risks. Part IV turns to the question of whether capitalism should be held responsible for the banking crisis; and Part V asks whether regulation should be held responsible.

The Limited Relevance of Federal Housing Policy

Chapter 6 attempts to pin the blame squarely on the government, not capitalism. The main culprits it identifies are the Community Reinvestment Act (CRA) and the government-sponsored enterprises (GSEs), Fannie Mae and Freddie Mac.

New regulations governing the enforcement of the CRA, issued in 1995, did cause subprime lending, but the question is, how much? First enacted in 1977 in an effort to rectify racism ("redlining") in mortgage lending, the CRA was revised in 1995 to require that all FDIC-insured mortgage-lending banks (for purposes of this introduction, "commercial" banks, including savings and loans) prove that they were making active efforts to lend to the underprivileged in their communities. Chapter 6 allows, however, that most subprime lending did not occur under CRA auspices. According to the Superintendent of Banks for the State of New York, only 6 percent of subprime loans were issued by banks subject to the CRA (Neiman 2009). This is because most subprime mortgages were originated in the "shadow banking system," that is, by mortgage specialists such as Countrywide and New Century rather than by commercial banks such as Wells Fargo, Citibank, and JPMorgan Chase (Gordon 2008).

However, Chapter 6 argues that the new CRA regulations were only one aspect of a government-wide effort to expand homeownership rates among minorities and the poor. The Federal National

Mortgage Association (Fannie Mae) and the Federal Home Loan Mortgage Corporation (Freddie Mac) were substantial contributors to this overall effort, under directives from the Department of Housing and Urban Development (HUD).

Fannie Mae had been created by Congress in 1938 to repurchase mortgages from commercial banks so that banks would be more willing to issue them. Fannie was pseudo-privatized in 1968 to move it off the federal government's budget; in 1970, it was joined off-budget by another congressional creation with a similar homeownership agenda, Freddie Mac. Although shares in these GSEs were owned by private investors after 1968, their congressional charters suggested that if they got into trouble, Congress would bail them out (as it did, in September 2008). This implicit federal guarantee enabled them to borrow money more cheaply than private competitors.

In 1995, HUD ordered Fannie and Freddie to supplement the FHA's efforts to expand homeownership, and eventually to far surpass them, by directing 42 percent of their mortgage financing to low- and moderate-income borrowers (Johnson and Kwak 2010, 112). In response, Fannie Mae introduced a 3 percent-down mortgage in 1997. Traditionally, non-FHA, GSE mortgages had required 20 percent down, giving them an initial loan-to-value ratio (LTV) of 80. (A mortgage requiring no down payment would have an LTV of 100.) But such large down payments were the biggest barrier to home ownership among the poor. Higher-LTV mortgages made housing more affordable.

Strictly speaking, the "subprime" label applies solely to the credit score of the borrower, not the terms of the mortgage. Fannie and Freddie were prohibited from making this type of subprime loan. But high-LTV loans were, at least when insured by the GSEs, designed to help impoverished borrowers with spotty employment histories and thus low credit scores. There was thus a great deal of overlap between high-LTV mortgages and subprime mortgagors. The average LTV of a subprime loan issued in 2006 was 95 (i.e., a 5 percent down payment). By that point, high-LTV loans had also been extended to borrowers with better-than-subprime credit scores, such as "Alt-A" mortgagors, who barely missed the criteria for a "prime" loan (or whose income or assets were under-documented). In 2006, the average Alt-A LTV was 89 (Zandi 2009, 33). Such "nonprime" mortgages played a significant role in what is more loosely called the "subprime" bubble. Unless the context calls for more precision, I will employ that looser usage here.

In 2000, HUD increased the GSEs' low-income target to 50 percent (Johnson and Kwak 2010, 112); in the same year, Fannie launched "a ten-year, $2 trillion 'American Dream Commitment' to increase homeownership rates among those who previously had been unable to own homes" (Bergsman 2004, 55). Freddie Mac followed, in 2002, with "Catch the Dream," a program that combined "aggressive consumer outreach, education, and new technologies with innovative mortgage products to meet the growing diversity of homebuying needs" (Bergsman 2004, 56). In 2004, HUD increased the target again, to 56 percent (Johnson and Kwak 2010, 112). In the end, as Chapter 6 shows, about 40 percent of all subprime loans were guaranteed by the GSEs.

In 2006, house prices began to level off and, in some places, fall. Subprime mortgagors began to default at higher-than-expected rates. By the summer of 2008, it was clear that this trend threatened the solvency of the GSEs, and on September 9, 2008, Fannie and Freddie were bailed out—just as had been expected, because of their government-sponsored status. However, precisely because they were bailed out, they cannot be said to have caused the worldwide financial panic that began a week later, when Lehman Brothers, the huge investment bank, declared itself insolvent. The bailout of the GSEs was certainly expensive—upward of $382 billion (Timiraos 2010)—but this expense merely added to the growing fiscal deficit of the U.S. government, which may cause a crisis in the future but did not cause the crisis of 2008. Indeed, the GSE bailout had the positive effect of removing the biggest risk that had been caused by the bursting of the subprime bubble: the possibility that commercial banks would become insolvent because they held $852 billion worth of mortgage-backed securities (MBSs) issued by Fannie and Freddie (Table 7.1). These securities bonds are called "agency" bonds to distinguish them from MBSs issued by investment banks (such as Lehman Brothers, Bear Stearns, and Goldman Sachs), which are called "private label" MBSs, or PLMBSs.

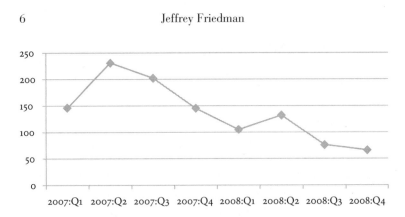

Figure 1.1. Decline in U.S. commercial lending during the crisis ($ billion). Real investment loans are intended for general corporate purposes, capital expenditure, or working capital. Data provided by Victoria Ivashina and David Scharfstein, compiled from DealScan database.

On the other hand, the post-Lehman panic was only the peak of a banking crisis that had been brewing for more than a year and a half. Figure 8.13 shows that doubts about subprime mortgages were already being reflected in the cost of insuring PLMBSs in January 2007. These doubts began to raise the cost of insuring the subprime securities predominantly held by commercial banks—the ones rated AAA—in June 2007. That is when commercial-bank lending to businesses began to decline, a decline that had more than halved new business lending by the end of 2007. It would be halved again by the end of 2008 (see Figure 1.1). The decline in lending is widely held to have been the direct cause of the Great Recession. It is quite possible that commercial banks were as worried about their holdings of agency securities as of private-label securities, and that until Fannie and Freddie were bailed out, this contributed to the banks' reluctance to lend, and thus to the recession. It is a ripe topic for future research.

What is more certain is that Fannie and Freddie used the borrowing advantages conferred upon them by their quasi-official status to pump up the housing bubble—not just the subprime portion of it. The GSEs accounted for 41 percent of all mortgages in the United States by the time the bubble burst (Table 7.1). This is important because the more buyers there are in a bubble, the higher prices go—and the farther they fall when the bubble deflates; and because the higher the price of a house, the larger the mortgage needed to buy it. (Thus "jumbo" loans, too big for the GSEs, became more common as the decade continued.) The higher the mortgage, the more tempting it is to put down a small down payment or to use the low initial rate offered by an adjustable-rate mortgage (ARM). Most important, though, the larger the mortgage, the more unaffordable it will be to the mortgagor if push comes to shove—for instance, if the interest rate on an ARM begins to rise, or the price of a home begins to fall.

Mortgage Securitization in the Private Sector

Private-sector lenders, including both commercial banks and mortgage specialists, originate all U.S. mortgages. Fannie and Freddie bought 41 percent of them for securitization, but the other 59 percent either stayed with the bank of origination or were sold for securitization to investment banks. Like the GSEs, the investment banks securitized mortgages—turning pools of hundreds of them at a time into mortgage-backed securities—by selling shares of the future principal and interest payments to investors around the world. From an investor's perspective, the main difference between an agency MBS and a PLMBS was that the latter, lacking the U.S. government's implicit guarantee, instead had various ratings to signify how safe it was. AAA is the highest rating a bond can get, and an MBS is an asset-backed bond. A bond is a promise to pay the bearer a certain interest rate over a period of years. An MBS is a bond in which the source of the interest payments is not, as with other bonds, a government or a corporation, but a pool of assets: the mortgages.

To produce the ratings on PLMBSs, investment banks worked with bond-rating agencies to divide the income from a pool of mortgages into different "tranches," or segments, which were assigned payment priority over each other, in what was called a "waterfall." Investors in the top, "senior" tranche would get paid before any other investors in the MBS; that tranche was rated AAA. (Sometimes there were even tranches that were senior to the triple-A tranche; these were called "super-senior" tranches.) After senior investors had received all of the payments promised to them, income from the pool would flow down to the AA tranche, then the A tranche, then the BBB tranche.

There was also an unrated equity tranche to provide extra safety to the investors; this was known as "overcollateralization." The mortgages in the rated tranches were the collateral that ensured payments to the bondholders; but if any of the mortgagors were delinquent (late) in their payments, or if they defaulted by stopping payments altogether, the extra collateral would pick up the slack before any investors suffered diminished income. After the overcollateralization was exhausted, if reselling foreclosed houses did not recover all the lost revenue, then investors in the juniormost (B) tranche would be the first to suffer interruptions in their guaranteed payments, since these investors were the last to be paid. In turn, these investors' income from the PLMBS would have to be completely halted by defaults or delinquent payments throughout the mortgage pool before investors in the next-most-junior tranche suffered any losses, and so on up the line, with the triple-A tranche being insulated from loss by all the subordinate tranches. Thus, in a typical MBS with a 2 percent equity tranche, investors in the BBB tranche would begin to experience reduced payments if more than 2 percent of the mortgage holders in the pool made late payments or stopped making payments altogether—except that even when a mortgagor "walks away" from a mortgage, the house is recovered and resold. Thus, when one adds the equity tranche to a typical BBB tranche covering 3 percent of the mortgage pool, an A tranche covering 4 percent, and an AA tranche covering 11 percent, it would be difficult for losses to reach the AAA tranche, even though this tranche typically covered 80 percent of the mortgage pool (IMF 2008, 60, Box 2.2). "It had been typical to assume that when a subprime mortgage foreclosed, about 65 percent of its outstanding balance could be recovered. Such a 35 to 50 percent loss-severity assumption implied that from 50 to 65 percent of the mortgages would have to default before losses would impact the MBS senior tranche" (IMF 2008, 59).

Given all the protection for the senior tranche, the obvious question is why anyone would buy a bond in a junior or "subordinate" tranche. The answer is that, in exchange for the higher risk they bore, investors in the subordinate tranches received higher rates of return, just as investors in junk bonds receive higher rates of return than do investors in "investment-grade" bonds. An investor could therefore choose to take a lot of risk on a subordinate tranche in exchange for a lot of income; or could instead minimize risk by investing in a senior tranche that paid less income.

The workings of structured securities have often been portrayed as being too complicated to understand, but they are really quite simple, and the reasoning is valid. Within any given pool of mortgages, even if 99 percent default, 1 percent of the investments in the pool would be justified (ex post facto) in being rated AAA. For this reason (and others to be discussed), tranching was extremely popular with investors. Eventually investment banks devised collateralized debt obligations (CDOs), which tranched tranches of PLMBSs and other asset-backed securities (ABSs), such as pools of student loans, car loans, and credit-card debt. The result of tranching these tranches was (in principle) an even greater minimization of risk, hence higher ratings, because of the broader and more diverse base of assets. High-grade CDOs possessed a "senior AAA" tranche that typically owned the rights to 88 percent of the income from the pool, with a "junior AAA" tranche claiming another 5 percent of the income and the remaining 7 percent divided among AA, A, BBB, and equity tranches. There were even "CDO-squared" bonds, which pooled tranches from several CDOs (each consisting of tranches from several ABSs, such as MBSs). Finally, when the possibility of a popped housing bubble called the value of mortgage-backed bonds into question, "synthetic" CDOs began to be traded. Here one party (such as a bank) bought from another the right to receive payments equivalent to those due to investors in a real CDO tranche. The two sides of this transaction disagreed about whether these payments would be diminished by a housing collapse; whichever side was wrong would lose money. (In the famous Goldman Sachs case, John Paulson bet against a synthetic CDO created by Goldman at his behest; a German bank bet in favor of it.)

The tranching system is easy to grasp, but it was not easy to execute. The problem was the width of the various tranches. That depended on predictions of future delinquency and default rates made by the three "rating agencies," which were actually private corporations: Moody's, S&P, and Fitch. The large triple-A tranches that were the norm were premised on these companies' low estimates of the probability of delinquencies and defaults in the underlying pools of mortgages. Everything rested on these estimates, which, in turn, depended on the rating agencies' mortgage-behavior models, which were based on historical data. But Moody's, for instance, had not bothered to update its "basic statistical assumptions about the U.S. mortgage market since 2002" (Jones 2008).[1] This meant that an unprecedented nationwide housing bubble had not been factored in.

The Federal Reserve and the Housing Bubble

Chapters 3, 4, 5, 7, and 8 argue that a major cause of the housing bubble was a flood of credit that pushed the interest rates paid on home mortgages (and on everything else) to record-low levels.[2] The Federal Reserve began to lower interest rates early in 2001, for fear that the tech bubble's bursting might lead to deflation; and after the September 11, 2001 terrorist attack, it kept interest rates low for another five years. Chapter 4 suggests that the Fed might not have needed to pump up aggregate demand with such low interest rates had not the Iraq war, which began in 2003, driven up the price of oil. By that year, the federal funds rate had fallen from 6.5 percent to 1 percent, where it stayed until gradual increases began in mid-2004. Prime mortgage rates followed, dropping from about 8 percent in 2000 to 5.25 percent in 2003, and then hovering between 5.25 and 6 percent until 2007 (Zandi 2009, 65). These were the lowest home-mortgage rates since the end of World War II.

Mortgage payments are almost always a family's largest financial obligation, and they are sensitive to small changes in the interest rate:

> The average home buyer in 2000 took out a $150,000 mort-
> gage. At the 18 percent mortgage rates of two decades earlier,
> such a loan would have required a $2,400 monthly payment,
> half the average household's after-tax income. At 8 percent,
> the payment would be $1,250; at 6 percent, the cost drops to
> a very manageable $1,050 per month. (Zandi 2009, 66)

Obviously, then, low interest rates are good for the housing busi-ness—but they have a downside, from a mortgage-banker's perspective. If a mortgage loan is made at 5.25 percent, based on a federal funds rate of 1 percent, but the latter rate rises, the bank is in danger of having to borrow money, and pay money to depositors, at higher rates than it is taking in from mortgagors. This is a quick route to insolvency.

Chapter 6 points out that the laws of the individual states often give mortgage borrowers the right to refinance their loans if interest rates go down—but mortgage lenders have no such legal right if interest rates go up, unless they put such a provision into the terms of the mortgage contract. Hence the adjustable-rate mortgage. It was obvious that the extremely low interest rates of the early 2000s would not last forever, so in 2004 banks began issuing a huge wave of ARMs with low two- or three-year teaser rates. These low initial rates compensated the borrower for assuming the risk of future interest-rate hikes, although surveys showed that many ARM borrowers were ignorant of this risk (Zandi 2009, 54). After the teaser periods, the mortgages would reset, and keep on resetting, to align with prevailing interest rates. By 2006, more than 90 percent of all subprime mortgages and 80 percent of all Alt-A mortgages were ARMs (Zandi 2009, Table 2.1). Once interest rates plateaued in 2006, ARM issuance fell. But in 2006 and 2007, ARMs issued in previous years began to reset at the higher rates, and subprime mortgage default levels began to spike. "From January 2007, the Moody's U.S. residential mortgage bond team began tracking a disturbing rise in the number of subprime mortgages going delinquent. . . . This was not in their models—nor anyone else's" (Jones 2008).

Something else that would be missing from a model that had not been updated since 2002 was the effect of a housing boom on the loan-to-value ratio of a mortgage. As the price of a house rises, its LTV ratio declines. A conventional 20 percent-down mortgage, which therefore has an initial LTV of 80, would reach 73, without any principal payments by the homeowner, if the price of the house simply rose by 10 percent. By the same token, a 25 percent price increase would push the initial 100 LTV of a no-downpayment mortgage down to the traditional LTV of 80. Therefore, low- or no-money-down loans—to both prime and subprime borrowers—became increasingly common as the housing boom continued. So, too, as

Chapter 6 points out, did second mortgages, in the form of home-equity loans, home equity lines of credit, and "cash-out refinancings,"[3] all of which effectively raise the LTV by increasing the size of the mortgage. This effect is counteracted, however, as the price of a house rises.

There are at least two reasons why low LTVs might correspond with lower default rates. The first is heuristic. A borrower who can put 20 percent down is likelier to be in better financial straits than one who cannot, and is likelier to be committed to staying in the house (instead of flipping it) and thus to making the required payments. Second, however, even if the financial condition of the borrower is shaky, when the LTV declines due to a housing boom, it means that the resale value of the house is going up. A financially stretched subprime borrower thus has an incentive to keep making difficult-to-afford payments until she sells the house, since she can then make a profit on it. The same reasoning applies even more to Alt-A borrowers, who generally have a better history of making payments on time; so as housing prices went up, so did Alt-A lending.

When house prices began to go down, however, these dynamics started to work in reverse. As an LTV rises due to the declining price of a house, the incentive to keep paying the mortgage declines, too. Even before a mortgage goes "underwater" (meaning that it has an LTV over 100), a borrower may decide that payments on a house with a plummeting resale value are not worth making, and she may simply "walk away" from the mortgage if she cannot sell the house. Chapter 6 shows that this is possible in many states, such as California, because of laws that give banks "no recourse" in case of default. And it is likeliest to happen with subprime borrowers, who can least afford to make payments in the first place.

Thus, the IMF (2008, 5) reported in April 2008 that "delinquency rates on subprime mortgage loans originated in 2005–6 have continued to rise, exceeding the highest rates recorded on any prior vintage." (The "vintage" is the year a mortgage was originated.) The IMF data showed graphically that delinquencies on subprime mortgages that were originated in 2000—before the housing boom—peaked four years later, with an average of 25 percent of the loan balance unpaid (6). By contrast, 2006-vintage subprimes had reached 25 percent delinquency values a mere year after they were issued, and as of March 2008, the slope of their ascent was nearly straight up (toward 100 percent default) and showed no sign of tapering off.

A model last updated in 2002 would not have predicted such changes—which is why they caused such consternation in the Moody's team that detected them in January 2007. The problem was not just with Moody's, however. According to the IMF (2008, 62), all three rating agencies underestimated "the joint effect of house price declines and high loan-to-value ratios."[4]

The Rating Agencies

While the rating agencies, like the government-sponsored enterprises, are privately owned, they are usually called agencies rather than companies for good reason—although the reason is not widely known. Chapter 9 shows that a welter of regulations going back to 1936 had, by the end of the twentieth century, conferred immense privileges on these corporations, effectively making them unofficial arms of the U.S. government. A growing number of institutional investors, such as pension funds and insurance companies, were prohibited from buying bonds that had not been rated investment grade (BBB− or higher) by these corporations, and many institutional investors were legally restricted to buying only the highest-rated (AAA) securities. So income from producing the ratings was guaranteed to the rating agencies. Moreover, in 1975, the Securities and Exchange Commission (SEC) effectively conferred on the three rating agencies that were then in existence—Moody's, Standard and Poor's, and Fitch—oligopoly status. In this ruling and subsequent actions, the SEC ensured that only these three companies were considered Nationally Recognized Statistical Rating Organizations (NRSROs)—and that only an NRSRO's ratings (oftentimes, two NRSROs' ratings) would fulfill the numerous regulatory mandates for investment-grade and triple-A ratings that had proliferated since 1936. The net result was that, while the three rating "agencies" remained in private hands and could use whatever rating techniques they wished, their financial success did not depend on the ability of these techniques to produce accurate ratings. Instead, their profitability depended on government protection. If the rating agencies used inaccurate rating procedures, they would not suffer for it financially—let alone would they go out of business.

Moody's and S&P, the oldest of the three agencies, had a proud history that is too often repeated as if it has any bearing on the quasi-governmental entities they have become. As a typical media report frames the story, it all started with

> Henry Varnum Poor's publication in 1860 of *History of Rail-roads and Canals in the United States* and John Moody's *Manual of Industrial and Miscellaneous Securities* in 1900. Since the Great Depression, U.S. agencies have relied on the companies to help evaluate the credit quality of investments owned by regulated institutions, gradually bestowing on them quasi-regulatory status. (Smith 2008a)

This story, like most media coverage of the rating agencies, goes awry as soon as it gets to the Great Depression. Since then, as Chapter 9 shows, the income of these legendary firms has depended increasingly on regulatory mandate, not the savvy risk assessment exemplified in the original Poor's and Moody's ratings books. Nor were (official) U.S. government agencies merely relying on the rating firms for "advice," as the reporter claims; both the federal government and the states were forbidding institutional investors from buying securities that these firms rated as below BBB− or, in other cases, AAA. Most important, however, the reporter omits mention of the 1975 SEC ruling that effectively forbade anyone else from competing with Moody's, S&P, and Fitch for the institutional investors' mandatory business. The effect of this ruling, combined with the others since 1936, was to license the three agencies to be sloppy, corrupt (as the currently popular theory has it), or simply inaccurate: no competitor could take advantage of their mistakes.

In assigning ratings to PLMBS tranches, the three agencies' cardinal error seems to have been their use of mathematical approaches to risk assessment, such as the "Gaussian copula" (Coval, Jurek, and Stafford 2009b; Jones 2009), to predict the default rates of the mortgages that were being pooled together. Nassim Taleb (2005 and 2007) has famously criticized such probabilistic bell curves for their naïve reliance on historical patterns, which cannot, by their very nature, reveal the likelihood of an unexpected event—a "black swan," such as the bursting of a housing bubble that virtually nobody realized was a bubble until it was too late.[5] In open competition with the Big Three, another rating firm might have exposed the foolishness of such models, or at least raised doubts. If one cannot imagine a rating firm run by the outspoken Taleb, there were plenty of disgruntled employees at the Big Three agencies who, as recently as 2000, might have been able to start a competitor firm if legal barriers to entry had not been in place. Frank Raiter, an S&P managing director, "and his counterpart at Moody's, Mark Adelson, say they waged a losing fight for credit reviews that focused on a borrower's ability to pay and the value of the underlying collateral" of the mortgage-backed securities—that is, the value of the mortgages themselves. "Adelson, 48, who quit Moody's in January 2001 after being reassigned out of the residential mortgage-backed securities business," told a reporter that in his view, "there is no substitute for fundamental credit analysis" (Smith 2008a). Nobody may have been able to foresee the bubble, but Raiter and Adelson certainly would have produced ratings that did not depend on historical inferences as heavily as the rating agencies' models did. Given the laws that protected the three NRSROs, however, competition with them was impractical. (In September 2006, Congress required the SEC to allow more companies to become NRSROs, and by the end of 2009 the number of them had expanded from three to ten; see Chapter 9. If this had been allowed earlier, the crisis might not have occurred.)

Even with the ratings oligopoly in place, major institutional investors such as banks could have studied the mortgage pools in which they were buying tranches so as to reach their own conclusions about how safe they were.[6] But there was a larger problem. Even the most sophisticated investors seem to have been ignorant of the fact that Moody's, S&P, and Fitch were protected by SEC regulations. The fact that the rating agencies were shielded from competition is, even now, not widely known among scholars, let alone financial reporters; and such obscure matters are unlikely to be well-known to investors—

even bankers—if they are not reported.[7] Thus, the investors usually chose to trust the agencies' ratings instead of spending time and money on their own research. An IMF report (2008, 80) concludes that "investors were in many cases too complacent about the risks that they were taking by . . . relying too heavily on rating agencies for assessing the risks to which they were exposed."

Nobody who knew about the legally protected status of the rating agencies would have been impressed by the ratings produced by an oligopoly, and they would not have been shocked if the ratings turned out to be unreliable. But when Moody's suddenly downgraded some of its triple-A PLMBS ratings in the second half of 2007, executives at such gigantic investment firms as Vanguard, Pimco, and BlackRock flooded their counterparts at Moody's with outraged e-mails:

> "If you can't figure out the loss ahead of the fact, what's the use of your ratings?" asked an executive with Fortis Investments, a money management firm, in a July 2007 e-mail message to Moody's. "You have legitimized these things, leading people into dangerous risk." (Morgenson 2008, 32)

If such investors had known that Moody's could prosper no matter how inaccurate its ratings, they surely would not have been stunned when its ratings turned out to be inaccurate, nor would they have been so reliant on its ratings.

Thus, if we are trying to explain the subprime boom—and bust—we need to keep in mind at least the following five factors:

1. HUD directives to Fannie and Freddie, beginning in 1995, which produced a gigantic spate of government-insured non-prime lending and subprime securitization, fueling the housing and subprime bubbles.
2. The innumerable regulations that had, since 1936, "canonized by decree" the judgments of the rating firms.
3. The 1975 SEC decision to confer legally protected status on the three extant rating agencies.
4. The loose-money policies of the central banks (not just in the United States, as Chapter 5 shows), which, in fueling the over-

all housing boom, also created a large but fragile subprime bubble.
5. "No-recourse" laws, entitling mortgagors to suffer little consequence if they defaulted.

The first four factors may explain why so many subprime, Alt-A, high-LTV, adjustable-rate, and even low-documentation, no-documentation, and "NINJA" (no income, no job, no assets) mortgages were issued during the 2000s: namely, so that they could be sold to Fannie, Freddie, and the investment banks for securitization. This reasoning might suffice to explain the demand for, and thus the supply of, subprime and nonprime mortgages. It would also explain why the underlying assets of so many GSE-issued and private-label MBSs—nonprime and subprime mortgages—were so vulnerable to delinquency and default (factor 5) once the housing boom ended.

This would mean that the five listed government policies, rather than capitalism, set the stage for a decline in the portfolios of investors in subprime securities. But as Chapter 3 emphasizes, declines in stock and bond markets reduce investors' portfolio values very frequently—without causing the world's financial system to seize up. So we cannot necessarily attribute the financial crisis to the listed government actions, even if they were necessary to produce the subprime crisis; and even if, in turn, the subprime crisis was necessary to trigger the financial crisis. Something is missing from this story—something that would explain why what turned out to be bad investments did not just cause a decline in PLMBS investors' wealth, but a decline in *commercial banks'* wealth so severe as to reduce their business lending—in the United States alone—from a peak of $231 billion per quarter in early 2007 to a mere $66 billion per quarter at the end of 2008 (Ivashina and Scharfstein 2010, Fig. 2), triggering the worst global economic downturn since the Great Depression.

Bank Deregulation, Bank Capital, and Bank Leverage

Glass-Steagall and the Financial Crisis

Chapter 5 is a revision of a paper by John B. Taylor that gained its fame[8] by targeting central-bank policy as the chief culprit in the housing bubbles of various economies, including that of the United States. But the chapter also suggests that the Fed got it wrong a second time by assuming, in September 2008, that the underlying cause of the collapse in interbank lending was a lack of liquidity (cash)—with which the Fed promptly flooded the economy. Taylor argues that this didn't help—at least not at first—because the reason banks were not lending to each other was not that they didn't have the cash on hand. The reason was that they feared for each other's ability to repay interbank loans, because they were uncertain about which banks were holding subprime securities; and because they were equally uncertain about how "toxic" these would turn out to be once the housing bubble had fully deflated. According to Taylor, then, the fear of mutual insolvency did lead to a liquidity crisis; but more liquidity was not the answer to the underlying problem. According to Juliusz Jabłecki and Mateusz Machaj in Chapter 8, the temporal sequence was reversed: the initial problem was liquidity, but the underlying problem was still insolvency.

The liquidity crisis, whatever its temporal order in the panic of September 2008, explains the collapse of Lehman Brothers. Like the main surviving investment banks, Goldman Sachs and Morgan Stanley, and like Bear Stearns, which had been bailed out in March, Lehman was a major private securitizer of subprime mortgages, and investment banks are extremely dependent on short-term loans from other banks. As Chapter 3 suggests, the investment banks had high quantities of subprime mortgages in their securitization pipelines (also see SEC 2009, 137; Gorton 2008, 70). Once doubts were raised about the accuracy of the ratings on these securities, and thus about their value, short-term lending to these investment banks dried up. The rates that banks charge each other for these loans began to rise in September 2007 (see Chapters 5 and 8)—six months before the demise of Bear Stearns, and a year before the bankruptcy of Lehman Brothers. In the week after Lehman failed, however, interbank lending froze everywhere, including among commercial banks (which, unlike investment banks, get their income from depositors, not investors).

The difference between how the panic among investment banks affected the economy and how the panic among commercial banks affected it is central to understanding both how the housing crisis turned into a financial crisis, and how the financial crisis turned into the Great Recession. It is also a reason to believe that the public debate over the effect on the crisis of financial deregulation has been misinformed.

The economy relies on commercial banks to lend not only to home buyers but to consumers and to businesses, large and small. Thus, the fortunes of the commercial banks have a much more direct effect on the "real economy" than do those of the investment banks, which underwrite bond and stock offerings for large corporations; manage the investments of large clients (and in some cases, such as Merrill Lynch, small ones); and buy stocks and bonds with their own funds—but which are not sources of financing for the mundane needs of consumers for credit, of home buyers for mortgages, and of businesses for loans with which to finance expansion. For example, as of March 2010, unemployment remained stuck above 10 percent even though investment banks were doing record business in under-writing large-business bond issues—because commercial bank lending was still at a virtual standstill, a full year and a half after the crisis peaked:

> As an alternative to seeking [commercial] bank financing, America's large corporations thankfully have had access to a healthy corporate-bond market [underwritten by investment banks]. They sold more than a trillion dollars in bonds in 2009, the most ever in a single year. But that has not been the case for medium- and small-size companies, and entre-preneurial start-up ventures, which have been credit-starved since the outbreak of the financial crisis. President Obama himself has said that these smaller firms and start-ups are responsible for 70 percent of our economy's net new jobs. (Smick 2010, 33)

Thus, commercial and investment banks remain very different in their functions and effects, despite the Gramm-Leach-Bliley Act (GLBA) of 1999, which is often said to have deregulated American banks by repealing the provisions of the Glass-Steagall Act (1933) that had prevented investment and commercial banks from being affili-

ated with each other. After 1999, a commercial bank and an investment bank could both be subsidiaries of the same bank holding
company; but they could not undertake the same types of activity.
GLBA made it possible for each of the major nationwide commercial
banks, such as JPMorgan and Bank of America, to be subsidiaries of
bank holding companies that also contain investment banks. But the
operations and functions of commercial and investment banks
remained separate.[9] Equally important, their capital levels were regulated in an entirely different way, and the regulation of commercial
banks' capital levels, according to Chapters 7 and 8, is the key to
understanding the financial crisis and thus the Great Recession.

The Concentration of Risk in the Commercial Banks

When the deflating housing bubble led commercial banks to fear for
each other's solvency they also, a fortiori, had to fear for their own
solvency—both because of their own holdings of MBS of dubious
value and because of the dubious MBS holdings of other banks to
which they had lent money. The logical reaction to such worries
would be for a bank to hold onto its cash, lest it wind up going broke.
So bank lending to businesses plunged. Chapters 7 and 8 suggest that
the underlying problem was that the commercial banks had invested
in the subprime securities that the investment banks (and the GSEs)
had securitized. By April 2008, American commercial banks (including savings and loans) constituted the largest single category of MBS
purchaser. In addition to $852 billion in agency MBSs, they held $383
billion in AAA tranches of PLMBSs and $90 billion in subordinate
PLMBS tranches, as shown in Table 7.1. U.S. commercial banks thus
held 23 percent of the entire world's supply of PLMBS tranches, and
20 percent of the supply of agency MBSs.

Unfortunately, Table 7.1 does not give a breakdown of the proportion of the $1.147 trillion in "overseas" MBS holdings that were
the property of non-U.S. commercial banks, as opposed to other
investors. However, a 2008 IMF study reports that as of March of that
year (even before the worst of the crisis, in September), the total losses
experienced by non-U.S. banks due to the declining value of PLMBSs
amounted to $161 billion, while the total of U.S. banks' losses

amounted to $144 billion (IMF 2008, 52, Table 1.6). In short, foreign banks' losses were slightly greater than American banks' losses, allowing us to add inferentially, to the 23 percent of the world's supply of PLMBSs held by American banks, at least another 23 percent held by non-American banks—upwards of $105 billion of the $458 billion listed in Table 7.1 as overseas PLMBS holdings.

Here, then, we find an explanation for why bad investments in housing had such a peculiarly devastating effect on the world economy: the world's commercial banks had made roughly half of all investments in private-label MBSs, as well as more than $852 billion in agency MBSs. The decline in the value of these securities forced banks to contract their lending into the "real economy" of consumers, home buyers, and businesses all over the world, starting in mid-2007.

The question, therefore, is why commercial banks bought so many MBSs. Chapters 7 and 8 conclude that the answer is found in the "Basel accords," named after the location of the Bank for International Settlements (BIS)—the standard setter for the world's banking regulators.

Bank-Capital Regulations

The first Basel accord (Basel I), reached in 1988, was subsequently implemented by the governments of more than 100 countries—each country implementing it at a different time and retaining the power to interpret and amend it. Basel I was implemented in the United States in 1991. Basel II was supposed to be implemented worldwide by January 1, 2007, but Basel I remains in effect for U.S. commercial banks as of this writing (June 2010), and Basel III seems to be imminent.

According to the Basel I rules, an adequately capitalized commercial bank must fund at least 8 percent of its assets with "capital." Capital is intended as a buffer against losses, but capital is not a supply of money sitting in a bank's vault in case of emergency. Rather, "capital" is a portmanteau term covering all of a bank's monies that are not owed to somebody else—that is, all of a bank's monies that are not debts. Most of a bank's monies *are* debts. A (commercial) bank's creditors include not only its "counterparties"—other banks that have lent it money—but businesses that have billed a bank for goods or services rendered; employees under contract; bondholders; and, most important, depositors into the bank's checking and savings accounts. If a bank were to repay all of these creditors, the money left over would equal the bank's "capital."

The most important source of this capital is "equity." Equity means, in this context, retained earnings and funds raised by selling shares in a bank to the public. The proceeds from selling stock to the public are the bank's, free and clear, as long as it remains solvent. This money, far from sitting in a vault, is deployed by the bank, alongside money borrowed from the bank's depositors and bondholders, to make loans, such as mortgages, and other investments, such as MBS purchases. Those loans and investments count as a bank's "assets," because they are expected to pay the bank returns of some sort (the interest payments on a mortgage or an MBS, for example).

On the other side of the ledger (literally; see Chapter 8) are liabilities, funds that are owed by the bank to its creditors (employees, bond holders, depositors, etc.). Any given quantity of liabilities is fixed—that is, a bank is legally obligated to pay its employees, bondholders, and depositors every penny these creditors are owed. Yet the value of the assets that will be used to pay these debts may fluctuate. Some proportion of mortgagors may default; some proportion of investments (such as MBS tranches) may not pay off as much as had been expected. So if a bank's assets were to match its liabilities exactly, then any decline in a bank's assets—brought about, perhaps, by a homeowner who cannot afford the full amount of his monthly mortgage payment—would instantly plunge the bank into insolvency. But if, say, 8 percent of the bank's mortgages are funded not by liabilities but by money the bank does not owe to anyone—its capital—then 8 percent of the bank's mortgages can default before the bank is again on the brink of insolvency. Bank capital is therefore an essential margin for error in accounting for the risks on the asset side of the ledger.

Issuing shares of stock is one way for a bank to come up with capital, but it is not the only one. Another way is to set aside a portion of earnings as a "loan-loss reserve": a rainy-day fund, as it were, against loans and investments that underperform the bank's expectations. However, under Basel I, loan-loss reserves are capped at 1.25 percent of a bank's assets; and they are categorized as "Tier 2" capital, which, in turn, is capped in relation to "Tier 1" equity capital. The only way for a bank to get around the first cap would be to increase its holdings of (inherently risky) assets, defeating the purpose of setting aside 1.25 percent of the assets' value as a cushion against risk.[10]

Another impediment to Tier-2 capital reserves is that

> current accounting standards for loan loss provisioning are based on the incurred loss model under which a bank can make a provision to the reserve only if it can document that a loss has been incurred, which means that a loss is probable and can be reasonably estimated. The easiest way to document those conditions is to refer to historical loss rates and the bank's own prior loss experience with the type of asset in question. (Wolters Kluwer 2009)

Thus, loan-loss reserves may be kept only for predictable losses—which are not true (unpredictable) risks. Consequently, in establishing loan-loss reserves, bankers are not allowed to provide for "unknown unknowns"—black swan events. Finally, the SEC demands the strictest documentation even when a bank attempts to provision against "known knowns." Simple prudence about the unpredictability of the future—that is, a banker's awareness of the fallibility of his own "risk model"—cannot be justified with historical documentation of the type the regulators require, since historical documentation necessarily justifies inferences only about what can be predicted.

In 1999, the SEC infamously penalized SunTrust Bank for keeping "excessive" loan-loss reserves, on the grounds that this "could be used to make earnings look less volatile" (Hopkins 2009). Since then, banks have avoided building up reserves when times are good because of the SEC's power to harass and penalize them if they do (Isaac 2009, 11; Rieker 2009). Banking analysts point out that in a long period of benign economic conditions, it becomes difficult to use acceptable documentation based on history and recent experience to justify significant [loan-loss] provisioning. Thus, when bankers were unable to produce acceptable documentation . . . auditors began to lean on them to reduce provisions or even take the more extreme step of reducing reserves. The result . . . was that the industry went into the current downturn without adequate reserves to absorb the wave of loan losses now being recognized. (Wolters Kluwer 2009)

Thus, in 2008,

amidst a bursting housing bubble that precipitated a severe recession, major U.S. banks . . . found themselves playing a game of catch-up. After being prohibited from procyclical reserve building beyond observable deterioration in their loan portfolios by accounting rules and S.E.C. regulations, banks [were] trying to catch up and get ahead of the steep asset quality deterioration. Weakening earnings are making this reserve build much more challenging. (Schwartz and Lister 2009)

The Basel I Accords in the United States

Capital requirements, such as Basel I's 8 percent, are as old as deposit insurance (FDIC 1984, chap. 6), which was enacted in the United States in 1933 at the height of the Great Depression. Initially, however, these capital requirements were flat minima that did not differentiate among how risky a bank's assets might be. An 8 percent capital minimum, for example, would be applied indiscriminately to all of a bank's assets, whether they were nearly riskless Treasury bills or, on the other hand, money lent to a precarious new business. The Basel accords, by contrast, linked the required amount of capital to differences in risk among various types of assets. The greater the risk perceived by the Basel Committee on Banking Supervision, the higher the capital requirement.

Cash, gold, and government bonds were judged by the Basel rule makers to have zero risk, meaning that under Basel I, a bank needed to deploy no capital to fund these assets. At the other end of the spectrum, commercial loans were given a 100 percent risk weight, requiring 8 percent capital: a bank had to devote $8 in capital to every $100 in loans to businesses, leaving $92 of the loans to be funded by money borrowed from the bank's depositors or bondholders. Individual or "whole" mortgages fell exactly in the middle, with a risk weight of 50 percent. Thus, a bank had to devote $4 of capital to every $100 in mortgages that it originated: $100 \times .08 \times .50 = 4$. Finally, the Basel rules assigned a risk weight of 20 percent to securities issued by "public-sector entities," which in the United States included the government-sponsored enterprises Fannie Mae and Freddie Mac. Therefore, a bank would have to devote only $1.60 of capital to buying $100 of such securities: $100 \times .08 \times .20 = 1.6$.

The net result of these regulations was that a bank that originated a $100 mortgage, sold it to Fannie or Freddie for securitization, and then bought it back as part of an agency MBS would reduce the amount of capital it needed to use from $4 to $1.60. Since $1.60 is 40 percent of $4, such transactions (known to economists as exercises in "regulatory arbitrage") would reduce the bank's need for scarce capital by 60 percent.

The GSEs were not allowed to securitize subprime whole mortgages, strictly speaking—mortgages to borrowers with low credit scores. But investment banks could buy subprime mortgages from commercial banks and mortgage specialists, securitize them, and then sell shares in the resulting PLMBSs to the GSEs for their own investment portfolios. Presumably these purchases helped fulfill the GSEs' mandate from HUD to expand homeownership opportunities for the disadvantaged. By April 2008, the GSEs held $308 billion worth of PLMBSs—second only to the American commercial banks' $473 billion in PLMBS holdings (Table 7.1). GSE purchases of subprime PLMBSs contributed to the profitability and the quantity of subprime lending. And purchases in the reverse direction—sales of GSE-issued MBSs to commercial banks—had a similar effect, encouraging the origination of nonprime mortgages (those with low downpayments).

Thus, Basel I, as implemented in America in 1991, may help to explain the size of the housing bubble—prime, nonprime, and subprime. However, it does not fully explain why the popping of the bubble caused the financial crisis, because, as noted, when the GSEs were bailed out, so were the $852 billion worth of MBSs that commercial banks had bought from the GSEs.

The Recourse Rule and the Basel
Accords outside the United States

The basic story of the financial crisis, then, is still incomplete. The missing piece is an amendment to the 1988 Basel accords, the Recourse Rule, that was issued a decade after the accords' 1991 implementation in the United States. This amendment, adopted in 2001 by the Federal Reserve, the Federal Deposit Insurance Corporation, the Office of the Comptroller of the Currency, and the Office of Thrift Supervision, added, to Basel I's assignment of a 20 percent risk weight to agency MBSs, the same risk weight for privately issued asset-backed securities, including mortgage-backed securities, that had received an AA or AAA rating from an NRSRO.

The Recourse Rule took effect on January 1, 2002, and seems to have produced a surge in demand for PLMBSs (including CDOs). Banks were now well advised to buy AA- or AAA-rated asset-backed securities if they wanted to conserve their capital. In 2000, a total of $150 billion in PLMBSs were securitized (IMF 2009, 84, Fig. 2.3). This figure roughly tripled in 2001, as one would expect of supply in anticipation of the demand once the Rule took effect. By 2004, the figure was nearing $1 trillion, and by 2006, it peaked at about $1.3 trillion. Figure 7.1 gives a picture of overall MBS issuance, including agency MBSs, that shows a similar trend.

Table 7.1 breaks down the roughly 23 percent of these MBSs that were held by American commercial banks (and thrifts, subject to the same capital regulations). One can see from the table that, of the $1.323 trillion in mortgage-backed securities held by these banks as of 2008, 100 percent either were rated AAA or were agency MBSs, thus meeting the Recourse Rule's criteria for capital relief.[11] Thus, all the banks' MBS exposure seems to have been acquired in pursuit of capital relief. To be sure, this was not the bankers' only motive, as can be seen by the 7 percent of their PLMBS exposure that took the form of AAA-rated CDOs ($90 billion worth), which by tranching mezzanine tranches of PLMBS achieved higher yields. We might say, then, that capital relief was the overall goal of the banks' MBS acquisitions, but that yield was a secondary consideration 7 percent of the time; but it was only secondary, since AA-rated CDO or PLMBS bonds would have garnered banks an even higher yield.[12]

Recall that, by an earlier inference, it appears that non-American banks may have held at least the same share of PLMBSs (including CDOs) as U.S. banks did. This raises a new question. The Recourse Rule did not cover non-U.S. banks, so why would those banks want to buy PLMBSs? There are at least two possible reasons.

First, under the original terms of Basel I, banks anywhere in the world could entirely escape capital minima by creating "structured investment vehicles" (SIVs) and other off-balance-sheet entities (OBSEs) to buy securities, as long as these were sustained by credit lines from the banks that lasted for less than one year. There was no Basel I specification of the ratings of these securities, but the Basel Committee on Banking Supervision reasoned that "commitments with an original maturity of up to one year, or which can be unconditionally cancelled at any time," deserved a 0 risk weight, because they "generally carry only a low risk" (BCBS 1998 [1988], 20, 12). Conceivably, the Committee believed this, in part, because OBSEs' assets were bought primarily with money borrowed from American money-market funds, which are required by law to place 95 percent of their investments in double-A or triple-A securities—another of the many regulations that had accreted to make the credit-rating firms into quasi-governmental "agencies" (Chapter 9).

OBSEs proved to be particularly popular in Europe, where 41 SIVs were established, compared to only 16 in the United States (seven of which were creatures of one bank, Citigroup; see Chapter 8). After all, the Recourse Rule made it possible for U.S. banks to gain capital relief for PLMBSs on their balance sheets. But there may have been a second factor encouraging non-American banks to invest in PLMBSs:

Basel II, which began to be implemented outside the United States in 2006, in advance of its target date of January 1, 2007.

Basel II extended the Recourse Rule's innovation to the rest of the world: now, double- and triple-A rated ABSs held on the balance sheet received a 20 percent risk weight in countries other than the United States. A promising avenue for future research would attempt to correlate, country by country, the date that Basel II was implemented and, on the other hand, the on-balance-sheet PLMBS holdings of those countries' commercial banks. At this point we don't know whether Basel II had time to significantly affect non-American banks' PLMBS investments before the crisis occurred.

Another uncertainty is whether Basel II contributed to the European debt crisis in May, 2010. Basel II assigned a zero risk weight to the sovereign debt of governments with AAA, AA+, AA, or AA– credit ratings, and a 20 percent risk weight to sovereign debt rated A+, A, or A–. The panic phase of the European crisis was triggered by a ratings downgrade from A– to BBB+ for Greek debt on April 21, 2010, forcing banks holding these bonds to come up with 60 percent more capital than they had held for them, since BBB+, BBB, and BBB- sovereign debt was assigned a 50 percent risk weight by Basel II. French and German banks alone held about $80 billion in Greek government bonds (Oakley 2010) plus $1.16 trillion in combined sovereign and private debt in two other countries that were at risk of ratings downgrades, Spain and Italy (Ewing 2010). On May 10, the European Central Bank bailed out European banks by agreeing to buy their bonds. The European banks' concentrated holdings of bonds issued by countries with low risk weights is exactly what was intended by Basel II, as the regulators considered these bonds to be ultra-safe.

Was It the Bankers' Greed, Then, After All?

It might seem that the role of the Basel and Recourse regulations lays the cause of the financial crisis at the feet of government, not capitalism, for without these regulations, commercial banks would not have overinvested in MBSs. And had they not done so, the dawning realization that these securities might be "toxic," despite their high ratings and implicit government guarantees, would not have caused bank lending to decline and eventually freeze. Yet if we look at the same process from a different angle, perhaps the bankers, and capitalism, should be held responsible after all. The Basel accords and the Recourse Rule were legally enforced government regulations. But these regulations did not *require* bankers to invest in asset classes with low risk weights, such as agency MBSs and triple- or double-A rated PLMBSs. The regulations mandated only that *if* a bank wanted to conserve its "regulatory capital," its most effective course would be to invest in asset classes with low risk weights. The only reason to conserve capital in this manner, however, was to increase the proportion of a bank's assets that was funded by debt.

Shifting out of business loans and whole mortgages into asset-backed securities or government bonds freed up capital under the Basel rules. But as we have seen, freed-up capital is then used to fund new assets—when the capital is combined with funds borrowed from a bank's depositors or bond holders. The effect of shifting a bank's assets into categories with low risk weights is, therefore, to allow the bank to increase its "leverage," meaning the ratio of borrowed funds to capital.

Consider a "well-capitalized" American commercial bank. Under American law, well-capitalized banks have certain privileges that "adequately capitalized" banks do not, so the American financial regulators require a 10 percent capital level for well-capitalized banks, compared to the 8 percent required of adequately capitalized banks (the Basel I capital minimum). Since 10 percent makes for easier arithmetic, the following thought experiment will assume a well-capitalized bank.

Suppose that this bank had $100 in capital on January 1, 2002, the day the Recourse Rule took effect. If it wished, it could have used this capital as the basis for $1,000 in commercial (business) loans—assuming it could attract checking and savings deposits and income from bond sales totaling $900—because the Recourse Rule's risk weight for commercial loans is 100 percent, or $1.00 \times$ the 10 percent capital level for a well-capitalized bank $\times \$1,000 = \$100$, the bank's capital. This bank would be leveraged at a ratio of 9:1.

To keep things simple, assume that this bank is able to make the same rate of return on all its loan and investment options (the various assets it can buy) under the Recourse Rule, and that it pays its depositors and bond holders the same interest rate. Thus, we can stipulate that the bank could make 5 percent on commercial loans, or else 5 percent on mortgages, or 5 percent on AA- or AAA-rated PLMBSs; and that its borrowed funds cost it 2 percent interest. At these rates, the bank would garner $50 in revenue on its $1,000 in commercial loans (.05 × $1000), less $18 in interest (.02 × $900), leaving a $32 profit.

Since the Recourse Rule's risk weight for mortgages is 50 percent—half the rate for commercial loans—the bank could instead deploy the same $100 in capital to make $2,000 in mortgage loans. This would make the bank twice as much revenue at 5 percent interest: $100 instead of $50. However, the bank could do this only by leveraging up to a ratio of 19:1; that is, by attracting a total of $1,900 in funds borrowed from its depositors or bond holders, costing it $38 in interest payments and leaving a profit of $62.

The bank's third option is to leverage up to 49:1 by using its $100 in capital to buy $5,000 of AA- or AAA-rated asset-backed securities carrying a 20 percent risk weighting: $5,000 × .20 × .10 = $100. The same $100 in capital would now yield $250 at a 5 percent yield, less $98 in interest payments, for a profit of $152. The bank would thus have made almost five times as much money by buying PLMBS as by making a business loan. Is it any wonder that mortgage-backed securities were so popular with the banks under the Recourse rule? (As Chapter 8 shows, the same process could be even more profitable off the balance sheets, as Basel I allowed.)

It might now seem that, after all, the most popular explanation of the crisis is true, although for a reason most people have never heard of. "Greedy bankers" were indeed at fault—because greedy bankers took advantage of the Basel regulations to bury themselves in debt, using the borrowed funds to buy risky subprime securities. Nobody made the bankers take these risks. Was it not the bankers' avarice, then, that caused the crisis?

The Red Herring of Leverage

A greedy banker may want to make more money, but he also doesn't want to lose it. With leverage comes not only the promise of large gains, but the risk of great losses. Avarice, therefore, can lead to leveraging down as much as it leads to leveraging up: if greed is a banker's motive, raising the bank's capital ratio (to reduce leverage) makes as much sense as lowering it—if the banker thinks the assets that could be purchased with extra borrowed money are risky enough to outweigh the greater profits.

To put the point differently: for all the peculiarly American moralizing about the evils of debt that has been heard since the crisis began, there is nothing wrong with debt per se, hence nothing wrong with leverage per se.

Consider the difference between debt and what is supposed to be, in contrast, its polar opposite: savings. Savings are rewards for past actions (such as laboring or investing) that are carried into the present to purchase goods or services. Debt is a reward for future actions (such as laboring or investing) that are carried into the present to purchase goods or services. Paying off a given amount of debt will require the same amount of work (in the future) as it took, in the past, to accumulate the same amount of savings—*more* work, actually, since the debtor must pay interest to the saver for the loan. Neither borrowing nor lending is inherently good or inherently bad, or inherently lazy or ambitious.

Debt, however, is inherently *riskier* because the future is unpredictable. A debtor who borrows from his future income to buy a house—courtesy of the savings borrowed, in turn, by a bank from its depositors, and then lent to the debtor in the form of a mortgage—does not know with certainty that he will earn enough money to be able to pay off his mortgage, because nobody can know the future with certainty. In contrast, if he were able to pay for the house in cash, he would be drawing on funds that he knows for a fact he has already saved. Likewise a banker who, courtesy of her depositors and bond holders, borrows from the bank's future income to buy a mortgage-backed security. She does not know for a fact that her investment will pay off.

That is why, *ceteris paribus*, it makes sense for any debtor to leave a margin of error. But just as with the rating agencies' judgments about the appropriate width of triple-A PLMBS tranches, nobody can say for sure how much of a margin for error one should leave: 10 percent, 8 percent, 5 percent, 2 percent?

In light of the uncertainty of the future, one might conclude that the best course is not to incur any debt at all: maintain a 100 percent margin of error, or in banking terms, a 100 percent capital cushion: zero leverage. This would achieve the aim of prudence but at the cost of prosperity. There is no good reason that a family should not be able to borrow from its future income to live in a house now, via money loaned from a bank (and, in turn, from the bank's depositors)—if it will turn out, after the fact, that the family was able to pay off its mortgage on time. By the same token, there is no good reason that a bank should not be able to borrow from its depositors, and from its own future income (paid out in interest to depositors and bond holders in the present), to make a mortgage loan, a business loan, or any other investment—if it will turn out, after the fact, that the investment enabled the bank to pay off its depositors, bond holders, and other creditors. To be sure, borrowing could not happen without lending, and thus saving; but just as lenders are rewarded for their past savings by borrowers, borrowers are rewarded for their future earnings by lenders. There is nothing undesirable about either side of this transaction.

Hence there is nothing wrong with leverage—or, for that matter, with gambling. The only relevant question is whether, in fact, the future will turn out the way the borrower (and, by implication, the lender—or the gambler) hopes that it will. What matters is whether one's bets turn out well or not, which depends on whether the future unfolds as one hopes that it will. If it does, then leveraging up to make a bigger bet on the future is a good thing. Only if the future does not unfold as hoped is leveraging up a bad thing. As the Basel Committee on Banking Supervision imperfectly recognized when it tied leverage levels to the predicted riskiness of asset classes, leverage ratios in themselves are meaningless, and the "right" ratio is impossible to determine in advance. A bet that turns out as predicted by the bettor should (in retrospect) have been financed with the most leverage conceivable; a bet that does not turn out as planned should not have been financed at all.

Moralizing aside, then, the problem with the bankers was not that they leveraged up. The problem was that they leveraged up to make what turned out to be a bad bet. That is because the only way they could leverage up economically, under Basel I and the Recourse Rule, was to buy asset-backed securities with a high rating; and the assets were mortgages that, it turns out, were constitutive of an asset bubble.

Imprudence Versus Error

The bankers bet wrong. But, of course, so did the regulators—by privileging asset-backed securities with a high rating. Should they be blamed as much as the bankers? Or more?

Assigning blame (a moral category) does not help us understand *why* the regulators or the bankers made their mistakes, as social scientists should do. But the blame game is very popular, even among the distinguished social scientists who have contributed to this volume— and it is especially popular in retrospect, when bad bets are easy to identify, and disastrously bad ones come to seem glaringly obvious. (Psychologists call this hindsight bias.)

The blame game is especially popular among economists, for deep methodological reasons. As Chapter 12 shows, economists use a model of human behavior in which genuine mistakes are effectively treated as impossible. "Homo economicus" is presumed to know everything that one needs to know in order to pursue self-interest "rationally." The inescapable conclusion is that what may appear to noneconomists to have been mistakes could not have been due to ignorance; therefore, they must have been deliberate, and thus not really mistakes. Those who ended up making bad bets must have *known* that they were bad bets with the same clarity that *we* know it in hindsight.

But why would anyone knowingly make a bad bet? They must (according to economists) have had an incentive to do so. The economists' attribution of omniscience to human beings has thus produced two incentives-based explanations of the financial crisis: the corporate-compensation theory and the too-big-to-fail theory. I will treat each in turn.

Bankers' Bonuses and the "Too Big to Fail" Problem

Those who espouse the corporate-compensation theory claim that bankers knowingly took excessive risks because the compensation structure of the banks, like that of most American corporations, gave bankers an incentive to disregard risk. Thus, bank executives received performance bonuses for profits; but if profits turned to losses and the executives were fired, they often had "golden parachutes" to protect them from financial damage. Meanwhile, lower-level employees got annual bonuses for their own profitable actions, even if their actions cost the bank huge losses the next year (Posner 2009, 93–100).

Corporate compensation arrangements do have a skew toward short-term risk. But banks also have employees who are paid to monitor and control the resulting risks. A bank's employees are also supervised by executives who are usually paid in stock, which declines in value if losses are incurred. Moreover, the employees may conceivably feel a sense of responsibility to each other, to their employer, and to society at large. In short, there are many cross-cutting "incentives" whenever human beings act in an institutional and cultural context; and when it comes to judging risk, there are many ways for fallible human beings to err. Whether the bankers' errors were genuine mistakes in judging the safety of the asset-backed securities that the Basel rules made so profitable or whether they were knowingly reckless risks is an empirical question that can be answered only with evidence, but the corporate-compensation thesis has been assumed as fact on the basis of almost no evidence at all.[13]

To date (August 2010), in fact, there have been just three studies of the matter, all of which appeared after the consensus in favor of the corporate-compensation thesis had already been reached. One study (Cheng, Hong, and Sheinkman 2009) tended to confirm the thesis. It found that financial companies that paid relatively large incentive bonuses tended to perform slightly worse during the crisis. This suggests that, to some extent, the economists' assumption is correct: the financial crisis was caused by employees who knew they were taking excessive risks, but went ahead and took them in pursuit of personal profit. The study has been criticized, however, on the grounds that most of the very small performance difference was among insurance companies (which the study counted as financial companies), not banks (Kaplan 2009). A second study (Fahlenbrach and Stulz 2009) found the opposite effect among banks that paid their top executives in stock. The higher the proportion of stock compensation, the worse the companies did. This suggests that the executives did not realize that their banks were taking excessive risks, or else they would have either put a stop to the risk taking or sold their stock. Thus, at Bear Stearns, executives collectively lost billions of dollars worth of stock when the bank went under; Lehman Brothers CEO Richard Fuld singlehandedly lost $1 billion; and Citigroup Chairman Sanford Weill lost half that amount (Cohen 2009). However, a third study pointed out that some of these executives did sell large quantities of stock in the eight years preceding the crisis (Bebchuk, Cohen, and Spamann 2009). James E. Cayne, chief executive of Bear Stearns, sold $289 million of stock in those years. The study does not consider, however, that payment in stock and stock options constitutes by far the greatest portion of executive compensation in America. One would not expect people who spend their lives trying to get rich never to cash in some of the riches and enjoy them. The fact that banking executives cashed in does not indicate that they knew that their firms were living on borrowed time, especially when they did *not* cash in the bulk of their stock compensation. Why would a banker who knew about risky behavior at his bank leave $1 billion worth of stock unsold, as Cayne did? As Bear Stearns was collapsing in March 2008, Cayne had to sell this stock for a mere $61 million.[14]

The evidence in favor of the corporate-compensation theory, then, is at best mixed. However, there are two decisive considerations *against* it.

First, if the bankers were insensitized to risk because they would be financially rewarded for gains but not penalized for losses, then they would have attempted to back their bets with the maximum leverage allowed by law, which is to say, in the United States, the maximum risk-weighted leverage allowed by Basel I and the Recourse Rule. But they didn't. In 2007, just prior to the crisis, the twenty largest U.S. commercial banks' regulatory capital ratio averaged 11.7 percent, nearly 20 percent above the 10 percent required of well-capitalized banks (Kuritzkes and Scott 2009). When one includes smaller commercial banks, the risk-based capital ratio as of mid-2007 was 12.85 percent (correspondence from FDIC), nearly 30 percent higher than the well-capitalized 10 percent level, and 60 percent higher than the adequately capitalized 8 percent level. Even the banks that actually went broke had significantly higher risk-weighted capital levels than required by law (Kuritzkes and Scott 2009).

Readers should keep in mind that our previous discussion of leveraging up was hypothetical. No commercial bank actually put all of its funds into asset-backed securities, as in our example, which would have produced a risk-weighted capital level of 2 percent for well-capitalized banks (10 percent × the .20 risk weight for asset-backed securities with AA or AAA ratings); or a risk-weighted capital level of 1.6 percent for adequately capitalized banks (8 percent × .20). The effect of the Basel regulations, even combined with the profits available from leveraging by their rules, was *not* to dramatically raise leverage among commercial banks, but was, instead, to shift leveraged assets into the Basel-approved risk categories. Tier 1 (equity) capital levels *unweighted* by risk category remained essentially unchanged throughout the years prior to 2008, as shown in the bottom curve of Figure 8.3. However, business investment declined in comparison with the 1990s (Duy 2009; cf. Johnson and Kwak 2010, 147), just as we would expect if banks reallocated their leverage away from business loans and into asset-backed securities.

Second, we know from Table 7.1 that all of the PLMBS tranches bought by the banks were rated AAA.[15] Setting aside the importance of AAA and AA ratings in the Basel and Recourse rules, it is undeniable that triple-A tranches paid lower returns than double-A and lower-rated tranches; high-rated bonds *always* pay less than lower-rated bonds. A study of 735 ABS CDOs issued between 1999 and 2007 puts the average yield of the AAA tranches at 3.4 percent and the average yield of AA tranches at 4.1 percent (Barnett-Hart 2009, Table 1). Buying double-A tranches would therefore have produced just the type of bonuses that the corporate-compensation theory alleges were the cause of the crisis—*and* it would have achieved precisely the same "capital relief" under the Recourse Rule. Yet none of the banks' PLMBS and CDO purchases were of lower-yielding AAA tranches; 100 percent of the time, banks bought either AAA PLMBS or CDO tranches or even lower-yielding agency debt (Table 7.1). Until this fact is explained away, it closes the case against the corporate-compensation theory of the crisis, because it demonstrates conclusively that, given the choice, bankers consistently chose the safest, lowest-yielding tranches of mortgage-backed bonds.

The fact that bankers did not leverage up nearly as much as they were allowed to, and the fact that they leveraged into the safest PLMBS and CDO tranches, also undermine the most popular of two extant versions of the too-big-to-fail (TBTF) theory.

Drawing on two historical instances in which the federal government bailed out financial institutions, the popular variant of TBTF posits bankers who deliberately made risky bets because they "knew" that they, too, would be bailed out if the bets turned sour. This theory does not make sense on its own terms, because the executives of the two institutions that were bailed out—Continental Illinois (a commercial bank) in 1984, and Long-Term Capital Management (a hedge fund) in 1998—were *not* bailed out. They were fired and, in the case of Long-Term Capital Management, the partners in the firm lost all $1.9 billion they had invested (Lowenstein 2000, 207–8). These instances therefore would have given no comfort to reckless bankers.

There is a subtler version of TBTF, however, which holds that because Continental Illinois's *depositors and bondholders* were bailed out, depositors and investors in the bonds of large banks knew from that point forward that they, too, would be bailed out if the bank to which they lent money (by depositing funds with it or by buying its bonds) were to become insolvent. (Small depositors already had a bailout guarantee, in the form of deposit insurance, but deposit insurance does not cover large institutional depositors.) Therefore, the big banks could offer bonds that paid a lower interest rate, because investors would accept a smaller yield in exchange for the safety implicit in the TBTF banks' implicit government backing. This, in turn, would increase the big banks' profits from increased leverage by widening the spread between the interest on their debt service (2 percent, in our previous example) and the revenue from their various investments (5 percent, in our example) (Johnson and Kwak 2010, 151).

The subtler version of TBTF is at least internally consistent and should be investigated empirically. Like the more popular version of

TBTF, the subtler version assumes that bankers knew they were taking big risks, such that only a higher profit margin would induce them to do so. However, many banks that were too small to be bailed out, and that did not enjoy the funding advantages of the big banks, also purchased mortgage-backed securities (e.g., Scism and Tamman 2010). *Prima facie,* then, it does not yet appear that any lower funding costs for such purchases enjoyed by the larger banks made a material difference in this case. Even the subtle version of TBTF, moreover, is difficult to square with the same two facts that falsify the corporate-compensation theory. First, the big commercial banks' legally allowed (i.e., risk-weight adjusted) capital levels were far above what they would have been if the banks had leveraged themselves to the hilt because of cheap funding from depositors and bond buyers who assumed that these banks would be bailed out. Second, it is hard to believe that bond buyers or depositors would have been alarmed by purchases of triple-A securities, even if they had been paying attention. The bankers themselves do not seem to have been alarmed.

Clearly the bankers misjudged the risk of those securities: they bet wrong. But their overwhelming preference for them shows that they, like almost everybody else, believed in the accuracy of the triple-A ratings, since they were trading the greater returns on AA (and lower) tranches for the supposed safety of AAAs.

As Mark Zandi (2009, 116) writes of subprime securities, "Banks themselves were the first in line, picking up most of the senior-rated segments." Returns on these were low, but greater than the banks were paying to their own depositors.

This behavior was nothing if not prudent. Notably, only eight corporations were considered, at the time, to be safe enough to warrant a triple-A rating; nobody would accuse a bank that invested in the likes of Berkshire Hathaway, ExxonMobil, or Johnson & Johnson (Johnson and Kwak 2010, 139) of imprudence. Yet the Recourse Rule deemed such investments *five times riskier* (risk weight 1.00) than investments in AAA or AA asset-backed securities (risk weight .20). More evidence that the bankers were not driven to imprudence by their greed can be found in their purchases of insurance on their

PLMBS holdings, both in the form of credit-default swaps (Chapter 10)[16] and insurance policies from "monoline" insurers, which promised 100 percent loss protection (Gorton 2008, 38n42) on some portion of the securities, generally 20 percent—equivalent to a 20 percent bank-capital level.

The evidence, then, suggests that bankers were not ignoring risks that they knew about, as both the corporate-compensation and TBTF theories suggest. Rather, the bankers were *ignorant* of the fact that triple-A rated securities might be much riskier than advertised.

The authors of Chapters 2 and 12 suggest that economists are poorly equipped to recognize ignorance because most economic models assume that economic actors are "rational representative agents" who know the correct "model" of the economy.[17] That mistakes are never made, that nothing is really accidental, is also the default theory of popular politics: major problems aren't caused by human error; instead, some self-interested person or cabal must be at fault—special interests, lobbyists, or, indeed, greedy bankers. Mistakes don't fit into standard economic and political models, because standard economic and political models take ignorance out of the human equation.

If, as I have been assuming (along with all of the contributors to this volume), the bankers bet wrong—a matter that is surprisingly open to question, even as of August 2010[18]—then, ex post facto, we can pass the judgment that their confidence in the value of mortgage-backed securities was "overconfidence." However, this is not evidence that they were imprudent in a meaningful (non-tautological) sense. They were trying to make money, but they were not being particularly greedy or hubristic. They, like the other investors and the rating agencies, were simply mistaken—or so it seems, with the luxury of hindsight. And the reason, apparently, is that they were ignorant of the true risk of the securities they were buying.

The same theme echoes through the available anecdotal evidence. "We were just told by our risk people that these instruments are triple-A, like Treasury bonds," says Peter Kurer, the former chairman of the huge Swiss bank UBS (quoted, Tett 2009a, 139). The UBS report to its shareholders and the Swiss government on its perform-

ance in the crisis bears Kurer out.[19] The UBS risk-management process was (in retrospect) woefully misguided,[20] but the results it
produced were reassuring, and there is no reason to think that Kurer
was less than reassured. Nor is there evidence that the risk managers
who generated these reports deliberately underplayed the risks (cf.
Chapter 7).

Even more telling is what we know about the two employees who
inadvertently brought down Bear Stearns, Ralph Cioffi and Matthew
Tannin, who ran two Bear hedge funds that invested in PLMBSs.
Cioffi's sales pitch to investors was compared to "a broken phono-
graph record . . . that basically says, 'The fund is 90 percent invested
in AA and AAA structured finance assets'" (Cohan 2009a, 311). Not
only did Cioffi's clients believe that these assets were safe;, so did he.
Thus, he was willing to risk a jail term by lying to them from December 2006 to February 2007, when news of subprime defaults was
spreading (Cohan 2009a, 311–12). To reassure his clients, Cioffi
reported that he was selling subprime CDOs during this period when
he was actually buying them. He must have been sure that there
would be no investigation, hence no jail sentence, if doubling down
on subprimes turned out well for his investors—so clearly he must
have believed that in buying them, he was not courting disaster.

Cioffi's partner, Matthew Tannin, seems to have held the same set
of beliefs. Tannin followed Alan Greenspan (Zandi 2009, 72–73) and
Ben Bernanke (Posner 2009, 90) in thinking that there was no nationwide housing bubble, as opposed to local bubbles in a few cities
(Cohan 2009a, 305). E-mails to Cioffi unearthed by the FBI show that
Tannin thought buying subprimes was a good idea as late as February
28, 2007 (Zandi 2009, 322), four months before the market price of
subprime, double- and triple-A rated PLMBS tranches dropped so
low that the parent bank had to bail out the hedge funds.

Both Tannin and Cioffi had millions of dollars invested in the
subprime hedge funds they ran, and Cioffi moved $2 million of his
$6 million investment out of these funds only on March 23, 2007—to
a new Bear fund over which he would assume oversight responsibility
on April 1, and to which he may therefore have needed to demonstrate his commitment (Cohan 2009a, 325). As of March 28, Tannin
was still in: "'I simply do not believe anyone who shits all over the

ratings agencies,' he wrote. 'I've seen it all before. Smart people being too smug'" (Cohan 2009a, 326). It was not until April 22, 2007—two months before the funds collapsed—that Tannin began to have doubts. A new internal analysis of subprime CDOs suggested that "the subprime market looks pretty damn ugly. If we believe the [new CDO report] is ANYWHERE CLOSE to accurate, I think we should close the funds now" (quoted, Cohan 2009a, 328). This was toward the end of a tortured letter that Tannin secretly routed to Cioffi through their wives' personal e-mail accounts (Cohan 2009a, 327), suggesting that the message reflected his true thinking. Tannin wrote that he "had no doubt 'I've done the best possible job that I could have done. Mistakes, yep, I've made them,'" he admitted, but "'all one can do is their [sic] best—and I have done this.'"

These are not the words, nor were Tannin and Cioffi's actions the behavior, of people who had deliberately taken what they knew to be excessive risks. If Tannin and Cioffi were guilty of anything, it was the mistake of believing the triple-A ratings. (A jury agreed, acquitting them of securities fraud in November 2009.) Yet Cioffi and Tannin were two of the best-placed bank executives in the world to know that there was excessive risk in triple-A tranches of subprime securities—if this fact, which we find it so easy to take for granted in retrospect, was obvious to anyone at the time. Bear Stearns annually securitized $61 billion of subprime loans in the peak period, 2005–6 (Luce 2009), and Tannin had spent seven years intimately involved in the securitization process itself before he joined Cioffi in buying PLMBSs for the two Bear Stearns hedge funds (Cohan 2009a, 283). By contrast, the commercial-bank employees who bought these securities typically would not have been in a position to know anything about them except that they were rated AAA. If Cioffi and Tannin were ignorant of the "true" risks,[21] then we have every reason to think that commercial bankers were just as ignorant of them.

This applies doubly to the executives at the top of the corporate hierarchies, supervising thousands of employees from afar. Early in 2007, as the problems with subprime mortgages became apparent, "members of the fixed-income department" of Merrill Lynch, an investment bank, "reported to [CEO E. Stanley] O'Neal that they were reducing the firm's subprime exposure, but no one in the department, or in the risk and finance departments, mentioned the CDOs accumulating on the balance sheet." A former Merrill executive told the *New Yorker*: "I can only believe that they saw the risk inherent in the CDOs in a different way. These securities were triple-A rated" (Cassidy 2008, 88). Similarly, when the market for the securities that Cioffi and Tannin were selling (and buying) dried up and Bear Stearns had to bail out the hedge funds, Paul Friedman, the CEO of the firm's fixed-income division, reports how bewildered everyone was: "At that point we still believed that an AAA rating meant an AAA rating, and we all believed that these things were reasonably well structured" (quoted, Cohan 2009a, 365)—just as did the infuriated executives at BlackRock, Fortis, Vanguard, and Pimco when Moody's downgraded the ratings.

A Crisis of Capitalism, or of Regulation?

"Regulators either did not have sufficient information to understand how concentrated risk was becoming, or if regulators had access to the information, they were unable to understand and identify the risks. (FDIC Chair Shelia Bair 2010, 28)

To the list of those who were, in retrospect, ignorant, we now must add the regulators.

The SEC had the same faith in Moody's, S&P, and Fitch that Cioffi, Tannin, and their superiors did. The regulators who enacted the Recourse Rule—at the FDIC, the Federal Reserve, the OCC, and the OTS—must have had the same faith, too, or they would not have given double- and triple-A rated securities the same risk weights that the Basel I rules assigned securities issued by GSEs. In turn, the regulators of all the governments that adopted Basel II were ignorant of the risk of relying on the NRSRO ratings. The Fed also misjudged the appropriate monetary policy; failed to notice the housing bubble; mismeasured inflation, according to Chapter 3; and, according to Chapter 5, mistook a crisis of doubt—doubt, ultimately, about the accuracy of all those triple-A ratings—for a liquidity crisis.

These regulatory errors indicate not only that the regulators *allowed* the crisis to develop (Chapter 4), but, furthermore, that the regulators *encouraged* the crisis by offering large advantages to banks that bought agency securities and double- and triple-A-rated PLMBSs— because the regulators were as ignorant of the risks of those assets as the bankers were. This is not surprising, as regulators are human beings, and therefore should not be expected to be any more omniscient than the people they regulate.

We seem to be left, then, with enough "blame" to go around: everyone was ignorant—investors, bankers, and regulators alike. But the story does not end so inconclusively.

When Capitalists Disagree

Along with the convention of assuming that the bankers bet wrong on high-rated PLMBSs, I have followed the convention of assuming that *all* banks did so. But in truth, they did so to very different degrees. As they competed against each other, they used different theories of where to find profit—and how to avoid loss.

At UBS, chairman Peter Kurer admitted, "people did not ask too many questions" about the triple-A ratings, so the bank invested heavily in triple-A subprime securities and suffered huge losses. Citigroup, too, accumulated gigantic quantities of mortgage-backed securities both on and off its balance sheets, and it went so far as to establish a securitizing arm that would transform mortgages originated in its commercial bank into PLMBSs. Thirteen percent of the adjustable-rate "jumbo" nonprime loans (too large for Fannie and Freddie to securitize) underlying Citi's 2007-vintage PLMBSs were delinquent by 2009 (Hagerty and Fitzpatrick 2009). So were 16 percent of those issued by Bank of America. However: that is twice as high as comparable PLMBSs issued by Wells Fargo, and four times as high as those issued by JPMorgan. Given the tranched structure of PLMBSs, such differences would have a huge impact on the safety of the senior tranches.

JPMorgan's CEO, Jamie Dimon, had decided that imitating Citi was too risky (Tett 2009a, 124–28), even though the cost of failing to do so was much lower profit levels (as illustrated by our example). He also raised the pay of Morgan's risk-monitoring personnel to try

to ensure that Morgan's own investments were safe (Tett 2009a, 115–
17). Years before his arrival, moreover, the Morgan employees who
originally developed CDO tranching had had the opportunity to
apply this technology to mortgage-backed securities. But they realized
that even though "the last time house prices had fallen significantly"
across the United States as a whole "was way back in the 1930s," a
similar event might make all the losses within a mortgage-backed
CDO "correlate" with each other, which "might be catastrophically
dangerous." Therefore,

> to cope with the uncertainties the team stipulated that a big-
> ger-than-normal funding cushion be raised, which made the
> deal less lucrative for J. P. Morgan. The bank also hedged its
> risk. That was the only prudent thing to do. . . . Mortgage risk
> was just too uncharted.
>
> The team at J. P. Morgan did only one more [such] deal
> with mortgage debt, a few months later, worth $10 billion.
> Then, as other banks ramped up their mortgage-backed busi-
> ness, J. P. Morgan largely dropped out. (Tett 2009b)

Morgan also "did not unduly leverage [its] capital, nor did [it] rely
on low-quality forms of capital." Instead of targeting a high leverage
ratio, as in the examples Chapter 8 uses to illustrate the behavior of
SIVs—of which Morgan established none—Morgan aimed for an 8
to 8.5 percent Tier-1 capital ratio. Since the Basel rules define Tier-1
capital as just half of the total (the other half being formed by Tier
2), this was twice the required Tier-1 level (Dimon 2009, 16)—despite
the higher costs of Tier-1 capital. With a higher Tier-1 capital level,
Morgan was also able to increase its level of loan-loss reserves in Tier
2 (Rieker 2010), since Tier 2 is capped in relation to Tier 1.

As a result of all of these moves, JPMorgan emerged from the
crisis as far and away the strongest of the nationwide American commercial banks. But it was not the only bank to behave differently from
the crowd. Goldman Sachs came to see the danger of its CDOs and
used credit-default swaps to escape serious damage (Chapter 3),
unlike the other investment banks. So did Morgan, which singlehandedly accounted for about 44 percent of the world's CDS expo-

sure (Slater 2009). CapitalOne eschewed the mortgage business altogether. Wells Fargo avoided the dangers well enough that it literally had to be forced by the government to take TARP money (Levy 2009).[22] There were also many smaller examples of what turned out to be prudent banking, ranging from regional giants BB&T, PNC, and U.S. Bancorp (Cox and Cass 2009) to tiny Beal Bank of Plano, Texas, which accumulated capital during the mid-2000s but avoided participating in what its president and chief stockholder, D. Andrew Beal, thought was credit-fueled craziness. In turn, his fellow bankers and the regulators thought he was crazy—literally (Condon and Vardi 2009).[23] When the crisis began, Beal was ready to take advantage of the mistakes of other banks, buying about $5 billion of distressed assets by April 2009 and angling to become a major bank by buying another $23 billion in short order.

Competition, Capitalism, and Heterogeneity

The Basel rules induced banks to invest in highly rated securities. For the most part, the bankers went along with the regulators' aim, which was to steer bankers' leverage in a "safe" direction. But since the regulations did not command anyone to take advantage of these inducements, it was still possible for bankers who disagreed with the rating agencies—and with the bankers who agreed with the ratings—to resist the herd, if they could absorb the competitive costs of doing so. In other words, there was enough leeway in the regulations that a determined banker with a different opinion from the regulators about which investments were prudent might be able to resist the tide for a period of time—if he happened to be standing on a large enough pile of cash.

That is what Beal, Dimon, and the other "dissident" bankers did. We are fortunate, then, that the regulations were not so tight that they forbade all heterogeneity in market behavior. But that is undeniably the tendency of economic regulation, and its danger.

By its very nature as a law, a regulation is imposed on every market participant. This means that even if, as with the Basel rules, the regulation takes the form of an inducement rather than a prohibition, it has a homogenizing effect on market behavior overall. The whole point of regulation is to get market participants to behave differently than they otherwise would; this is why regulations have the force of law. Through the power of government, every regulation imposes one opinion—the regulators'—on all market participants, even if only by advantaging those who go along with it.

When companies are in competition with each other, advantages conferred on those who do what the regulators want are functionally equivalent to penalties imposed on those who do not. It should not be surprising, then, that most banks participated, in one way or another, in the origination and securitization of nonprime and sub-prime mortgages and the purchase of the agency and private-label securities that resulted. The whole cycle of origination, securitization, and purchase was made artificially profitable by the Basel rules—even though the rules were sufficiently flexible to allow different degrees of participation, depending on the ability of a given nonparticipant to withstand competition from its artificially advantaged competitors.

It must surely be true that, as among the bankers, there was dis-agreement among the regulators about the wisdom of placing so much power in the hands of the rating agencies, or about the precise 20 percent risk weight that the regulations assigned to AA- and AAA-rated asset-backed PLMBSs and agency bonds. But heterogeneous opinions among regulators do not matter in the end. Only one regu-lation becomes the law in any jurisdiction (regarding any given activ-ity), regardless of whatever arguments occur among regulators before the decree is issued. This renders heterogeneous opinions among reg-ulators fundamentally different from heterogeneous opinions among capitalists, for when capitalists disagree, they can (in effect) test their discordant theories against each other through market competition. Therefore, capitalists' heterogeneity need not take the form of actual, verbal disagreement. Instead, it takes the more concrete form of dif-ferent enterprises structured by different theories (from an analytical perspective—not necessarily from the deliberate perspective of the managers of the enterprises): theories about how best to compensate executives and other employees, theories about which products or services to offer, theories about how to avoid bankruptcy.

For example, JPMorgan had, for half a century, cultivated an ethos that worked against any temptation to disregard known risks:

"While at other banks, the emphasis had turned to finding star players, offering them huge bonuses, and encouraging them to compete for preeminence, at the Morgan Bank the emphasis was on teamwork, employee loyalty, and long-term commitment to the bank" (Tett 2009a, 15).[24] Each capitalist enterprise tacitly combines any number of such practices, with the enterprise as a whole embodying (from an analytical perspective) a meta-theory about what the firm should do, and how to do it, in order to make profits and avoid losses. If an enterprise loses out in competition to others, then one or all of the theories contained in its meta-theory have been falsified in that particular time and place.

The greatest advantage of covert competition among capitalists' theories is that it places relatively low cognitive demands on the "theorists." The "theories" in question need not have actually been thought up or written down by any of the participants for competition among them to take place. The success of competition does not require that the competitors understand the reasons for their success or failure, any more than members of a species who carry a genetic mutation need to know why it is that (it will turn out, in the future) their progeny will, or won't, proliferate more than the progeny of other members of the same species.

By the same token, economic competition, like biological evolution, need not have some master note-taker standing above it and learning its lessons if the process is to do its work. This is crucial because such a synoptic preceptor, being human (hence fallible), could not be relied on to learn the right lessons from the process being observed. The process of competition "learns" these lessons as mechanically as evolution does—not by anyone thinking about them, let alone engaging in debate about them, but instead by eliminating, through bankruptcy, the erroneous theories embodied in loss-making firms (Alchian 1950).[25] (The TBTF theorists have misused a good idea: that any business should be allowed to fail. As a normative rule of capitalist practice, this is important; but the absence of the threat of failure does not explain the errors of bankers prior to the bailouts of 2008.)

The participants in a capitalist system need not be well informed, prescient, or even particularly intelligent. The low demands made on any single capitalist decision maker, due to the competitive mechanism for sorting good decisions from bad ones, is arguably the sole advantage of capitalism over alternative systems. Regulators, by contrast, *are* required to be brilliant synoptic preceptors, codifying in law their predictions about which practices will avert market failures. If they err in this analysis, the mistake is imposed homogeneously on the entire system. They need, therefore, to be able to grasp the complexity of the system they are trying to regulate—which no *participant* in the system needs to do. A system of regulation is therefore much more cognitively demanding than a system of competition. Consider how hard it would be to reverse-engineer *in detail* a complex biological organism, such as a human being, by observing and theorizing about human behavior. Yet the design of all complex biological organisms was produced by a completely noncognitive process: natural selection among competing genes. The only requirement was heterogeneity, in the form of genetic variation. Certainly the results of natural selection are not perfectly adaptive, but just as certainly, they are more adaptive than could have been produced by "intelligent design"—unless the designer were omniscient and thus infallible.

The regulators were neither omniscient nor infallible. Only their errors can explain why the banks regulated by them proved, on the whole, to be so homogeneously susceptible to the lure of agency bonds and high-rated PLMBSs in comparison to other classes of investors. Agency MBSs and PLMBSs were bought in quantities by banks of every size, and in immense disproportion to their purchases by other institutions. Pension funds, hedge funds, mutual funds, general (as opposed to monoline) insurance companies—they, too, invested in MBSs, including PLMBSs, but their investment portfolios were sufficiently diversified that none of these financial sectors, as sectors, were wiped out. However, they were not subject to Basel I, the Recourse Rule, or Basel II

Regulation and Systemic Risk

Fallibility does not entail error. All-too-human regulators may still get it right. Conversely, market competition does not entail good outcomes. Consumers may not know what they want, at least not at first—and, ultimately, consumer purchases are the systemic filter that screens out mistaken businesses' "theories." Consumers form the environment to which businesses will or will not prove to be adaptive.[26] Likewise, the entrepreneurs with access to capital—or the bankers and investors who supply it—might tend homogeneously to make the same error.

However, where there are competing powers, as in a capitalist economy, there is more chance of heterogeneity than when there is a single regulator with power over all the competitors. At worst, in the limit case of a market that, through herd behavior, completely converged on an erroneous idea or practice, unregulated capitalism would likely be no worse than regulated capitalism, since an idea or practice that is homogeneously accepted by all market participants in a given time and place is likely to be accepted by the regulators of that time and place, too. But at best, competing businesses will embody different theories, with the bad ones tending to be weeded out.

All of this is assuming, however, that the only source of error—whether on the part of capitalists or on the part of their regulators—is cognitive. This assumption is inherently unfriendly to regulation, because there is no plausible reason to think that regulators will be smarter or better informed than those they regulate. This fact tends to be invisible to citizens, legislators, regulators, and economists, however, when, in their preoccupation with infallible "incentives," they overlook the possibility of human error. If the polity blames capitalists' greed for whatever errors they make, then it will seem perfectly sensible for the polity to demand regulation of the greedy, reckless capitalists by regulators who—however greedy they might be—are not rewarded for taking recklessly self-serving actions, unless they are corrupt. Since it is relatively easy to police corruption among a handful of regulators who are, in addition, enjoined by cultural norms to be honest, then it is logical to entrust them with the job of restraining the misdeeds of avaricious capitalists—if avarice, rather than error, is the source of their misdeeds.

However, if we take seriously the possibility that market participants are making cognitive errors—grounded in their ignorance, not their incentives—then the case for regulation loses considerable force, because regulators, however well-motivated, are as likely as anyone else to be ignorant. Moreover, market competition limits even incentives-based error by conferring losses on those firms that, for example, use compensation systems that encourage too much risk taking.[27] So the main case for preferring regulation to competition arises when market participants' self-interest can be served only at the expense of consumers.

That may seem to be the norm until one considers the fact that, in the absence of regulatory intervention, capitalist self-interest is usually served by selling consumers things that the consumers think make them better off. In short, capitalists' and consumers' incentives are normally aligned. However, even those who, like economists, do recognize this concede that there are cases in which the self-interest of a business and its customers may be served, but may have deleterious systemic effects. In such instances, there is a good case for "systemic" regulation.

To evaluate the case for systemic regulation, however, it needs to be recognized that all regulations are already, by their very nature as laws, systemic; so one must find out why systemic regulators made the decisions that seem to have caused the crisis. Perhaps these decisions indicate cognitive difficulties in regulation that are so great that they might be expected to thwart effective systemic regulation, even when a good "economic" (noncognitive) case could be made for regulation on grounds of the regulators' untaintedness by market self-interest.

The Regulators' Ideology

In Chapter 4 Joseph Stiglitz blames the free-market ideology of the regulators (such as the libertarian Chairman of the Fed, Alan Greenspan) for having restrained them from using regulatory powers they already had or easily could have gotten. This notion is problematic since Greenspan's successor, Bernanke, no libertarian, acted no differently than his predecessor. Granting Stiglitz's point, however, does not strengthen the case for systemic regulation. Ideology is one of many heuristics through which fallible, ignorant human beings try to make sense of the world, and it seems to be much more prevalent among relatively well-informed political elites, who are trying to make sense of more political information than people with other concerns (Converse [1964] 2006). If people, not gods, are going to be making public policy, then we have to accept that they will be guided by their ideologies (and other heuristics). To blame a regulator's ideology for a regulatory mistake is merely to emphasize that regulators, like entrepreneurs, depend on theories to guide their actions. Ideologies provide such theories. The problem, again, is that only one regulatory theory is imposed on everyone, so if the regulator's ideology is flawed, everyone pays the price.

In this particular case, the true ideology at work seems to have been economism, not libertarianism. The regulators' actions were based on what academic economists judged to be the best economic theories. Thus, when regulators chose not to exercise their power—for example, when they chose not to allow for the regulation of credit-default swaps—it was because economic theory tended to endorse the benefits of these instruments. Deputy Treasury Secretary Lawrence Summers, a John Bates Clark Medalist of the American Economic Association, tenured member of the Harvard economics faculty, future Clinton administration Treasury Secretary, and future head of the Obama administration's economic council, helped kill the Commodity Futures Trading Commission's proposal to study the regulation of credit-default swaps (Chapter 3)—presumably because, like economists generally, he thought that swaps were an invaluable way to reduce systemic risk (see Chapter 10). For the same reason, as noted in Chapters 2, 7, and 8, economists firmly believed in the benefits of securitization. From a "scientific" perspective, one could not have asked more of economic regulators than that they encourage securitization by giving lower risk weights to securitized assets than they gave, say, to whole mortgages.

Likewise, as Chapter 11 points out, contemporary economics places great reliance on companies' good reputations as important barriers to unnecessary risk taking. What could be better, then, than to rely on the rating agencies' desire to maintain their good reputations? Thus, in a report issued in 2005 by the Bank for International Settlements, a team of economists analyzed whether, in light of the rise of structured finance, Basel II should incorporate the NRSROs' ratings into the risk-weight formula, as the American authorities had

already done by issuing the Recourse Rule. The BIS researchers'
answer was yes, and their recommendation was enacted in Basel II.
In concluding that this was the wise course, the BIS researchers
acknowledged the possibility of error by the rating agencies, but they
could imagine no systematic reason for errors to occur other than the
fact that, as had been true since the 1970s, the securitizers of asset-
backed securities paid the rating agencies to rate the securities. In
short, like contemporary economists generally, the BIS team effectively reduced knowledge problems to incentives problems, and they
became preoccupied with whether the "issuer-pays" system of com-
pensating the rating agencies made for a conflict of interest. They
overlooked the possibility that even without a conflict of interest, the
rating agencies might be mistake-prone simply because they were
shielded from competition.[28]

Indeed, like virtually everyone else, the authors of the report
appear to have been *ignorant* of the fact that the agencies were
shielded from competition. Thus, they reached the naïve conclusion
that "the agencies appear to be sensitive to the value of their reputational capital for future business and to market sanctions that would
be associated with poor management of conflicts of interest" (BIS
2005, 25–26). Since in fact the agencies' "future business" was guaranteed by the various regulations outlined in Chapter 9, the agencies
would have had no reason to worry about their "reputational capital." But that is not where the real naïveté lies. For it is conceivable
that employees of the rating agencies were themselves ignorant of the
legal status of their "firms," and thus that they did their level best
to maintain their firms' reputations—just as if their firms' existence
depended on it, due to interfirm competition. Assuming that the
employees did try to preserve the agencies' reputational capital, however, the question they would have faced is How? What is the best
rating method? In answering that question cognitive errors may
occur, such as using historical data rather than judging the quality of
the underlying collateral (the mortgages). If there is no competition
to weed out rating agencies that make such errors, then the intention
of the employees to maintain the agencies' reputations is irrelevant.

On the other hand, once we set aside that cognitive question, then
even a rating firm that was highly incentivized to maintain its reputa-

tion (perhaps by potential competition from the other two members of the oligopoly)[29] would already have been using the "best practices" available, and no BIS research would have been needed to confirm it. The research makes sense only if the main question in the researchers' minds was whether the issuer-pays model might have led the rating agencies *knowingly* to use bad models. But the "market sanctions" in which the BIS team professed confidence do not penalize only deliberate errors of the sort that might be brought about by self-interest. Markets sanction any errors, regardless of the motive behind them—and regardless of whether they are not motivated at all, but are simply accidental—as long as there are competitive enterprises that can capitalize on these errors. Mark Adelson and Frank Raiter, the dissident employees at Moody's and S&P, disagreed with their superiors'—and the BIS researchers'—notions of best practice. They thought that the methods used by the rating agencies would lead to errors. But the regulations detailed in Chapter 9 precluded competition, by them or anyone else—which rendered "market sanctions" a moot point. In turn, the banking regulators, from the BIS team on down, seem to have been so thoroughly absorbed in the incentives-obsessed ideology of economists that they could see none of this.

The banking regulators' decision to encourage banks to invest in asset-backed securities that were highly rated by the NRSROs, like Summers's opposition to CDS regulation, reflected the best social science of the day. But even social science can be ideological: like libertarianism or Marxism, for example, economism can make otherwise unintelligible complexities appear to be orderly and legible by means of oversimplification. Like the claims of political ideologies, moreover, social-scientific theories are difficult to subject to controlled experimentation, which might otherwise check their oversimplifying tendencies. As Chapter 12 emphasizes, contemporary economic theories are rarely subjected to such tests. Without testing, however, social science may be worse than ideology, because it appears to be precisely the opposite of ideology.

Given the regulators' ideology, it will not do to blame the crisis on capitalism. If there was homogeneous thinking among capitalists about the accuracy of the rating agencies and the safety of securitization and credit-default swaps, the same thinking was shared by the regulators. This is not only why the latter failed to stop—or even anticipate—the crisis, but why their own actions inadvertently encouraged it. With that in mind, the participation of the bankers in the crisis is beside the point. We are not asking, after all, whether it is logically possible that imaginary bankers might have created a crisis like the one we just experienced if they had decided to do, en masse, when it so happens that a series of actual regulations gave them ample reason to do. It is logically possible, but that is not what happened in the real world. Judgments about "capitalism" and "regulation" are being made now by citizens, scholars, legislators, and regulators based on what they take to be the lessons taught by the actual financial crisis of 2008. But there is no reason to think that subprime securities (or mortgages) would have been issued in such volume, or that they would have been so highly concentrated in the hands of the banks, in the absence of the Basel rules. Indeed, what may have saved the world from complete economic chaos in 2008 was the fact that the regulations were loose enough that some bankers resisted buying the "safe" securities that most banks seem to have bought. Heterogeneous behavior like that, however, is allowed for, encouraged, and rewarded by capitalism; it is either discouraged or prohibited by regulation, depending on how tight the regulations are.

Regulation and Disagreement

There is no better emblem of the comparatively high epistemological burden on the regulators than the continued disagreement, years after the crisis began, over the value of those supposedly toxic assets. Until well after the housing market bottoms out, nobody will know the final default rate of subprime mortgages; nor the final value of mortgage-backed securities containing them; nor which banks made the wisest decisions; nor how unwise the other banks were. As of April 2009, seven months after triple-A PLMBS tranches had come to be seen as worth, at best, 40 percent of their face value (Figure 8.13), these tranches were, in fact, still paying off their investors, and in consequence, several banks vowed that they would not sell them to the government even at the subsidized prices that were to be offered under a new Treasury bailout plan (Dash 2009). A few experts (e.g.,

Stanton and Wallace 2008) had been saying all along that widespread estimates of the value of these assets were far too low, and that they were not "toxic" at all.[30]

Disagreement of this type is, of course, what occurs almost every time an asset is bought. The buyer thinks the asset will be worth more than the seller does.[31] If the difference of opinion is too great, there is no sale. It would be hubristic to predict in advance which side in such a dispute is correct. But that is exactly what the lead regulator—Treasury Secretary Timothy Geithner—had no choice but to do when confronted by the banks. At an early April 2009 "breakfast with a dozen or so corporate and banking executives in New York," he said that "many banks believe the investments and loans on their books are worth far more than they really are"—which is to say, far more than Geithner thought they were worth. In short, he disagreed with the bankers about the securities' correct valuations. But this disagreement, according to Geithner, was "unacceptable. The banks, he said, will have to sell these assets at prices investors are willing to pay, and so must be prepared to take further write-downs" (Dash 2009).

Geithner may have been right or he may have been wrong. He, too, is human. But as much as he may have recognized his fallibility, his role as regulator compelled him to act, in his confrontation with the banks, as if he were omniscient.

Systemic Risk in a Social Democracy

Systemic "contagions" with purely psychological causes are certainly conceivable under capitalism. But there is no evidence that the financial crisis was one of them, and there is plenty of evidence on the other side (Posner 2009, 82–92). The financial crisis instead seems to have been caused by the much more likely source of systemic failure: systemically imposed rules.

If the contributors to this volume are to be believed, what happened in 2008 was the culmination of a series of regulatory actions (and inactions) that, taken together, had the unintended effect of concentrating (what came to be seen as) especially risky investments in the financial sector. While bubble psychology may have been at work in the housing market, no contagion of "irrational exuberance"[32] infected "the" banks—not even the banks that put triple-A subprime securities in their portfolios. What actually seems to have happened was less sexy and more disturbing. The Basel rules interacted with the legal protection of the three rating firms by SEC regulations in unexpected ways—*as if* some "exuberance virus" had indeed been injected into the air ducts of (most of) the world's commercial banks.

These regulations were a few of the literally millions of rules that have been imposed under "social democracy"—a clumsy term to describe the status quo in all the developed capitalist countries.

The rationale of social democracy is to solve what the *demos* perceives to be important social problems, including economic problems. These solutions necessarily occur on a case-by-case basis as the mass media bring the problems to public attention. After a public outcry has been raised, the legislature redistributes wealth to solve the problem, or it creates the authority for specialist bureaucrats to solve the problem.[33] This case-by-case, problem-solving approach is universal in the West and, arguably, is the key difference between social democracy and communism.[34]

In the United States, the case-by-case approach was first articulated by the Progressives (Friedman 2007), although it had been practiced at the state, local, and occasionally federal level since the founding of the republic. It has always been considered the height of pragmatism. Yet if social democracy is to be truly pragmatic—if it is to solve social problems without creating new, worse ones—then the designer of a new problem-solving law or regulation needs (1) to be able to predict the unintended consequences of the new rule, considered in isolation; and (2) to be able to predict its unintended interactions with other rules. These requirements would fulfill the legislator-regulator's one systematic advantage: the motivation to preserve or improve the system as a whole.

Ideally, of course, the second requirement would mean predicting the new rule's unintended interactions with rules that have yet to be promulgated—rules that will be crafted as solutions to problems that have yet to arise. That being impossible, the most we can realistically hope for in the way of systemic regulation is that, when a new rule is being designed, possible interactions with previously enacted rules are fully considered. As time passes, however, that becomes increasingly difficult, as the number of rules that have been enacted rises.

Currently, after more than a hundred years of social democracy, a regulator cannot possibly know how a contemplated regulation might interact with previously enacted regulations, since no human being can master the contents of the Code of Federal Regulations, in which all permanent federal regulations are recorded. The Code contains more than 150,000 pages and grows by thousands of pages a year. A competent systemic regulator would also have to master the state, local, and international equivalents of the Code. Moreover, no human being, or group of human beings, has anything close to a detailed, accurate grasp of the workings of the modern societies that all those regulations are designed to improve. Thus, even if large numbers of researchers and computers set to the task of collating the hundreds of thousands of regulations that have already been issued, they would not be able, in advance, to correlate them with the problems they might cause. They would not know what to look for.

Consider, in this light, the regulatory contributions to the crisis listed at the end of Part I:

1. HUD directives, beginning in 1995, which spurred subprime and nonprime lending and securitization by the GSEs.
2. Regulations that had, starting in 1936, mandated minimum ratings for a growing number of investments.
3. The 1975 SEC decision to confer NRSRO status on the three extant rating firms.
4. The loose-money policies of the central banks.
5. "No-recourse" laws passed by different states over the years.

We should of course add, from Part II:

6. The Basel accords, as promulgated across the world in 1988, as amended in the United States in 2001, and as redesigned and implemented outside the United States in 2006–7.

How would one collate or categorize these regulations? Items 1 and 5 would seem to be "housing regulations," items 2 and 3 "securities regulations." Item 4 is "monetary policy," item 6, "banking regulation." There is no "natural" or obvious connection among these categories, but without understanding how they intersect categorially, and thus may interact causally, one cannot understand the greatest economic crisis in eight decades.

No matter how vast the resources of a super-systemic regulator, the main problem he or she would face—the main problem (other than mortality) that we all face—is a superabundance of information, which needs to be dramatically reduced and generalized if it is to be comprehensible. But simple categorization exercises like the one just conducted show that, while it is easy to organize information, it is well-nigh impossible to organize it in a manner that might contribute to effective systemic regulation. Categorizations reflect preconceptions and theories. But if regulators' preconceptions and theories were good enough, then they would never write bad regulations.

In 1936, when the regulations encompassed by item 2 began to be issued, they seemed to be more than reasonable injections of prudence into the "retirement system," for example, as exemplified by pension funds that were now required to invest only in high-grade bonds. Nobody could have predicted that "retirement" regulations might, thirty-nine years later, contribute to the perceived need for item 3. But by 1975, so much legal weight had been placed on bond ratings in different "areas" (categories) that it seemed imperative— and it was reasonable—to delineate who was qualified to issue them. Nobody in 1975 could have predicted the effects of conferring NRSRO status on a small, fixed universe of companies if, twenty-six years later, item 6 made those firms' ratings the basis of bank-capital regulations, because nobody could have predicted item 6.

With this last link in the chain, it is at least logically possible for someone at the Basel Committee on Banking Supervision, at the Federal Reserve, at the FDIC, at the OCC, or at the OTS to have looked backward, selected item 3 out of the vast sea of regulations that had been enacted during the late nineteenth and twentieth centuries, and recognize the danger of directing so much bank capital into securities that had merely won the approval of a legally protected oligopoly. But as a practical matter, we can hardly fault them for failing to notice the potential problem. Nobody else—not investors, not reporters, not scholars, not bankers—noticed the problem either.

The Shadow History of Systemic Failure

The problem-solving function is one of two foundational legitimating principles of modern government (the other being democracy itself). It is also the raw political basis for the success of any politician or party in a jurisdiction where vote buying has become a scandalous exception, and problem-solving promises have become the accepted political practice. The modern politician or party promises solutions to whatever problems seem pressing at a given time. There is usually no practicable way to attempt to keep this promise other than by authorizing bureaucrats to issue putatively effective regulations to fill in the details (the job being far too big for a legislature to handle). The regulators are compelled to rely on their understanding—their theory—of the cause of the problem they are trying to solve.

Thus, every regulation has its own shadow intellectual history, in which legal responses to perceived social problems have their parallels in arguments won or lost in "what is loosely called 'the history of ideas'" (Converse [1964] 2006, 66). Perhaps that is putting it too loosely, however, since the ideas with which we are concerned are not just the "broad or abstract contextual information about . . . society that educated people come to take for granted" (Converse [1964] 2006, 65); they are the particular views about society—the theories— that are accepted by the small subset of the educated population that, in a particular time and place, is charged with designing a regulatory response to a perceived social problem.

If these theories are mistaken or simply incomplete, the regulations to which they lead may produce unintended consequences that, later on, in principle, may be recognized as mistakes and rectified. But this does not seem to be the usual course of events, since regulations are rarely repealed. Whatever cultural or cognitive factors made the theory behind a mistaken regulation seem sensible in the first place make it likely that its unintended effects will not be recognized as such in the future, given a general continuity in human psychology and in the history of ideas. Other things being equal, then, subsequent social-democratic regulators will tend to assume that the problem with which they are grappling is a new excess of capitalism, rather than being an unintended consequence of an old mistake in the regulation of capitalism. Thus, instead of repealing the old regulation—of whose effects the regulators are, *ex hypothesi*, ignorant—they add a new one, creating fresh possibilities for the process to repeat itself.

Consider item 6. It is the latest version of capital minima that were adopted to protect against what would now be called the "moral hazard" of mandatory deposit insurance, which was instituted in 1933 in the United States. The theory was that, absent the threat of a run on the bank (which was effectively removed by deposit insurance), nothing but capital minima could keep bankers from making wild, speculative investments. This is still the leading view. On March 26, 2009, for instance, Treasury Secretary Geithner said that "stronger standards on bank leverage are needed 'to protect against the moral hazards presented by [deposit] insurance'" (Graham 2009). The original, economistic current in the history of ideas is still running strong.

In turn, deposit-insurance legislation was thought, in 1933, to be necessary to guard against banking panics such as those that had just swept through the United States. That theory may well have been wrong. "Historically it does not appear that panics are an inherent feature of banking generally" (Gorton 2008, 2). "The United States experienced panics in a period when they were a historical curiosity in other countries" (Bordo 1985, 73; cf. Selgin 1994). And this unfortunate case of American exceptionalism may, in turn, have been due to a series of earlier American regulations, dating back to the Civil War, that impeded bank-note issuance, branch banking, and nationwide "clearing houses" (Selgin 1988, 12–14; Dowd 1992; Schuler 1992; Gorton 2009n27).[35] Thus, at the onset of the Great Depression, while the United States underwent the greatest "contagious" banking panic in history, Canada experienced no panics or bank failures at all. Like the United States, Canada did not yet have deposit insurance; but Canada also lacked the American laws that inhibited flexible banking (Friedman and Schwartz 1963, 353ff.; Carlson and Mitchener 2006).

In this light, deposit insurance, hence capital minima, hence the Basel rules, might all have been mistakes founded on the New Deal public's, legislators', and regulators' ignorance of the fact that panics like the one that had just gripped America were the unintended effects of previous regulations. But having reached the conclusion that deposit insurance was needed to forestall bank panics that they thought were endemic to capitalism, the rule makers had little choice but to institute mandatory capital requirements to guard against the risky behavior in which they thought that bankers, now protected from bank runs, would be even more likely to engage. Three-quarters of a century later, with different versions of "bankers gone wild" constituting the mainstream narrative of the financial crisis, we will surely see new regulations that raise these minima higher and tighten their grip.[36]

Compare this account to the diagnosis of the crisis presented by the head of the FDIC, Sheila C. Bair, to the Financial Crisis Inquiry Commission in 2010. Among other regulatory failures, Bair (2010, 21) cited "the regulatory capital requirements for holding . . . rated instruments," which "were far lower than for directly holding these toxic loans" (21). This, Bair noted, was a result of the reduction by regulators "in 2001" of "capital requirements for highly rated securities" (29)—i.e., it was due to the Recourse Rule. Clearly, the regulators "were unable to understand and identify the risks" (28).

Bair does not, however, go on to conclude that capital minima are a fool's errand, in that they attempt to impose one a priori categorization of risks on the entire banking system, rather than letting different theories of risk, embodied in different banks, compete with each other. Indeed, she blames the crisis on the fact that "the market, abetted by the alchemy of rating-agency assisted securitization, did not prevent the growth of excessively easy access to credit and the resultant massive economic loss," for "markets are not always self-regulating and self-correcting" (Bair 2010, 23). She seems not to recognize that the regulations whose effects the regulators did not understand *structured* the markets. Certainly one might argue, against the position I took in section IV, that bankers should be blamed for succumbing to the immense profits offered them by the Recourse Rule if they leveraged into highly rated mortgage-backed securities. But in disputing the idea that markets are so "self-regulating and self-correcting" that whatever the regulators do doesn't matter, Bair is knocking down a straw man. Markets cannot correct for regulatory errors unless market participants are willing to break the law.

Perhaps, however, Bair means that omniscient agents, of the type modeled by economists, would have known what regulators did not: that it would be disastrous to invest in mortgage-backed securities during a housing bubble that was widely misperceived as a mere housing boom. Had they known that, then they would have resisted the lures of the Recourse Rule's 20 percent risk weight on AAA/AA PLMBSs. If bankers were omniscient, then what the regulators had done really wouldn't have mattered. Therefore, in Bair's economistic understanding of "markets," the crisis was a market failure *to undo the mistakes of the regulators*—yet future crises must be prevented by more of the same types of regulation whose effects the regulators did not understand in 2001, and whose effects markets did not magically reverse.

Bair is in an intellectual trap, but her way out of it—wishing for better regulation—follows the same path that has always been followed after regulatory failures. The only difference is that Bair is actually aware of the contribution of a regulatory failure: item 6.[37]

Systematic Systemic Regulation

Even though each regulation covers the whole system because each regulation is a law, the pragmatic, case-by-case proliferation of regulations accumulates piecemeal, and this may inhibit regulators from taking a properly systemic view. It may stop them from seeing how the different pieces fit together, or fail to fit together—and it may well stop them from knowing about the existence of the relevant pieces. It might therefore be better to start over and write a comprehensive set of regulations, which would better allow the regulators to address our second requirement for good regulation. That is a lesson one might draw from the second half of Chapter 2, which shows that deposit insurance and capital minima were just parts of a more comprehensive set of financial-industry reforms enacted in 1933 and 1934, among which were ceilings on the interest rates that banks could pay depositors. Perhaps, then, a more comprehensive regulatory overhaul, like the one in 1933–34, is needed every once in a while.

However, Chapter 2 also shows that in the 1970s a new development—money-market funds that paid higher interest rates than the ceilings set by the New Deal regulations—disturbed the overall structure of the New Deal financial reforms, eventually causing the system to fall apart. The difficulty of squaring comprehensive regulatory systems with new developments such as money-market funds underscores one of the problems in equating systemic stability with *systematic* regulation. A comprehensive reform in response to each new problem would either be impractical in upsetting all the arrangements and expectations that had grown up around the old system; or it would devolve into the piecemeal regulation that makes systemic effects hard to predict.

A second problem is the tension between the democratic and the regulatory aspects of social democracy if, as the history invoked by Chapter 2 suggests, any change—including one that arises from popular discontent—is liable to undermine the whole system of financial regulation. If money-market funds had not arisen, it is hard to imagine that depositors would have tolerated the low interest rates paid by their banks as inflation increased during the 1970s. They might then have demanded the very thing that eventually disrupted the finely tuned system that had been imposed in the 1930s. No politician would respond to such demands by insisting that his or her constituents suffer for the sake of the regulatory system. The relief of suffering, in the form of the solution to social problems, is the *raison d'être* of the regulatory system.

Of course, in this instance one might justly blame the Fed for letting high prices outstrip the interest rates paid to depositors (Samuelson 2008)—but that is only to say that the success of "financial regulation" is heavily dependent on "monetary policy." Perhaps a truly comprehensive set of regulations would cover the central bank, too. But the more types of policy that have to be coordinated into a single comprehensive framework, the greater the cognitive burden placed on the super-regulator, and on the super-legislator charged with designing the whole system—which brings us back to the overriding problem: the all-too-human ignorance that plagues everyone, in both the political and the economic realms.

Thus, the first half of Chapter 2 shows how even sweeping regulatory programs may be plagued by their designers' ignorance of unanticipated effects. A comprehensive package of equities-market reforms was also enacted during the New Deal, and the effect, Chapter 2 suggests, was not only to make mass equities investing possible—as intended—but to make responsible corporate governance, and thus systemically beneficial investing, much more difficult. This was obviously not what the designers of the regulations intended.

Mark-to-Market Accounting and Regulatory Dynamics

In the tradition of closing with a call for future research, there is a glaring need for historical scholarship on the "dialectics" of regulatory failure.[38] Among the types of dialectic that such research might uncover, the simplest would be where an initial regulation "fails" in the sense of producing an unintended negative consequence, leading—out of sheer ignorance of the fact that today's problem is the result of yesterday's regulatory failure—to the addition of a new regulation, which may, in turn, create new (real or perceived) problems that require still newer regulations (see Ikeda 1997). Perhaps the most relevant lesson of the crisis, though, is a different one: namely, that regulations designed to address different social problems may interact in unexpectedly disastrous ways, as did, arguably, items 3 and 6.

Another example might be the interaction of item 6 with rule 115 of the Financial Accounting Standards Board (FASB 115), which in 1993 imposed mark-to-market or "fair value" accounting on all American corporations—including commercial banks. This rule requires corporations to write off paper losses as if they were permanent, even when the losses are caused by what turn out to be temporary declines in the market price of an asset.

In conjunction with bank-capital minima, mark-to-market write-downs reduce banks' regulatory capital. Mark-to-market paper losses may have caused a $1 trillion contraction in U.S. lending capacity during the earliest phase of the crisis, from the summer of 2007 through the first quarter of 2008, when the market valuation of mortgage-backed securities had only begun to fall.[39] This may explain why banks contracted lending as soon as there were signs of a burst housing bubble (Figure 1.1) in the summer of 2007, even though it was likely that the government would bail out Fannie and Freddie (if it came to that), and unlikely that losses on private-label mortgage-backed securities would be so great as to seriously damage their senior tranches. Mark-to-market accounting mandates quarterly write-downs for commercial banks based on current market sentiment, and the rising cost of CDS insurance (Figure 8.13) in early 2007 shows that market sentiment had begun to turn sour. Since market prices for mortgage-backed bonds declined even more precipitously after the first quarter of 2008, there is good reason to think that mark-to-market writedowns for the rest of the year were even greater than $1 trillion, again reducing lending capacity by reducing regulatory capital levels. The translation of a banking panic into a worldwide recession may therefore stem from the conjunction of an accounting regulation and bank-capital regulations. The question has, however, attracted no research attention of which I am aware.

The task of researching such interactions illustrates the practical difficulties of minimizing the disasters to which such interactions might lead. Just as a major problem that regulators may face is their ignorance of the effects of their actions, especially in conjunction with past regulatory actions, the main problem scholars of regulation may face is that there are so many regulations, and so many historical circumstances explaining them—and so many theories about their effects—that inevitably the scholars will, here as everywhere, be compelled to overspecialize. The predictable cost is that most scholars will overlook interactions between the rules in which they specialize and the rules studied by specialists in a different subfield—even if they are deliberately attempting (like a supersystemic regulator) to see the big picture.

The problem of the regulator and the scholar—and of the citizen of a social democracy—is essentially the same: there is too much information. This is why modern societies seem "complex." And it creates the special kind of ignorance with which modern political actors, from citizens to regulators, are plagued: not the costliness (scarcity) of information, but its overabundance. This is a curse because, as a practical matter, it becomes impossible to pick out, from the blooming, buzzing profusion of data about previous political actions and their effects, precisely the things we would need to learn if we were to arrive at the theory that would allow us to avoid a political decision that might contribute to a systemic catastrophe.

PART I

The Crisis in Historical Perspective

Chapter 2

An Accident Waiting to Happen: Securities Regulation and Financial Deregulation

AMAR BHIDÉ

The specific missteps that triggered the current financial debacle have been extensively criticized. The easy-money policy of the Greenspan Federal Reserve after 2000, misaligned exchange rates that sustained large global financial imbalances, a housing bubble inflated by Fannie, Freddie, and subprime lenders, forays by insurance companies such as AIG into activities outside the purview of insurance regulators, AAA ratings bestowed by rating agencies on securitized debt obligations, and the comprehensive recklessness of the large banking houses have received their due reproach.

This chapter looks at some longstanding underpinnings of the crisis: factors that helped turn the recent lapses of bankers, rating agencies, and mortgage brokers into a crisis of extraordinary proportions and scope. Finance, I will argue, has been on the wrong trajectory for more than half a century. Its defects derive from academic theories and regulatory structures whose origins date from the 1930s, which encouraged financiers to rely on blind diversification as a substitute for due diligence and ongoing relationships.

As with any "structural" explanation, my analysis cannot tell us why problems unfolded in a particular manner. Yet without such an analysis we cannot understand basic defects in the foundation of our financial system.

The Effect of Make-Believe Models on the Real World

Until the 1930s economists had two views of uncertainty. Frank Knight, who dominated the University of Chicago economics department through the late 1940s, and John Maynard Keynes highlighted uncertainties that could not be reduced to quantifiable probabilities. On the other side, followers of the Reverend Thomas Bayes developed theories in which all uncertainties were quantified, like the odds of hitting a number on a roulette wheel. The two views didn't necessarily conflict: economists used whichever best suited their problem and approach. But the Bayesian view became dominant[1]—not because it was established that people can, do, or should always think probabilistically, but because this notion allowed economists to build seemingly scientific mathematical models that more or less drove the old "literary" or "narrative" style of analysis to the fringes of economics.

Further mathematical convenience was purchased by assuming that because everyone is omniscient, all individuals form identical probability estimates. Even though this assumption had no "microfoundations" (Elster 2009)—we have no reason to think that everyone would form the same estimates—and even though it led to what philosopher Jon Elster (2007) calls "science fiction" economics, it came to underpin basic theories of modern finance. The Capital Asset Pricing Model (CAPM), for instance, assumes that all investors place exactly the same value on all stocks. This is self-evidently false: without buyers who believed that IBM's shares were cheap and sellers who thought them dear, there would be virtually no trading of IBM stock.[2] Yet CAPM has "become the backbone of modern price theory of financial markets" (Lindbeck 1990).

Worse, when the assumption of identical probability estimates conquered the theoretical journals, it provided a springboard from which make-believe modeling could extend its sway over financial practice, too.

In the real world of old, faced with unquantifiable uncertainty, sensible investors, bankers, and borrowers made subjective judgments in the holistic manner of a common-law judge, considering all the relevant precedents and features of the case at hand, and anticipating the possibility of mistake and ignorance. Or, as John Kay (2009) puts it, they tried to construct a coherent narrative to guide their decisions. Too, their concerns about unforeseeable developments encouraged the development of ongoing relationships that facilitated the judgments necessary for mid-course changes. If all uncertainty can be reduced to probability distributions, however—and if (assumed) omniscience ensures that market prices always accurately reflect the risks—then case-by-case judgments and ongoing relationships are unnecessary. Returns are maximized for the least risk and negligible cost simply through diversification.

In 1974 Paul Samuelson, who had spearheaded the theoretical triumph of mathematical economics, issued investors a "Challenge to Judgment" in the first issue of the *Journal of Portfolio Management*. The world of "practical operators," Samuelson wrote, was giving way to a "new world of the academics with their mathematical stochastic [probabilistic] processes." The academics understood that valuing individual securities was a wasted effort. Ordinary investors should understand this too, Samuelson counseled. Eschew stock picking— just buy a diversified market portfolio and throw away the key.[3]

Of course, it is imprudent for investors to put all their eggs in one basket; and conversely, as formalized in the CAPM, the sum of many independent gambles may not involve great risk. Similarly the Samuelsonesque hypothesis that market prices are "efficient" provides a useful starting point for investors: hasty judgments that market prices are too high or low are unwise. But, except in an imaginary universe of known probability distributions, relying on diversification to substitute for due diligence and ongoing oversight is delusional. Backing twenty thieves or buying a basket of 500 inflated bubble stocks does not produce higher returns than going with a single Madoff or WorldCom.

Moreover, blind diversification involves free riding, so it can't work if it becomes widespread. Dispensing with the costs of active investment management seems astute—even high minded. But, like littering or not voting, it's unsustainable en masse: if everyone eschews judgment, who will make market prices even approximately right, or exclude from the diversified portfolio the offerings of thieves and promoters of worthless securities? Sensible investors, who are predisposed to believe that well-functioning markets price assets accurately, must at least make an ongoing effort to assess whether the other players are doing what it takes to keep the markets well functioning.

Nonetheless, the Samuelson prescription proved enormously influential. Reading "Challenge" inspired John Bogle to launch the first stock index fund in 1976, and by November 2000 it had become the largest mutual fund ever, with $100 billion in assets. Case-by-case investing didn't completely disappear, of course. Venture capitalists who invest in young, unlisted companies continue to use the "common-law," due-diligence approach and maintain close ongoing relationships with the companies in their portfolios. But this active style was progressively banished to the margins. The standard formula for institutional investors comprised a core holding of the Standard and Poor "500" stock index, with peripheral investments in venture-capital funds and other such "alternative" vehicles.

Free riding through blind diversification took off in the credit markets as well. Bruce Bent launched the first American money-market fund in 1970. Now nearly 2,000 funds manage about $3.8 trillion. Like stock-index funds, money-market funds eliminated the costs of case-by-case judgment and of maintaining ongoing relationships: they simply bought a diversified portfolio of short-term instruments certified as high quality by a rating agency—a certification that cost the money-market fund nothing. The traditional relationship model of bank lending, encumbered by the overhead of loan officers and committees, faced significant cost disadvantages.

The emergence of ingenious schemes to take advantage of money-market funds that depend entirely on free double- or triple-A certification by Standard and Poor's and Moody's (which themselves have come to rely on stochastic modeling processes rather than on costly shoe-leather due diligence) was also unsurprising. Losses on debt issued by Lehman Brothers broke Bent's pioneering reserve money-market fund in September 2008. The debt was, of course, rated AA or AAA; that is the law governing money-market funds. But not all highly rated securities homogeneously deserve high ratings.

How Regulation Encouraged Mass Equities Trading

The regulatory apparatus whose origins date back to the 1930s was designed to protect bank depositors and investors in publicly traded securities. It has also unwittingly undermined due diligence and ongoing relationships, but, as we will see, in quite different ways: protection of securities markets has become too strong and regulation of banking too weak.

Federal securities regulation involves a subtle tradeoff. It sustains the unparalleled liquidity and breadth of U.S. stock markets, but it also fosters antagonistic, arms-length relationships between shareholders and managers (Bhidé 1993, 1994a). The foundations of this regulatory system can be traced to the extensive losses suffered by the public during the Crash of 1929. Between September 1, 1929, and July 1, 1932, stocks listed on the New York Stock Exchange lost 83 percent of their total value, and half of the $50 billion in new securities that had been offered in the 1920s proved to be worthless. The losses were widespread: according to the SEC, the Crash followed a decade in which some 20 million shareholders "took advantage of the postwar prosperity and set out to make their 'killing' on the stock market," giving "little thought to the inherent dangers in unbridled market operation." Responding to "the outraged feelings of voters," Congress passed the Securities Act of 1933, and in 1934 its Securities Exchange Act created the SEC (SEC 1984, 7).

Prior to the early 1930s, the response to stock-market panics had been to let the victims bear the consequences of their greed and to prosecute frauds and cheats. The new legislation had a revolutionary preemptive orientation: it sought to protect investors *before* they incurred losses, in three ways.

First, to help investors make informed trading decisions, the acts required issuers of securities to provide information about directors, officers, underwriters, and large shareholders, and about the organization and financial condition of the corporation. Issuers were also required to file annual and quarterly reports, following rules prescribed by the SEC. Over the years, SEC efforts substantially increased the length and quantity of the reports companies had to file. For example, companies had to disclose management perks and overseas payments and provide replacement-cost and line-of-business accounting. The laws backed the disclosure rules by providing criminal penalties for making false or misleading statements and by empowering the SEC to suspend the registration of securities.

Second, to discourage insider trading, the laws required every officer, director, and 10-percent equity owner to report the securities they owned. Such insiders had to turn over short-term trading profits (from purchases and sales within any six-month period) to the company. The laws provided criminal sanctions for failure to report such transactions. The SEC has zealously prosecuted the insider-trading provisions of the law and helped send offenders to jail.

Third, the 1934 Securities Exchange Act sought to eliminate the "manipulation and sudden and unreasonable fluctuations of security prices." The law prohibited several practices, such as engaging in transactions to manipulate prices or to create an illusion of active trading, making material false and misleading statements, and spreading rumors about market rigging. Stock exchanges had to register with the SEC and help enforce compliance by exchange members with the securities acts. The SEC could deny registration to any exchange that failed to comply with its rules, and it rapidly used its powers to close nine exchanges. In the late 1930s, Chairman William O. Douglas virtually threatened the New York Stock Exchange with takeover if didn't reform.

Over the years, Congress also sought to protect investors by regulating the financial institutions that manage funds. For example, the Investment Company Act of 1940 set minimum levels of diversification for mutual funds and precluded them from holding more than 10 percent of a firm's stock. Complaints about the self-serving management and underfunding of corporate pension funds led Congress to pass the Employee Retirement Income Security Act of 1974 (ERISA). ERISA prohibited pension plans from holding more than 10 percent of the sponsor's own stock or 5 percent of any other firm's stock.

Wall Street's traders, who reflexively resist any form of regulation, in fact owe a great and unacknowledged debt to rules that protect the small shareholder, mutual-fund investor, and pension-fund beneficiary. The SEC reassures the speculators—whose trading is essential to maintain the liquidity of markets—by certifying the integrity of the exchanges. Casinos with reputations for rigged games eventually drive away patrons. Penalties for insider trading similarly undergird a liquid market in which many buyers bid for stocks offered by anonymous sellers. The fear of trading against better-informed insiders would otherwise lead buyers to demand access to the company's books and to investigate the motivation of the sellers. Do they know something bad about the business or do they just need money? Without insider-trading rules, stock trades, like used-car or real-estate transactions, would probably require protracted negotiation between known parties.

Disclosure rules similarly facilitate trading of the stock of companies that neither buyer nor seller has examined from the inside. The SEC's vigorous and well-publicized prosecutions of inaccurate or incomplete statements reassure traders that they can buy stocks without independent, time-consuming audits.

The laws that protect mutual-fund investors and pension-plan beneficiaries by enjoining broad diversification of portfolios also subtly contribute to market liquidity. The more investors diversify, the more fragmented the stockholding of any firm. And fragmented stockholding promotes liquidity by increasing the odds of a trade because someone needs the money or believes that a stock is mispriced.

The historical evidence suggests that, without regulation, stock markets would be marginal institutions. Financial markets in Europe and the United States developed around debt, not equity. "Prior to 1920," Jonathan Baskin (1988, 222) writes, "there were no large-scale markets in common stock. . . . Shares were viewed as akin to interests in partnerships and were simply conveniences for trading among business associates rather than instruments for public issues." Promoters of canals and railroads—the few businesses organized as joint-stock companies—restricted ownership to known investors whom they believed to be "both wealthy and committed to the enterprise." The public at large perceived equities as "unduly speculative," and "tales of the South Sea fiasco evoked instant horror" (216).

Public markets for high-quality *bonds*, however, can be traced

back to the 1600s. The first financial instrument to be actively traded
in Britain was the national debt, and in the United States, as well,
most publicly traded securities consisted of government issues until
1870. Later, railroad debt became popular, and, at the turn of the
century, preferred issues financed the great merger wave. It is noteworthy, too, that, unlike the public-equity markets, which would
evaporate for long periods following speculative bubbles, debt markets bounced back from serious crises.

The contribution of U.S. regulators to the growth in equities markets can also be inferred from the historic illiquidity of European
markets, where restraints on insider trading, disclosure requirements,
and manipulative practices were traditionally weak. In the Belgian
market, described in 1984 as "a sad, largely deserted place" (Bertoneche 1984), insider trading was considered unethical but not illegal.
Most other countries in Europe did not have statutes against insider
trading until the mid-1980s, when the European Community directed
member countries to adopt a minimum level of shareholder-protection
laws. U.S. occupation forces instituted laws against insider trading in
Japan after World War II, but officials exercised "benign neglect" of
the rules.[4] And indeed, as American-style securities regulation and
enforcement caught on in the rest of the world, the liquidity of stock
markets around the world also improved.

Mass Equities Markets and Out-of-Control Capitalism

Unfortunately, there is a catch to the rules that sustain stock-market
liquidity: they also drive a wedge between shareholders and managers.
Instead of yielding long-term shareholders who concentrate their
holdings in a few companies where they provide informed oversight
and counsel, we see diffused, arms-length stockholding. Pension- and
mutual-fund rules that require extensive diversification of holdings
similarly make relationships with a few managers unlikely. ERISA further discourages pension managers from sitting on boards, for if the
investment goes bad, Labor Department regulators may make them
prove they had expertise about the firm's operations. Concerned
about overly cozy relationships between unscrupulous fiduciaries and

company managers, the regulators have effectively barred all but the most distant relationships.

Similarly, the insider-trading rules place special restrictions on investors who hold more than 10 percent of a company's stock, serve on its board, or receive any confidential information about its strategies or performance, and require them to report their transactions, forfeit short-term gains, and try to avoid any hint of trading on inside information. But why should investors become insiders and be subject to these restrictions just so that everyone else can enjoy the benefits of a level trading field? They don't: institutional investors with fiduciary responsibilities usually refuse to receive any private information from managers. They may grumble about a firm's performance, but they will not sit on its board for fear of compromising the liquidity of their holdings. Institutions also make sure they stay below the 10 percent ownership limit that puts them under the purview of insider-trading restrictions. The rules thus make large investors resolute outsiders. In a free-for-all market, the same institutions would likely demand access to confidential information before they even considered investing.

Disclosure requirements also encourage arm's-length stockholding. For example, rules that mandate the disclosure of transactions with insiders make a firm's banks, suppliers, and customers less willing to hold large blocks of stock or serve on boards. Disclosure rules also make anonymous shareholding safe. If companies' reports were sketchy or unreliable, shareholders would likely demand an inside role and ongoing access to confidential information.

Market liquidity itself weakens incentives to play an inside role. All firms with more than one shareholder face a free-rider problem. The oversight and counsel provided by one shareholder benefits the others, with the result that all of them may shirk their responsibilities. This is particularly relevant if a company faces a crisis. In illiquid markets shareholders cannot run away easily and are forced to pull together to solve any problem that arises. But a liquid market allows investors to sell out quickly and cheaply. In economist Albert Hirschman's terms, investors prefer a cheap "exit" to an expensive "voice."

Diversification rules that cause institutions to fragment their portfolios and the stockholding of the firms in which they invest compound the free-riding problem. The chance that a 20 percent stockholder will expend resources for the benefit of the group is much greater than a 0.1 percent stockholder doing so.

Thanks to these extensive rules, transient outsiders now own a significant share of most publicly held stocks in the United States. The typical institutional investor's portfolio contains hundreds of stocks, each of which is held for less than a year. Institutional investors follow the so-called Wall Street rule: sell the stock if you are unhappy with management. In countries where American-style rules don't exist, aren't enforced, or have been adopted relatively recently, the situation is different. There we see large investors whose holdings are immobilized by special classes of stock, long-term financing, or other business relationships.

Richard Breeden, a former chairman of the SEC, claims that the "closed nature" of foreign governance systems "contradicts U.S. values of openness and accountability" and is "not appropriate to U.S. traditions." However, the historical evidence suggests that investor-protection rules, not deep-rooted traditions or values, have fostered the unusually fragmented and anonymous stockholding that we find in America today. Before the New Deal, investors who took an active inside role in governance played a major role in financing U.S. industry. Du Pont family money helped William Durant—and later Alfred P. Sloan—build General Motors. Investors represented by J. P. Morgan helped Theodore Vail build AT&T and enabled Charles Coffin to create the modern GE. These investors were in it for the long haul—the du Ponts fought Justice Department efforts to make them sell their GM stock—and they played an important oversight role. Pierre du Pont watched over the family investment in GM as chairman of its board; he reviewed "in a regular and formal fashion" the performance of all its senior executives and helped decide on their salaries and bonuses. Although he left the details of financial and operating policy to executives, du Pont "took part in the Finance Committee's critical decisions on important capital investments" (Chandler and Salisbury 1971, 573, 580).

Even today, investors in *private* companies continue the du Pont tradition. Partners in venture-capital firms, for instance, serve as active board members of their portfolio companies, help recruit and compensate key employees, work with suppliers and customers, and help develop strategy and tactics (Gorman and Sahlman 1989). The investment strategy of Berkshire Hathaway's Warren Buffett also suggests that Pierre du Pont's careful overseer approach conflicts more with U.S. regulations than with the traditions or values that Breeden invokes. Buffett isn't subject to the same regulatory pressures to diversify as the typical pension-fund manager; he and his long-term partner and vice-chairman Charlie Munger own well over half of Berkshire's stock. Berkshire seeks to "own large blocks of a few securities we have thought hard about," writes Buffett (1987, 83). Buffett serves as a director of the companies that constitute Berkshire's core holdings and will, in a crisis, intervene to protect his investments. For example, during the government bond-auction scandal at Salomon Brothers, he stepped in as chairman to help effect sweeping changes in management. Apparently, Buffett's large holdings of Berkshire stock (and the tax consequences of realizing gains) make him more willing than other institutional investors to submit to the liquidity-reducing rules that insiders face. His favored holding period is "forever. . . . Regardless of price, we have no interest at all in selling any good businesses that Berkshire Hathaway owns, and are very reluctant to sell sub-par businesses. . . . Gin rummy managerial behavior (discard your least promising business at each turn) is not our style" (52).

The absence of close, long-term manager-shareholder relationships that has become the norm in publicly traded companies in the U.S. has significantly impaired their governance. The basic nature of executive work calls for intimate relationships; anonymous masses of shareholders cannot provide good oversight or counsel and often evoke mistrust and hostility.

Managers are not like agents who execute specific tasks under the direction of their principals. Like doctors or lawyers in relationship to their patients or clients, they have a broad responsibility—a fiduciary one—to act in the best interests of stockholders. As with other fiduciaries, their performance cannot be assessed according to a mechanical formula. Shareholders, on the other hand, must weigh the outcomes they observe against their guesses about what would have happened if managers had followed other strategies. Losses do not necessarily establish managerial incompetence because the alternatives might have been worse. If concrete performance objectives are set, shareholders have to judge whether managers are playing games with the targets: for example, if they are meeting cash-flow goals by skimping on maintenance.

To make fair evaluations, therefore, shareholders must maintain a candid dialogue with managers. But a candid dialogue between managers and arm's-length shareholders is impossible. Practically speaking, diffused shareholders cannot have much contact with senior executives: in the typical public company, most retail shareholders have no idea who is running the company, and most institutional investors catch, at best, only an occasional glimpse of the CEO in a carefully staged road show or a presentation to analysts. Neither can managers share sensitive data with shareholders at large; indeed, managers must *conceal* strategic information from them. If a company wants to convince potential buyers that its new product is here to stay, its managers cannot reveal to stockholders that early sales have been disappointing. Managers are forced to be circumspect; they can't discuss critical strategic issues in public, and insider-trading rules discourage private communications. Almost inevitably, their dialogues with the investment community revolve around quarterly earnings-per-share estimates, even though both sides know well that those figures have little long-run significance.

How wholeheartedly managers will advance the interests of anonymous shareholders is also questionable. Basic honesty and concern for their own reputations, as well as fear of public censure, inhibit flagrant disloyalty and fraud; but the abuses that shareholders must worry about are often more subtle. CEOs who use corporate jets to fly their dogs around patently abuse shareholders. But having CEOs wait in airports for standby seats more subtly ill serves shareholders. Where and how do managers draw the line?

The identity and values of the particular people whose approval managers seek has a great influence on these choices. CEOs who want to impress other CEOs, and who have no contact with their shareholders, will find it easier to convince themselves that well-appointed corporate jets will make them more productive. Executives who know their stockholders and value their esteem will probably provide more careful stewardship. Similarly, shareholders are more likely to ascribe poor performance to managerial incompetence than to bad luck if their perceptions have been shaped by colorful reports in the press instead of personal relationships with a company's managers.

Unfortunately, thanks to the rules, American managers and shareholders now regard each other with suspicion. CEOs complain that investors are fixated on quarterly earnings and are ignorant of companies' markets, competitive positions, and strategies. Investors see many CEOs as entrenched, overpaid, and self-serving. As Peter Lynch, former manager of Fidelity's Magellan Fund, half-jokingly remarked, "I only buy businesses a fool could run, because sooner or later one will." Conversely, CEOs could well have asked how Lynch even remembered the names of the 1,000 or so stocks in which his fund invested.

The alienation of stockholders and managers makes public-equity markets an unreliable source of capital. Surprisingly, the exceptional liquidity of U.S. markets apparently does not compensate for the problems that come with issuing equity shares. Thus, American corporations are no different from the large public corporations of other major industrialized nations in issuing common stock to raise funds "only in the most exigent circumstances," and "the quantity of funds raised by new equity issues—especially by established firms—appears to be relatively insignificant" in all countries, regardless of the liquidity of their stock markets (Baskin 1988, 213). The stock market does, on occasion, allow firms in fashionable industries to issue stock at lofty prices. But such instances usually represent episodes of "market mania," which underwriters call "windows of opportunity." When the window closes, investors dump the stocks wholesale and don't give the category another chance for a long time.

On the downside of issuing shares, arm's-length stockholding subjects managers to confusing signals from the stock market. It isn't that Wall Street is short sighted—in fact, the market often values favored companies at astonishing multiples of their future earnings. But companies fall in and out of favor unpredictably: the market abruptly switches from a rosy long-term view of biotechnology to a fascination with Internet companies. Understandably so, for without inside knowledge of companies' strategy and performance, investors have little choice but to follow the crowd.

Managers, in turn, pursue strategies to protect "their" companies against apathetic or fickle investors. Uncertain about access to capital when the firm might need it, managers avoid paying out earnings to stockholders even when it does not. They reinvest profits, sometimes in marginal projects, and outside shareholders can do little about the situation.

In the 1960s, for example, managers of cash-rich companies in mature industries made acquisitions in businesses that were unrelated to their core capabilities. The result was many conglomerates of unmanageable size and diversity. As historian Alfred Chandler (1990) observes: "Before World War II, the corporate executives of large diversified international enterprises rarely managed more than 10 divisions. . . . By 1969, many companies were operating with 40 to 70 divisions, and a few had even more." Top management often had "little specific knowledge of or experience with the technological processes and markets of the divisions or subsidiaries they had acquired." In more recent periods, the managerial propensity to retain earnings has led to investment in businesses that should be shrunk. "In industry after industry with excess capacity," Michael Jensen (1993) writes, managers "leave the exit to others while they continue to invest," so that they will "have a chair when the music stops." Thus, the workings of a stock market that supposedly facilitates capital flows actually helps immobilize capital within companies.

Investor indifference and hostility are also reflected in operating inefficiencies. Apparently, many managers don't try very hard to please anonymous shareholders. Several studies have documented dramatic improvements in profit margins, cash flows, sales per employee, working capital, and inventories and receivables after leveraged buyout transactions that replaced diffused public stockholders with a few private investors.

What about the so-called "market for managerial control"? How can CEOs who provide poor stewardship survive the unsolicited tender offer, which supposedly represents "the most effective check on management autonomy ever devised" (Rappaport 1990)?

Actually, unsolicited tender offers comprise a tiny fraction of takeover activity. Most mergers are friendly affairs, negotiated by executives of established companies seeking well-managed, profitable targets for which they are willing to pay premium prices. The managerial club frowns on hostile offers. The few profit-motivated raiders serve as a check only against flagrant incompetence and abuse. This is because they operate under significant constraints. They have to raise money, much of it in the form of high-yield debt, deal by deal, making their case from publicly available data. Even at their peak, in the mid-1980s, raiders posed a threat only to a small number of targets: those diversified firms whose break-up values could be reliably determined from public data to be significantly higher than their market values. They could not and did not go after turnaround candidates any more than friendly acquirers do.

Outside shareholders, analysts, and takeover specialists cannot easily distinguish between a CEO's luck and ability. Again, Warren Buffett, because he was a director and major investor in Salomon Brothers, could much more easily assess the culpability of Salomon's CEO and the consequences of replacing him than outside shareholders could. Judgments of managers are necessarily subjective and require considerable confidential and contextual information.

By contrast, the case of IBM dramatizes the inadequacies of external scrutiny. Between the summers of 1987 and 1993, IBM stock lost more than 60 percent of its value while the overall market rose by about the same degree. The magnitude of IBM shareholders' losses was comparable to the GDP of several OECD countries. But while its stock price relentlessly declined, IBM management did not face the least threat of a hostile takeover or proxy fight. Outsiders had no way of knowing whether managers were struggling, as competently as they could, with problems beyond their control. Ultimately IBM fortunes turned—not because of a new strategy demanded or imposed by a raider, but because of the fortuitous appointment of Lou Gerstner as its CEO.

Banks and other financial service firms, it is important to note, are virtually immune to even the limited restraints imposed by hostile takeovers. As mentioned, raiders use high-yield debt (aka "junk") to finance their takeovers. But relying on a bank's "unused" debt capacity to take it over is difficult, because most banks are already very highly leveraged: they have just a small sliver of equity in their capital structures. The takeover of a financial institution also has to be approved by bank regulators, and they will not approve a transaction that involves loading on more debt. As a result, there is no recorded instance of a large U.S. financial institution that has been the target of a serious tender offer by a raider. Bank CEOs usually lose their jobs only when calamitous performance has forced their boards of directors into action.

Another noteworthy consequence of the reassurance provided by the rules (and academic theories) encouraging diversification has been the increase in what is euphemistically called market "breadth." Differently put, in the 1980s and 1990s, the ranks of publicly listed companies were swollen by businesses that simply didn't belong. After 1979 IPOs increased from about 140 to nearly 600 per year, a process that culminated in the Internet bubble, when companies with no profits and tiny revenues famously went public. But it wasn't just dot-coms. Investment banks such as Salomon Brothers, Morgan Stanley, and Goldman Sachs that had flourished as private partnerships also went public. After centuries of having to worry about their own capital, bankers were free to play "Heads we win, tails public stockholders lose." That became an important source of the recent crisis.

Making—and Then Breaking—the Banks

Defective regulation of the classic function of banks—deposit taking and lending—has done even greater harm to the financial system than the impairment of shareholder-manager relationships. Here the problem has been half-heartedness, not the overzealousness that has characterized the SEC.

The case for deposit insurance in conjunction with tough regulation of bank lending was and remains strong. There is a lot to be said for the enforcement of prudence by a steadfast regulator rather than by many fickle depositors. But thanks to the progressive weakening of the rules, the system has little depositor monitoring or regulatory oversight. The weakening of banking rules has undermined long-term relationships between borrowers and lenders and fostered an arms-length securitized credit system—just as the strengthening of securities laws has undermined close stockholder-manager relationships.

The classic structure of a bank, offering liquid demand deposits on one side and making illiquid loans on the other, has been a puzzle to economists: why staple these two functions together? Various ingenious rationales have been suggested for the existence of the organizational form (Rajan 2006, 325–26), but in reality the form is inherently fragile. While it can play a valuable economic role in channeling saving, it does tend to collapse without careful regulation. The "free-banking" era of the nineteenth century was inherently unstable. In good times, unfettered competition between banks encouraged a race to the bottom in lending. But at the slightest whiff of trouble, depositors (who knew that most of the bank's assets were illiquid) would rush to withdraw funds before someone else emptied the limited cash in the till that was held as reserves. The problem of retaining depositor confidence was especially acute in a rapidly industrializing economy. In small agrarian communities, depositors often personally know their bankers and can assess the prudence of their lending practices; with borrowing by large dispersed organizations, that's impossible.

The banking system was ultimately stabilized in the United States by New Deal rules that protected depositors from imprudent bankers—and bankers from jittery depositors. A cornerstone of the new rules, the Banking Act, established the Federal Deposit Insurance Corporation in 1933—the same year as the first Securities Act. Its provisions were controversial. According to an official FDIC history, opposition to the Banking Act "had earlier been voiced by the President, the Chairman of the Senate Banking Committee and the American Bankers Association" because "they believed a system of deposit insurance would be unduly expensive and would unfairly subsidize poorly managed banks." Public opinion was "squarely behind a federal depositor protection plan," however, after the failure of more than 9,000 banks between the stock market crash in October 1929 and March 1933, when President Roosevelt had declared a bank holiday (FDIC 1984, iii).

Unlike the preemptive approach to investor protection taken by the Securities Acts, the idea of deposit insurance wasn't revolutionary.

Starting in 1829, according to the FDIC (1984, 3), New York and then the thirteen other states had experimented with guaranteeing deposits, but the schemes "had proved unworkable" and all had ceased operations by the early 1930s. At the federal level, 150 proposals for deposit insurance had been made in Congress between 1886 and 1933, many prompted by the financial crises and bank runs that were a recurring feature of the time (3).

Nor was the notion of regulating banking practices novel. In the early 1800s, state legislators required banks to submit financial reports that were used to monitor banks' compliance with their charters. New York's 1829 Safety Fund established both a system for regular bank examination and the first system of deposit insurance. Because New York banks had to pay for the insurance, they had a stake in limiting losses by means of good supervision. But later, as the state insurance schemes ended, so did their supervisory complements. States did, however, create systems of bank supervision that were not tied to deposit insurance, and by 1914 every state was conducting regular bank examinations. Federal supervision of banks started with the National Currency Act of 1863, which authorized national banks and created the Office of the Comptroller of the Currency (OCC) to supervise them. Legislation creating the Federal Reserve System in 1913 created a second federal agency with the right to examine banks that were members of the system. The Federal Reserve was more concerned with its role as central banker, though, and did not exercise these powers until the 1930s.

But although deposit insurance and bank supervision were not new, the ambition and scope of the 1933 and 1935 banking acts were unprecedented. Besides establishing a national system of deposit insurance, the 1933 so-called Glass-Steagall Act ordered the separation of investment from commercial banking. In order to "forestall ruinous competition among banks," it outlawed payment of interest on demand deposits, and it authorized the Federal Reserve Board to set ceilings on time-deposit rates. The 1935 Banking Act expanded the FDIC's supervisory powers, set more rigorous standards for deposit insurance, and extended deposit-rate controls to banks that had been exempted in the 1933 Act.

Out of the large and inevitably uneven menu of New Deal initiatives, the banking legislation was arguably the most effective. The rate of bank failure "dropped precipitously" (FDIC 1984, iii); in 1934, only nine insured banks failed. Improvement in economic conditions also helped stabilize banks: unemployment fell sharply after 1933, and real GDP expanded at an annual rate of 9.5 percent from 1933 to 1937. Banks faced another test in the second leg of the Depression, in 1937–38, but came through without difficulty. During World War II, when business activity was vigorous and banks financed the federal government's war effort, loan losses and deposit outflows were negligible. Only twenty-eight insured banks failed during the war years (ibid.).

Banks were well positioned to finance the "spending spree" that occurred after the war. Some questioned whether banks would resume their traditional lending instead of buying the government's war bonds, but "these concerns proved groundless" (FDIC 1984, 6). Bank lending increased by nearly two and a half-fold in the 1950s, growing at an annualized rate of over 9 percent a year. Apparently, satisfying bank examiners rather than jittery depositors was liberating. Yet there were very few bank failures: only five banks failed in 1955, the high-water mark of the 1950s. In fact, the low failure rate concerned some. In a 1963 speech, Wright Patman, the Chairman of the House Banking Committee, came out in favor of more bank failures. "The record of the last several years of almost no bank failures and, finally last year, no bank failure at all," said Patman, "is to me a danger signal that we have gone too far in the direction of bank safety" (FDIC 1984, 7). In fact, however, the proportion of bad loans had increased. The ratio of loan losses to total loans grew from .16 percent in 1950 to .25 percent in 1960. But even the higher ratios did not jeopardize the solvency of the banking system.

The Beginnings of Deregulation

In the 1960s, according to the FDIC's history (1984, 7), banks started to change. A new generation of bankers who hadn't experienced the Depression "abandoned the traditional conservatism that had characterized the industry" and "began to strive for more rapid growth in assets, deposits and income." Large banks led the trend toward "aggressiveness and risk taking" and "began pressing at the boundaries of allowable activities," expanding into fields involving "more than the traditional degree of risk for commercial banks." Depression-era rules to limit "ruinous" competition were also relaxed: states liberalized branching laws and bank holding companies were created as vehicles for multi-office banking and for entering new product markets. Banks did face some new rules, but these were intended to improve consumer protection and securities disclosure rather than prudence. Nonetheless, banks weren't "noticeably harmed" by increased risk-taking in the 1960s. Loan-loss ratios did not grow in spite of another two and a half-fold increase in lending because, according to the FDIC, "favorable economic conditions" allowed "marginal borrowers to meet their obligations. With the exception of relatively mild recessions, the economy produced high levels of production, employment and income during most of the period."

Loan losses and bank failures jumped in the 1970s. The ratio of loan losses to total loans had never exceeded .27 percent in the 1950s and 1960s. In the 1970s the ratio never fell below .33 percent, and in 1975 and 1976 the ratio exceeded .65 percent. The frequency of bank failures likewise increased, as did the size of the failing banks.

The greater severity of economic downturns was an important reason for higher loan losses and bank failures in the 1970s. The increased risk-taking that hadn't hurt banks in the more forgiving climate of the 1960s now resulted in more defaults. Large banks and banks with large real-estate exposures were particularly hard hit. Banks were also squeezed between new competition from "securitized" credit and unprecedented inflation. Money-market funds, the first of which was launched in 1970, attracted deposits away from banks and purchased short-term instruments that substituted for bank loans. Because these funds didn't incur the costs of due diligence or maintaining loan-officer relationships, they had a natural advantage in attracting deposits from banks because they could pay higher rates. Recall that, thanks to the Banking Acts' efforts to control "ruinous" competition, regulators had imposed ceilings on the rates that banks could pay.

As non-banking entities, money-market funds enjoyed other subtle advantages. They didn't have to pay the FDIC for deposit insurance or maintain non-interest-bearing reserves to cover losses or unexpected withdrawals. They weren't subject to regular examination by multiple regulators. And they didn't have to comply with consumer-protection rules, or demonstrate their contribution to the local community. True, they couldn't offer deposit insurance, but they did carry a regulatory imprimatur: they were supervised by the SEC under the 1940 Investment Company Act. Apparently this was good enough for many depositors, either because they couldn't understand the difference between FDIC insurance and SEC regulation, or because they astutely realized that whatever the legal differences, the government would make them whole if disaster struck.

Inflation amplified the funds' advantages. In 1971, the United States went off the gold standard and adopted a regime of floating exchange rates. In 1973, Arab states placed an embargo on oil exports to the United States and other Western countries in response to their support of Israel in the Yom Kippur War—and possibly to try to recoup the losses they had suffered from the reduced value of a freely floating dollar. Oil prices rose substantially, from $3 a barrel to $12, triggering first a recession and then, after significant monetary easing by central banks, high inflation. High inflation, in turn, encouraged the flow of funds from banks to money-market funds, because depositors earning low nominal rates of interest in banks faced a loss in the real value of their savings. At the same time, banks couldn't get rid of their thirty-year mortgages and other loans that had been made at rates below the new rate of inflation. Even if the borrowers were sound, therefore, these loans were effectively "underwater."

The banking problems of the 1970s, like those of the early 1930s, elicited a vigorous legislative and regulatory response. Congress passed five relevant laws between 1980 and 1991[5] and considered significant bills in nearly every session. Regulatory change was equally extensive. Federal banking agencies proposed and implemented new changes under the new laws as well under the authority of old statutes (FDIC 1997, 87). But there was a basic philosophical difference between the New Deal rules and those adopted during and after the

1970s. The 1933 and 1935 Acts sought to limit competition and other stimulants and opportunities for imprudent lending. The reformers of the Carter administration—and their allies in Congress—believed in the curative and prophylactic benefits of deregulation and market mechanisms in several fields, including trucking, commercial aviation, and finance. The same approach was even more vigorously pursued by the Reagan administration and continued during the Bush I, Clinton, and Bush II presidencies.

In the new orthodoxy, banks weren't the victims of predation by free-riding money-market funds. Rather, banks had "earned monopsony profits by being able to acquire deposit funds at below-market rates," while money-market funds were "market innovations" that helped undercut these excess profits and paid depositors attractive rates (Berger, Kashyap, and Scalise 1995, 61). What was needed was even more competition for depositor funds. Similarly, commercial paper and other such securitized forms of debt, such as the "junk bonds" pioneered by Drexel Burnham Lambert's Michael Milken in the late 1970s, were thought to offer better risk-bearing than the loans they replaced. While a bank would bear the entire risk of a loan it made to a company, the risks of commercial paper issued by the company could be widely distributed across many purchasers. And by facilitating the diversification of credit risks, securitization reduced borrowing costs. The policy implication was that rather than shield banks from securitization, the rules should be changed to allow banks to participate in the revolution by scrapping provisions of the 1933 Banking Act that separated commercial and investment banking.

To the degree that banks couldn't securitize and sell off all their assets, fans of new finance advocated more diversification of their activities and better use of innovative risk-management technologies and markets. For instance, it was argued that banks could have mitigated the 1970s problem of holding fixed-rate mortgages when interest rates were rising if they had been more diversified and had used interest-rate futures (which had then just started trading in Chicago) to hedge their risks. Again, the solution was allowing banks to enter new lines of business more freely, and easing regulatory constraints on the development of new risk-management tools and markets.

The first major legislation of the 1980s, the Depository Institutions Deregulation and Monetary Control Act (DIDMCA), was signed into law by President Carter on March 31, 1980. The DIDMCA allowed banks to start offering competitive rates on checking accounts and mandated that all other interest-rate limits (administered through "regulation Q" ceilings) be eliminated by March 1986. The Depository Institutions Act (known as the Garn-St. Germain Act), enacted in 1982, allowed banks to offer accounts that, like money-market funds, had no reserve requirements or restrictions on rates. Garn-St. Germain also eliminated statutory restrictions on real-estate lending by national banks that had imposed maximum loan-to-value ratios and required repayment of the principal within thirty years for many kinds of loans. Instead, the 1982 Act delegated the authority to set such rules to the OCC. In response, the OCC proposed a regulation that imposed no limitations on real-estate loans, because it believed limits had hampered banks' ability to respond to changes in real-estate markets, and believed also that decisions about lending policies were the responsibility of bank management.

A controversial proposal to grant commercial banks new powers to underwrite securities and deal in mutual funds, and thus repeal important provisions of the Glass-Steagall Act's separation of commercial and investment banking, didn't make it into the final version of Garn-St. Germain. The Reagan administration was strongly in favor, as was Jake Garn, who had just become chairman of the Senate Banking Committee. In fact, Senator Garn made the expansion of banks' powers a priority of his chairmanship. But the securities and insurance industries lobbied against legislation that would allow banks to enter their businesses. And some influential voices in Congress, notably senators John Heinz and William Proxmire and representatives Fernand St. Germain and John Dingell, argued that expanded banking powers would inject too much risk into the system.

No effort was made to dilute the deposit-insurance provisions of Glass-Steagall. The 1933 legislation limited insurance coverage to $2,500 for each depositor. The coverage limit was then raised to $5,000, effective June 30, 1934. Subsequent increases, to $10,000 in 1950, $15,000 in 1966, $20,000 in 1969, and $40,000 in 1974, usually reflected changes in price levels. As a practical matter, though, there was no limit, because of the way the FDIC handled bank failures. Rather than close down a failed bank and pay off depositors up to the limit of their insurance, the FDIC facilitated its merger with a healthy bank, which would pay off the failed bank's deposits. The de facto unlimited coverage concerned the FDIC (and others), who believed that it discouraged large depositors from scrutinizing the lending practices of their banks, and thus deprived regulators and small depositors (who were presumably entitled to a free ride) of an additional level of monitoring. One of the goals of deregulators in the early 1980s was to increase the level of monitoring by depositors (which was regarded as "market based") and thus reduce the role of regulators. Yet in spite of concerns about depositor complacency, the 1982 Garn-St. Germain Act more than doubled the insurance limit, from $40,000 to $100,000. The chairman of the FDIC had testified that an inflation adjustment could justify an increase to $60,000, and the initial proposal in the Senate bill was for an increase to $50,000. This was increased to $100,000 at a late-night House-Senate Conference. The beleaguered savings and loan industry had lobbied for the increase in the hope that it would help attract and keep large deposits that would otherwise go into money-market funds (FDIC 1997, 93).

The assurance provided by high de jure and de facto deposit-insurance limits also likely had the unintended consequence of facilitating the use by banks of new markets and instruments. This had both good and bad consequences. With more stringent depositor discipline, it is unlikely that banks could have used the futures markets that emerged in the 1970s to hedge the risks of making long-term loans with short-term deposits. Without generous insurance limits most depositors, even sophisticated ones, would likely have shunned banks that traded futures. Paltry passbook rates simply wouldn't compensate for the risks. Later depositor complacency also allowed banks to take their chances with much racier and more opaque derivatives.

After 1982, the main objective of proponents of deregulation was to "repeal Glass-Steagall and expand the powers of banks." But a thrift and banking crisis intervened and none of the subsequent bills enacted in the 1980s had significant deregulatory provisions. "Deregulation remained an undercurrent" in Congress, however, and some skeptics were converted to the cause. In 1988 for instance, Senator Proxmire promoted legislation that would undo some of the limitations on banking powers (FDIC 1997, 88). Federal regulatory agencies—the OCC, the FDIC, and the Federal Reserve Board—increasingly interpreted existing statutes to grant banks under their jurisdiction entry into new areas. During the early 1980s, national banks were authorized to offer discount-brokerage and investment-management services, operate futures brokerages, and underwrite credit life insurance. A 1990 article in *Banking Law Journal* argued that, for all practical purposes, most Glass-Steagall restrictions on bank powers had been repealed by "regulatory and judicial reinterpretation" (Kaufman and Mote 1990).

State legislators and banking authorities also contributed to the deregulation movement. State chartered non-member banks (those that didn't belong to the Federal Reserve System) had always been exempt from Glass-Steagall. In the 1980s, states increasingly allowed state-chartered banks to enter into securities, insurance, and real-estate activities not permitted by federal statutes. By the end of the decade, 29 states had given state-chartered banks at least some power to underwrite securities, and all but seven states allowed banks to engage in securities brokerage. Half the states permitted some form of real-estate development, and six allowed insurance underwriting beyond credit life insurance.

A 1995 Brookings Institution paper described the "transformation" of U.S. banking over the previous fifteen years—which the authors attributed mainly to regulatory changes such as the deregulation of deposit accounts and the expansion of bank powers, which led to a "tremendous explosion" in the number of products, such as derivatives, that banks could hold and offer. In this transformation, U.S. commercial banks lost about a third of their share of total credit-market debt from 1979 to 1984; apparently, in spite of the deregulation of interest rates, the process of "disintermediation" by non-bank competitors and the replacement of bank loans by securitized debt that had started in the 1970s did not abate.

As the share (and profitability) of traditional lending declined, banks significantly increased their derivatives activity. Megabanks were at the forefront: in 1983, the notional value of their derivatives positions amounted to 82.3 percent of the value of their assets, whereas in 1994 they amounted to more than eleven times the value of their assets. Correspondingly, "other non-interest income," such as fees earned from issuing counterparty guarantees and derivative instruments earned by megabanks, increased from 7.0 percent of operating income in 1979 to 20.9 percent in 1994 (Berger, Kashyap, and Scalise 1995, 68).

The second half of the 1990s and the first few years of the new century, which spanned the Democratic Bill Clinton and Republican George W. Bush administrations, saw much more of the same. New forms of multilayered debt securitization took off. The early forms of debt securities had been issued by large businesses as a substitute for bank credit, and thus had helped disintermediate the banking system. For instance, General Motors would issue commercial paper directly to investors instead of securing a short-term loan from its bank. Later, securitized debt was issued not by the ultimate users of the funds but rather by intermediaries who used the proceeds to extend credit. The origins of these so-called intermediated "asset-backed securities" (ABSs) go back to the 1970s, when federally sponsored agencies such as Fannie Mae and Freddie Mac pooled residential mortgages and sold interests in these pools to investors (using the proceeds to make more mortgage loans). Eventually other kinds of financial assets were pooled into ABSs. By the late 1980s, ABSs had become a viable means for commercial banks and other private lenders to package and sell off other kinds of debts such as car loans, credit-card balances, mortgages on commercial properties, and lease receivables. By 2002, privately issued ABSs accounted for about a quarter of the entire corporate-bond market. ABS issuers also became dominant issuers of short-term paper: in 2002, securitized pools of loans represented nearly half of commercial paper outstanding. Other kinds of short-term paper issued by financial institutions had also grown, so that in 2002 the share of commercial paper accounted for by industrial companies (and other nonfinancial entities) had fallen to a fifth of the total.

The widening range of ABSs involved a progressive increase in the riskiness of the assets that backed the securities and an increase in the number of layers between the ultimate users and investors. In the

1980s ABSs mainly comprised packages of low-risk loans issued by "brand-name" intermediaries with high credit ratings. The creditworthiness of an ABS was also typically "enhanced" by guarantees, provided by banks or insurance companies, that they would pay for some or all of the losses arising from the default of the loans. Later, new techniques involving complex structures were used to securitize increasingly high-risk loans. For instance, the loans might be placed in a "special-purpose vehicle," which would then issue multiple classes of securities with different levels of risk and return. The top level, for instance, would have first claim on the cash flows generated by the loans, enabling that security to get a high credit rating from the rating agencies. Interest rates paid to investors in this secure, "senior," or "super-senior" tier were accordingly low. The cash flows left over for the lower levels were of course riskier, had low credit ratings, and paid higher interest rates. Famously, this sort of slicing and dicing enabled supposedly rock-solid AAA securities to be extracted from highly risky subprime mortgages.

The new kinds of securities, which were then often packaged and repackaged, also spawned new derivative contracts that could be used to hedge them—and, to an even greater degree, to take speculative side bets on the prices of the securities. The now-notorious credit-default swaps (CDSs), for instance, were sold as insurance (by companies like AIG) against events such as missed payments or credit downgrades. Often the insurance purchased amounted to ten or more times the value of the underlying security, suggesting that most of the purchasers were buying CDS contracts just to bet on bad things happening to the security.

Speculative side-bets typically dominate hedging transactions in traditional agricultural and interest-rate futures markets. In fact, the frenetic buying and selling of futures by day traders is necessary to provide liquidity to these markets, and contracts that fail to attract day traders are dropped from the exchanges, whatever their value might be as hedging instruments. Examples of contracts that failed to survive because they could not attract the necessary volume of day trading (in spite of considerable promotion by the exchanges) are the Consumer Price Index contract (championed by Milton Friedman), contracts on a corporate-bond index, and contracts on an index of municipal bonds. And hedgers have to cope somehow with the mismatch between the popular contracts that survive and their own positions. For instance, those who use futures to hedge the risks of their bond holdings have to live with the fact that the prices of their specific issues may not correlate perfectly with the limited menu of futures traded on the exchange.

Thanks to lobbying by their promoters, CDSs and other such derivative products escaped regulation by the Commodities Futures Trading Commission,[6] and instead were traded in the unregulated "over-the-counter" (OTC) market. One obvious result was the absence of the daily settling up of gains and losses through an exchange. In OTC markets, buyers and sellers settle up with each other according to the terms of their bilateral agreements. This can create counterparty risks: if the bilateral agreements are not well drafted or diligently adhered to, one or the other party may not be able to collect what it is owed by a trading partner who goes bust. The OTC market also provided a home for a much larger number of contracts than could the commodities exchanges. The large number meant that speculators and hedgers could find instruments that more precisely fit their preferences. With exchange-traded contracts, participants have to adapt to whatever contract best suits their needs from a relatively small menu. For instance, a speculator or hedger who would like to trade a thirty-year U.S. government bond may have to make do with a futures contract that is actually best linked to a bond with a twenty-year maturity.

At the same time, the dispersion of whatever interest day traders might have had in OTC derivatives meant that the liquidity in any one type of them was low. Direct transactions between buyers and sellers rather than through an exchange also contributed to illiquidity and settling-up problems in the following way: in exchange-traded contracts, anyone who can post the necessary margin can buy or sell. Direct trading in CDSs limited the players to a relatively small number of professionals; within this circle, anyone who could pay the premiums could buy insurance on the default of a security, but not everyone had the credibility to sell insurance. This asymmetry further limited active trading. The absence of a deep secondary (or "resale") market did not seem to hold back buying derivatives in huge volumes, however: credit-default swaps were reportedly invented in 1997. Ten years later CDSs outstanding had grown to about $62 trillion.[7]

Large commercial banks and bank holding companies played an important role in the growth of the ABS and derivative markets ever since they first packaged and sold off their auto and consumer loans. Regulatory reinterpretations and new laws continued to expand the role banks could play in such nontraditional activities thereafter. In 1996, for instance, the OCC reinterpreted its "incidental" powers, granted under the National Banking Act of 1864, to permit operating subsidiaries of national banks to underwrite municipal revenue bonds, corporate bonds, and even equity securities. The OCC also decided that some products, like annuities, were banking rather than insurance products and could thus be sold by banks. The November 1999 enactment of the Gramm-Leach-Bliley Act (GLBA) formally repealed the long-eroded Glass-Steagall prohibitions on the mixing of banking with securities or insurance businesses. GLBA, for instance, permitted the creation of a new kind of holding company: one that could own, as subsidiaries, banks and other entities that could engage in a variety of financial activities (including underwriting and dealing in securities; sponsoring and distributing mutual funds; insurance underwriting and agency activities; and merchant banking) that banks or their subsidiaries might be otherwise forbidden from performing.

Megabanks and their holding companies, like Citigroup and J. P. Morgan, were at the forefront of taking advantage of deregulation. CDSs, in fact, were invented by a J. P. Morgan team, not by a traditional investment-banking firm. The ratio of non-interest income to banks' total operating income continued to rise at the same rapid rate in the ten years after 1994 as it had in the previous decade, thanks to the continued rapid growth of activities such as securitization and trading. As before, the largest banks took the lion's share: the top five banks accounted for more than 80 percent of total trading revenues earned by all commercial banks in 2001 and nearly two-thirds of all securitization income.

The profits of the commercial banking sector as a whole rebounded strongly in the second half of the 1990s, as it recovered from problems it had faced in the early 1990s because of falling real-estate prices and a recession. Commercial banks' share of finance and insurance-industry profits, however, fell as investment banks' share rose. As a 2004 FDIC research paper (Samolyk 2004, 54) observed, in the 1990s, while banks were "returning to record-setting earnings," investment banks and other financial-service providers were regaining their even higher prior earnings levels. But in the early 2000s, as banks continued their expansion into nontraditional domains such as securitization and the trading of derivatives, the growth in their profits "outpaced that of other financial sectors."

The profits from securitization and derivatives, however, came with much higher risks, although the subtle nature of these risks may have caused banks and their regulators to ignore them. For instance, banks were more willing to offer "subprime" mortgages to borrowers who would not qualify for regular mortgages, because these mortgages could be packaged and sold instead of being held to maturity. Although banks wouldn't receive interest payments, they would earn underwriting fees for originating subprime mortgages, and possibly ongoing fees for servicing them—without taking the risk that the borrower would default. Involvement in securitization posed several other kinds of risks, however. Banks would sometimes provide "credit enhancements" to ABSs, which created exposure to defaults. There was also the risk of financing warehouses of loans awaiting securitization. Loans that went into ABSs could not be securitized as soon as they were made, and besides carrying their own loans, banks sometimes extended credit against the inventory of other originators. In principle, these were well-secured short-term credits. But as banks were to discover in the financial crisis, when the ABS market seized up, they could find themselves locked into warehouses containing large quantities of low-credit loans.

In complex, sliced-and-diced ABSs, banks would often have to keep the thinner but most risky slices in order to encourage others to buy the thicker, less risky ones (as Rajan 2006 emphasized). And even as banks sold off to investors low-risk slices of packages of loans they had originated, they would often turn around and buy slices of someone else's packages. Thus, banks were simply swapping the credit risks of the loans they had originated for the credit risks embedded in an ABS.

New derivatives such as CDSs created opportunities to speculate with virtually unlimited leverage and could thus generate huge profits or losses. Yet, as we have seen, with a large number of derivatives traded over the counter (instead of the small number that typically survive the Darwinian selection of trading on an exchange), liquidity was low. Low liquidity made highly leveraged trading especially risky. For instance, speculators could—and often did—purchase default insurance amounting to many times the total issuance of a security. But in the absence of a liquid market, they could not easily reverse the trade. Risk management was also challenging. In a liquid market, positions can be accurately "marked to market" by the minute. With illiquid derivatives, however, traders could hide losses by asserting, like the Red Queen, that the value of their positions was whatever they said it was. Unreliable prices also made end-of-the day settling-up of gains and losses more difficult and exacerbated the counterparty risks that are an unavoidable feature of OTC trading. Banks were therefore exposed not only to their own trading mistakes but also to the missteps of their trading partners: if a hedge fund (such as Long-Term Capital Management) or an investment bank (such as Bear Stearns) couldn't honor its trading obligations, commercial banks would often be left holding the bag.

The Interaction of Equities Regulation and Banking Deregulation

Here, at last, the tight regulation of equities markets, leading to diffuse, hands-off monitoring of corporate management, comes together with financial deregulation: commercial bank CEOs weren't concerned about the escalation of risks. Freed of stockholder restraints (thanks to the Securities Acts) and depositor restraints (thanks to the Banking Acts), banks became sprawling, too-complex-to-manage enterprises whose balance sheets and trading books were but wishful guesses. Moreover, turning a blind eye to reckless bets wasn't a bad policy for executives with limited personal downside (Bhidé 2008).

American industry—businesses in the real U.S. economy—had long ago learned hard lessons in the virtues of focus. In the 1960s, the prevailing wisdom had favored growth through diversification. Many benefits were cited. Besides synergistic cost reductions offered by sharing resources in functions such as manufacturing and marketing, executives of large diversified corporations allegedly could allocate capital more wisely than could external markets. In fact, the synergies often turned out to be illusory and corporate executives out of touch. (Super-allocators like Jack Welch and Warren Buffett were exceptions.) The weaknesses of diversification were sharply exposed by the recession of the early 1980s and by Japanese competition. Later in the decade, raiders used junk bonds to acquire conglomerates at deservedly depressed prices and sold off their components at a handsome profit.

Banks missed the 1960s conglomeration party. Prohibitions on interstate banking and the separation of investment and commercial banking severely limited diversification in the financial industry. But as the rules were dismantled, financial institutions plunged right in.

The early results weren't promising. Efforts to sell stocks and socks at Sears went nowhere, as did the Prudential Insurance Company's foray into the brokerage business and Morgan Stanley's venture into credit cards. But the forces that had curbed diversification in the industrial sector did not restrain financial institutions. Low-cost Japanese competitors did not show up inefficiencies; and in many financial businesses, the driver of long-run profits lies in the prudent management of risks and returns, not in cost control. Raiders couldn't use junk bonds to dismantle conglomerates: financial institutions are too highly levered for regulators to allow them to be taken over with borrowed money, and compensation arrangements made conglomeration irresistible anyway. Many financial firms pay out nearly half their gross profits as bonuses—even if these profits are secured by loading up on risk. Bonuses paid are paid forever, even if the bets ultimately go bad. Conglomeration offered CEOs the opportunity to make ever larger bets—and to earn staggering personal returns without much personal risk.

Bank regulators were more concerned than bank executives about the growing risks. But they apparently succumbed to the idea, peddled by financiers and modern finance theorists, that if a little financial innovation was good, a lot must be great. Instead of curbing the issuance of ABSs or the growth of derivatives that were far outside their capacity to monitor, regulators tried to adapt: they required banks to hold more capital for riskier assets and to disclose what proportion of their trading positions could not be marked to market. The Federal Reserve pressed dealers to improve the processing of trades in over-the-counter derivatives. Unsurprisingly, given the asymmetry of resources and incentives, these measures proved inadequate: the regulators could not keep up.

Former president Clinton, whose administration midwifed the first large-scale production of financial toxins, blames the current crisis primarily on the absence of good investment opportunities besides housing in the Bush administration. Others have indicted the Federal Reserve monetary policy, the rating agencies, and even the SEC for abolishing the uptick rule, which discouraged short selling. But the analysis I have outlined above suggests that elected officials and appointees from both political parties—and respected economists—had so undermined the banking system that anything could have triggered a collapse.[8]

The Revolution Reconsidered

According to the prevailing wisdom, the crisis was the result of a regulatory apparatus that had fallen behind the development of modern financial theory and practice. There were too many gaps in the regulation, and these need to be filled. But there is little recognition of the role that regulation actually played in fostering the crisis. Thanks to the regulations, the wizards of Wall Street can lever up their balance sheets—and their bonuses—to levels far beyond what private lenders would tolerate. Without FDIC insurance, for example, banks that engaged in highly levered speculation—or extended credit to investment banks and hedge funds that engaged in such speculation—would have faced great difficulty in attracting the deposits they needed.

The conventional wisdom is also defensive: it holds that by filling the right regulatory gaps, the financial status quo can be saved from its excesses. But is the new financial technology really worth saving? How does the securitization of the credit that was previously extended by banks, and how do the derivative instruments and the trading based on this securitized debt, contribute to economic prosperity?

In 1987 Lowell Bryan, a McKinsey & Company director, wrote that "a new technology for lending—securitized credit—has suddenly appeared on the scene. This new technology has the capacity to transform the fundamentals of banking, which have been essentially unchanged since their origins in medieval Europe." Bryan predicted that traditional lending might soon become obsolete: "About half of all debt in the national economy is raised through securities; that number might increase to 80 percent in the next decade." The new technology, he argued, offered more checks and balances than traditional banking:

> Under a securitized credit system, in which an outside agency assigns a rating to the issue, credit risk will likely be properly underwritten before investors will buy an issue. In many cases, another third-party credit underwriter (a bank, a finance company, or an insurance company) must guarantee a portion of the credit risk in the issue. So at least one and often two skeptical outside parties review the credit underwriting before the issue can be placed with investors.

In contrast, he suggested, "loan risks depend entirely on self-definition by the institution making the loan." Similarly, the rates of securities were set by an objective market, not by subjective judgments of bankers. And securitized debt was "attractive to individuals, pension funds, and other investors who either can't or won't assess credit risk and would rather let rating agencies do the job."

In a now celebrated paper given at the annual Jackson Hole conclave of central bankers in 2005, Raghuram Rajan warned that, in reality, financial innovation had made the economy riskier. But his critique was aimed mainly at the perverse incentives of financiers, and did not question the value of the new financial technology Bryan had celebrated. In fact, according to Rajan (2006, 321), financial innovations had produced "beneficial, real effects, increasing lending, entrepreneurship, and growth rates of GDP, while reducing costs of financial transactions." For the new technologies had made "hard" information on firms and individuals from "centralized sources" such as Dun and Bradstreet widely available, allowing loan officers to cut down on regular visits to borrowers. Some "soft information that is hard to collect and communicate," such as judgments of character, was certainly lost when regular visits were ended (319–20). But the increased availability of hard information more than compensated for the loss of soft information. Moreover, unlike soft information, hard information (for instance, credit histories and accounting data) could be automatically processed, further reducing costs and raising the productivity of lending.

The productivity-enhancing technologies also changed the nature of borrower-creditor relationships: many transactions had moved from being "embedded in a long-term relationship between a client and a financial institution to being conducted at arm's length in a market" (Rajan 2006, 321).[9] To be sure, there was a tradeoff: long-term relationships produced "greater trust and understanding." But they also constrained each party's choices. Thanks to technological changes (and their knock-on effects on regulatory and institutional arrangements), the tradeoff favored long-term relationships mainly for "the most complicated, innovative or risky financial transactions" (321).

This chapter suggests a different set of inferences.

The claim that the automated processing of hard information provided by a centralized source is usually a superior substitute for the subjective judgments of a banker—F. A. Hayek's "man on the spot" —ignores the unquantifiable uncertainty that is an important feature even of seemingly routine lending decisions. Using a credit score produced by feeding a few items of hard data into a mathematical model to assess the likelihood of default assumes that all risks are quantifiable. And that is just one of the many assumptions at work. For instance, credit-scoring formulas also assume that the probability that all loans of a certain kind will default derives from exactly the same risk factors; that these risk factors are all combined or "weighted" in exactly the same way; and that somehow an omniscient modeler knows the right weighting scheme.

Such assumptions would be risible in other walks of life: replacing "routine" felony trials with a scoring model is inconceivable, what-

ever the cost savings might be. Nor do economics departments economize on the costs of hiring even entry-level faculty or Ph.D. students
by using predictive quantitative models (save in countries like France
where faculty are hired on the basis of objective scores in a competitive national exam).

Like criminal trials and faculty hiring decisions, the traditional
lending process implicitly took into account unquantifiable uncertainties and the uniqueness of individual circumstances. The difference between the information produced by a loan officer's visits and
that offered by Dun and Bradstreet is more than just a matter of soft
rather than hard. Visits produce information that is wider in its range
(and can cover private information that is not available to Dun and
Bradstreet) and better tuned to the specific circumstances of the borrower. For instance, a commercial loan officer may take note of
changes in the number of cars in the visitors' lot of an industrial
distributor, but ignore such changes for an Internet retailer. Similarly,
loan officers and committees traditionally used a wide range of information (including both quantitative data on past and projected
financial performance and qualitative observations about competitors
and customers) to construct a coherent "case" or "narrative" rather
than plug data into a formula. This may have amounted to overkill
in certain kinds of lending: mortgages with high down payments in
stable housing markets, for instance. But it is hard to imagine that
mechanistic lending is an appropriate rule for most credit decisions,
and that case-by-case ought to be reserved just for unusual situations.

Similarly, embedding financial transactions in long-term relationships instead of conducting them at arm's length in an "objective"
marketplace has merit in many seemingly mundane contexts, and not
just for "the most complicated, innovative or risky financial transactions." Banks whose lending far exceeded their base of long-term
depositors have discovered that it is dangerous to rely on funding
by fickle strangers in wholesale money markets. Similarly with the
extension of credit: a financial institution that underwrites securitized
credit for resale becomes, to a significant degree, a sales agent for the
borrower. Of course, sensible sales agents who value their relationships with customers will exercise some care in what they sell; nonetheless, the degree of care is diluted by the expectation that customers

will do their own analysis, and by the absence of any direct financial risk to the sales agent. Thus, an underwriter of debt cannot be expected to exercise the prudence of a banker making a loan that will remain on the bank's balance sheet.

Long-term relationships between lenders and borrowers have great value even after credit has been extended, akin to the benefits of shareholder-manager relationships. Borrowers can share private information with lenders just as corporate "insiders" could (if not barred by law), and thus have a greater opportunity to send early warnings of danger. In addition to self-interested restraints on opportunistic behavior, because the parties know they are stuck with each other—a banker cannot dump a thirty-year loan as easily as a mutual fund can sell a bond—there may develop an additional sense of mutual solidarity. A banker may thus renew a line of credit in hard times where an arm's-length purchaser would not roll over the same issuer's maturing commercial paper. Renegotiating the terms of a loan with one banker is easier than corralling many dispersed bond-holders to discuss the modification of bond covenants. One of the consequences of the slicing and dicing of mortgage loans is that it is now often practically impossible for homeowners in default to work things out with their lenders, as they might if their mortgage had a single owner, especially one located at the nearby branch of their bank.

Why was there such a mass displacement of long-term, relationship-and judgment-based lending by arms-length securitization? In the narrative offered by Rajan and several other economists, exogenous technologies played a deterministic role, inexorably forcing changes in regulation and financing arrangements. But technology might, instead, have facilitated relationship banking. For instance, collaborative software (such as Lotus notes) could have improved the capacity of large lending teams serving far-flung borrowers to share a wide range of data, observations, and judgments. The outcome was not predetermined. In fact, in the story I have told here, the increased share of securitized financial assets was driven mainly by the beliefs of financial economists and regulators.

Economics has underpinned securitization through its embrace of mathematical models to the exclusion of other perspectives, and through a complementary tendency to ignore the downside of liquidity and arms-length relationships. Regulation has brought this way of thinking into the world of practice in two paradoxically related streams: the increasing scope and effectiveness of the New Deal securities acts and subsequent rules that fostered the growth of arms-length transactions in corporate control; and the progressive dilution of New Deal banking acts, which nurtured and protected long-term relationships. This is the complicated story that may explain why developments in mortgage banking, of all things—traditionally the plodding, conservative bread-and-butter of depository banking—should have led to the implosion of the world economy.

Chapter 3

Monetary Policy, Credit Extension, and Housing Bubbles, 2008 and 1929

STEVEN GJERSTAD AND VERNON L. SMITH

Asset price bubbles have been common for hundreds of years, from the Dutch tulip mania in 1636 to the South Sea bubble in 1720 and on through the years until the recent dot-com and housing bubbles. Indeed, bubbles occur quite predictably in the laboratories of experimental economists under conditions that—when we first studied them in the 1980s—we thought were so transparent that bubbles would not be observed. We were wrong. Even when every trader in an asset market is provided with complete information on the fundamental value of holding an asset, and is provided with regular reminders of that value, large price deviations from that value in the form of bubbles occur routinely. A sufficient condition for a bubble to arise and be sustained is when some agents buy not on any discount from fundamental value, but on price trend or momentum. When the momentum-trading sentiment increases, the bubble becomes more pronounced. If momentum traders have more liquidity, either in the form of higher endowments of cash or access to margin buying, they can sustain a bubble longer.

Momentum trading and liquidity can fuel a bubble, but the factors that spark the formation of ebullient price expectations both inside and outside the laboratory—in a "crowd"—and those that trigger the sudden turnaround in those expectations, resulting in a crash, remain mysteries. We can model price bubbles, and we have learned much about the conditions that exacerbate or dampen them. But the sparks that ignite them, and the myopic, self-reinforcing behavioral mechanisms that sustain them, remain unpredictable.

Moreover, as common as they are, most bubbles do not bring down an entire economy when they pop. Something more than "irrational exuberance," and something in addition to momentum trading, must have been responsible for the financial crisis and the great recession of 2008. Thus, beyond asking what triggered the recent bubble and what sustained it, we want to address another crucial question. Why does one large asset bubble—such as the dot-com bubble—do no damage to the financial system, while another bubble leads to its collapse?

Lest we be misunderstood, we hasten to add that the behavioral features of laboratory asset markets do not apply to the ordinary day-to-day markets—prominent in all modern economies—that sustain the flow of goods and services from producers to consumers and that represent efficient decentralized mechanisms for wealth creation through specialization and innovation. This important distinction is echoed in the crisis of 2008 and the events that led up to it. The housing asset-market bubble collapse was transmitted into mortgage, financial, and banking markets, and this disrupted an economy that had been performing quite well.

If we add key characteristics of housing markets to the standard bubble story, we can offer a fairly complete and simple hypothesis for why first the financial system, and then the wider economy, were pulled down when the bubble popped. Moreover, we will present some data on parallel developments in the 1920s suggesting that we have experienced similar circumstances before.

The Housing Bubble in Outline and in Theory

Housing markets go through long swings. In just the past forty years in the United States, there were two other nationwide housing bubbles, with peaks in 1979 and 1989.

We think that the upward turn in housing prices that began in 1997 was probably sparked by rising household income (beginning in

1992), combined with a very popular bipartisan political decision in 1997 to eliminate taxes on capital gains of up to a half million dollars for residences. A rising price path in any asset market is likely to draw the attention of investors, and the early stages of the housing bubble had this potential for nourishing a self-reinforcing continuation of rising prices.

The recession in 2001 might have brought the housing bubble to an early end, but the Federal Reserve—with its eye focused not on any one sector, but on the overall economy—decided to pursue an exceptionally expansionary monetary policy in order to counteract the recession.

Naturally, when the Fed opened its liquidity valve, the money flowed to the fastest expanding sector of the economy. House prices were already rising, and both the Clinton and Bush administrations pursued the goal of expanding home ownership; public policy and private incentives combined to erode mortgage-underwriting standards. Mortgage lenders, the government-sponsored enterprises (Fannie Mae and Freddie Mac), and investment banks that securitized mortgages used rising home prices to justify loans to buyers with limited assets and income. Rating agencies also accepted the notion of ever-rising home values, so they gave large portions of each securitized package of mortgages an investment-grade rating, and investors gobbled them up. Everybody in the chain thought that risk was being reduced by the fact that the asset values underlying loans were growing.

The availability of housing finance and the relaxation of lending standards provided a flow of new buyers into the market that even rapid investment in new housing construction couldn't fully accommodate, so house prices rose dramatically. When even subprime lending couldn't keep new buyers arriving fast enough to sustain the price increases, the financial wizards turned to the interest-only adjustable rate mortgage (ARM). When that stopped working, they had one more magic potion: the negative-equity option ARM. These innovations were responses to the incentives that arise naturally in an environment of rising home-price expectations. But housing expenditures in the United States, and in most of the developed world, have historically accounted for about 30 percent of household income. If housing prices double in a seven-year period without a commensurate increase in income, eventually something has to give.

The price decline started in 2006, and with it all the policies designed to fulfill the American dream turned into unintended nightmares. Trillions of dollars of mortgages had been written to buyers with slender equity, and when delinquencies and defaults started, the borrowers' risk was limited to their small down payments. Hence, the lion's leveraged share of the risk was transmitted directly into the financial system. Uncertainty about which banks holding the securities would fail impaired the credit-intermediation capacity of the financial system, and its subsequent collapse abruptly ended the fine performance of the broader economy.

As straightforward as this story is, analyzing each step more closely yields parallels to the Roaring Twenties—and the Great Depression.

Consumption Markets Versus Asset Markets

In an early experimental study modeled after consumer goods and services markets—in which items disappear after being bought and consumed—Smith (1962) showed that these markets are far more efficient, under conditions of strictly private information, than economists had expected. Since then, hundreds of other experimental studies have demonstrated the robustness of this competitive equilibrium discovery process in repetitive-flow markets for goods and services. Moreover, Williams et al. (2000) and Gjerstad (2007a) showed experimentally that convergence to competitive equilibrium in single-commodity supply-and-demand markets also extends to more complex interdependent commodity markets, where what people are willing to pay for good A depends on the price of good B, and vice versa. For the single-commodity markets first studied experimentally in Smith (1962), Gjerstad and Dickhaut (1998) developed a model of heuristic learning by buyers and sellers about the prices that are likely to be accepted by the other side of the market; and they showed, in artificial-intelligence simulations, that when traders follow strategies based on these beliefs, market prices converge to the competitive equilibrium. (Gjerstad 2007b also showed, by mixing algorithmic and human traders in the same market experiment, that these heuristic traders can perform as well as, and even better than, human buyers and sellers.)

Taken together, all these results demonstrate just how well markets function when the items traded are not retraded later, but are produced, purchased, consumed, and disappear, and when this process is repeated over and over.

But in asset markets where the item can be resold, value can depend on how a buyer thinks others will value it in the future. Vernon Smith, Gerry Suchanek, and Arlington Williams (1988) showed that human behavior in asset-trading markets leads to dramatically different convergence results from those in commodity-flow markets, even under conditions of high transparency. In their experiment, assets pay dividends over many periods. In early periods, prices rise and soon exceed the expected stream of dividend payments that the asset will yield. Halfway through an experiment session, asset prices are often 50 percent or even 100 percent higher than the expected dividend payments.

While under stationary conditions, a market consisting of people who have previously been through two complete experiment sessions—such that they've had the same experience twice before—finally converges to fundamental values (rational equilibrium) in the last session, it will tend to generate substantial bubbles in the earlier sessions. Although baffling at first, these results were replicated with widely different groups of traders—college students, small-business owners, corporate-business executives, and over-the-counter stock traders—and by skeptical new experimenters. (Initially, Smith, Suchanek, and Williams had been skeptical of their own findings.) But the phenomenon is at the heart of human behavior. Twenty years of experimental research on asset-market bubbles shows that, under a wide variety of treatments, asset prices typically deviate substantially from those predicted by the rational-expectations market model (Postrel 2008).

Economists first had to overcome the shock that laboratory markets, like those of daily consumer life, proved the "wisdom of crowds" when people—informed only about their private individual values (as buyers) or of their private costs (as sellers)—sell, buy, and consume items in a process that is replicated over time. But the next shocker was that in asset markets, the wisdom of crowds failed decisively. The key difference in asset markets was the prospect of resale, with no immediate endpoint consumption.

Houses and securities can be retraded, unlike hamburgers, plumbing repairs, haircuts, and all manner of consumer and producer services. People rely on their investments in asset markets, including the chief asset of many—their houses—to meet retirement and other significant life-cycle needs, and, naturally, they desire high yields on those investments. Firms rely on asset markets for the effective allocation of savings toward productive new investments and innovative technologies. When bubbles emerge, the effect is to distort prices and yields, interfering with both objectives.

Caginalp, Porter, and Smith (2000) modeled asset-market bubbles by assuming that they form out of the interaction of two kinds of investors: (1) fundamental-value traders, who buy in proportion to the percentage discount below, and sell in proportion to the premium above, underlying asset value; and (2) momentum traders, who buy (or sell) in proportion to the current percentage increase (or decrease) in price. Plainly stated, a momentum trader gets into the market when prices are rising because he believes that he'll be able to sell later at a higher price. Fundamental traders have long-term rational-expectation-supported objectives, while momentum traders are driven by myopic expectations that cannot be indefinitely sustained.

The Caginalp-Porter-Smith model of bubbles also shows that momentum traders can sustain their buying longer as a bubble expands when there is more liquidity in the capital market. A larger credit market allows buyers to sustain their momentum trading longer, and at higher and higher prices, so the bubble diverges ever farther from fundamental values.

The factors that initiate bubbles remain a mystery, but once one is underway, we have a basic understanding of its mechanics. The expectations that people have of future price changes, and the provision of liquidity to an asset market, are integral elements in understanding how bubbles grow and are sustained.

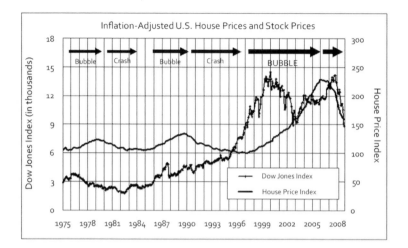

Figure 3.1. Three housing bubbles, 1975–2008. Dow Jones Industrial Average; Freddie Mac CMHPI, 1975–1987; Case-Shiller 10-city composite index, 1987–2008. See note 3 for details on these indices. All three series are deflated by the Consumer Price Index (CPIAUCNS).

Public Policy and the Housing Bubble

Over the last four decades, the United States has passed through three national housing-price cycles, the last of which has been the largest housing bubble in U.S. history. During the same period, the stock market registered several bubbles and crashes comparable in percentage magnitude to those in the housing market, but the two market time paths appear to move independently, to a considerable extent (see Figure 3.1). Moreover, they seem to have distinct causes and effects. Six years of relatively tight money, from 1995 to 2000, failed to preclude a large rise in stock prices from 1995 through 1999. The same period saw the start of the current housing bubble (in 1997); but the surge in house prices continued well after the stock market decline of 2000–2002.

This divergent behavior may be explained, in part, by a new factor introduced in 1997: the Taxpayer Relief Act, which for the first time exempted housing assets (up to $500,000) from the capital-gains tax.

Housing and corporate securities each make up about one third of all U.S. wealth. Since, historically, about 30 percent of household income is spent on housing, one would expect housing wealth to account for about the same fraction of total wealth. An asymmetric reduction in taxes on homes implies that a larger fraction of wealth will eventually flow to home investment, away from other forms of capital investment. Insofar as overinvestment in housing diverted capital away from new-product and cost-reducing technologies, it reduced the growth of productivity per labor hour and, therefore, diminished future (i.e., at this writing, present) wealth-creation capacity. Smith (2007) argues that the 1997 tax law, which favored houses over all other investments, would have naturally led more capital to flow into the housing market, causing an increase in demand—and a takeoff in expectations of further increases in house prices (see also Bajaj and Leonhardt 2008).

If the Taxpayer Relief Act helped trigger the run-up in housing prices, a significant sustained change in monetary policy, beginning in 2001, appears to have dramatically strengthened it.

In January 2001, after four years of real house-price increases averaging 7.2 percent per year in the Case-Shiller ten-city composite index (about 6 percent above the inflation-adjusted trend for the previous eighty years), the Federal Reserve started to ratchet down the federal funds rate (see Figure 3.2). By December 2001, the federal funds rate had been reduced to its lowest level since 1962. The average rates in 2003 and 2004 were lower than in any of the years since the Fed began reporting this rate in 1955; the average had been lower than the average rate of 2002 in only one year since 1955: the recession year of 1958. In other words, the years 2001–2004 saw the longest sustained expansionary monetary policy in half a century.

The combined effect of the Taxpayer Relief Act and loose monetary policy as inflators of the housing bubble is revealed in the fact that the path of house prices from 1997 through 2005 is convex: House prices were increasing at an increasing rate. The effect of the sharp easing of monetary policy between 2001 and 2004 is evident in the continued acceleration of home-price increases between 2002 and 2005, shown in Figure 3.1.

We find equally persuasive the fact that, during the expansion

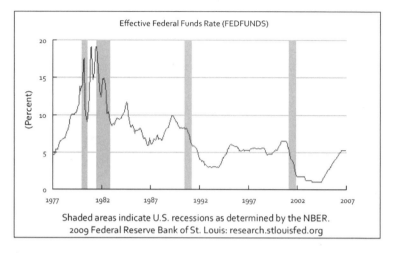

Figure 3.2. Monetary policy over the period including the three housing bubbles. Board of Governors of the Federal Reserve System.

phases of the two earlier bubbles (1976–79 and 1986–89), the Fed was increasing the federal funds rate, and those two bubbles were much milder than the current one. In short, when the Federal Reserve was "leaning against the wind," the bubbles were far smaller than when, at the beginning of this century, monetary policy pumped credit into the economy.

How the Bubble—and Inflation—
May Have Escaped Official Notice

Monetary policy, in conjunction with mortgage securitization and tax-free capital-gains status for housing, appear to have added up to an astonishing housing-market stimulus: mortgage-loan originations increased from $1.05 trillion in 2000 to $3.95 trillion in 2003, or 56 percent annually. By the time the Federal Reserve slowly began to raise the federal funds rate in May 2004, housing prices had been increasing by 2.8 percent per month in Las Vegas for the previous year (39 percent over the twelve-month period June 2003–May 2004); by 2.3 percent per month in Los Angeles (31 percent over the twelve-month period); and by 1.5 percent per month in Washington, D.C.

(20 percent over the twelve-month period). The Case-Shiller twenty-city composite housing-price index increased 15.4 percent during that twelve-month period.

Yet the housing portion of the Consumer Price Index (CPI) for the same period rose only 2.4 percent. How could this be? The answer reveals the dramatic effect that loose monetary policy was having—despite effectively escaping official measurement.

Starting in 1983, the Bureau of Labor Statistics began to use the price of equivalent rentals in estimating the housing portion of the CPI for homeowner-occupied units. Between 1983 and 1996, the ratio of house prices to rental equivalents increased from 19.0 to 20.2, so the change had little impact on measured inflation: the CPI underestimated inflation by about 0.1 percentage point per year during this fourteen-year period. Between 1999 and 2006, however, the ratio shot up from 20.8 to 32.3, creating a whole new structural relationship between house prices and their "rental equivalents."[1] With home asset-price increases effectively excluded from the CPI and the price-to-rent ratio rapidly increasing, an important source of inflation escaped inclusion in the CPI. In 2004 alone, the price-to-rent ratio increased 12.3 percent. Since homeowner-occupied housing accounts for about 23 percent of the CPI, inflation for that year was reported as being 2.9 percentage points lower than it would have been if home-ownership costs were folded back into the CPI: the reported CPI increase was 3.3 percent instead of 6.2 percent.[2]

With nominal interest rates around 6 percent and actual inflation around 6 percent, the real interest rate approached zero. With continuing expectations of rising prices, people borrowed in response to this strong incentive. As measured by the Case-Shiller ten-city index, the accumulated surge in home ownership prices between January 1999 and the peak, in June 2006, was 151 percent—but the CPI measured an accumulated increase of a mere 25 percent.[3] As the Federal Reserve monitored the economy for signs of inflation during the early 2000s, housing price increases were no longer so visible in the CPI. Consequently, the Fed saw no reason to curtail its lax monetary policy.

Even after the Fed began to raise the federal funds rate in May 2004, the housing bubble grew for two more years, due, we would argue, to self-reinforcing expectations of rising resale prices and to overgenerous mortgage financing in the form of low down payments, interest-only loans, negative-equity loans, and adjustable-rate mortgages (ARMs), enabled by the Fed's loose-money policy.[4] Surely such financing unintentionally encouraged momentum buying. But the liquidity that sustained subprime and ARM lending was about to evaporate.

Subprime Mortgages and the Bursting of the Housing Bubble

The collapse of the housing market is in many ways the most fascinating—and certainly the most painful—part of the story.

In 2006, the median price of existing homes fell from $230,000 in July to $217,300 in November. By the beginning of 2007, the Case-Shiller Boston and San Diego price indices had been falling for over a year; the indices for San Francisco and Washington, D.C. had been falling for six months. In thirteen of the other sixteen cities in the Case-Shiller index, too, prices were falling. Only the housing markets in Miami, Seattle, and Portland had not turned down by December 2006.

Serious mortgage delinquencies spiked noticeably at about the same time, especially for subprime ARM loans. In the second quarter of 2006, 6.52 percent of these loans were seriously delinquent; by the third quarter, the figure was 7.72 percent; by the fourth quarter, it reached 9.16 percent.[5] The mortgage market collapse had not yet begun, but the warning signs were there for any alert observers.

Kelly (2007) tells the story of how Goldman Sachs avoided the fate of many of the other investment banks. In January 2006, a small group in Goldman's mortgage department—the structured-products trading group—began trading Markit ABX credit-default swap indices. In December 2006, Goldman's CFO, David Viniar, pushed these traders to hedge the firm's long positions in mortgage-backed securities by using the same indices. They loaded up on an issue called ABX-HE-BBB − 2006–2. This asset, which started trading in July 2006, is tied to the performance of subordinate (BBB −) tranches of an index of twenty mortgage-backed securities issued in the first half of 2006. When the price of an ABX index falls, the cost of insuring mortgage-backed securities rises. The price of an ABX index is approximately 100 minus the expected percentage of the losses on the twenty mortgage-backed securities in the index. If the index stands at 100, the aggregated market belief is that there will be no losses at all. If it falls to 90, the market believes that losses on the security will be 10 percent. But this is only an approximation, because a Markit ABX index also has a coupon, which is an annual premium. For the ABX-HE-BBB— 2006–2 issue, the coupon was 242 basis points. Thus, insuring $10 million of mortgage-backed securities rated BBB— cost $242,000 per year when the index was first issued. Every price drop of one unit below the par value of 100 adds a fixed cost of $100,000 to the cost of $10 million of insurance.

Goldman anticipated large losses on these assets and began to purchase insurance (with Markit ABX credit-default-swap indices) when their prices reflected market-expected losses that were well below the losses that Goldman expected.[6] As the prices of ABX derivatives collapsed, the cost of insuring new mortgage-backed securities skyrocketed. Goldman had invested heavily in these derivatives—that is, it had increased its insurance against declines in the underlying value of their mortgage-backed securities—between the beginning of December 2006 and late February 2007, as the price dropped from 97.70 on December 4 to under 64 by February 27. Normally, buying an asset with a falling price is not a good idea, but the ABX index pays off when mortgage-backed securities suffer losses: at a price of 97.70, it cost $230,000 plus the annual premium of $242,000 to insure $10 million of BBB— tranches; at a price of 64, the same insurance cost $3.6 million (plus the same annual premium).

By getting into this market early, Goldman Sachs had obtained the insurance at a much lower fixed cost. With insurance premiums on new residential mortgage-backed securities (RMBSs) skyrocketing, mortgage financing from these securities rapidly declined. In 2006, $483 billion in new subprime RMBSs were issued. By the fourth quarter of 2007, the figure had fallen to $11.9 billion.[7] Other measures of new loan originations were falling at the same time.[8] As the liquidity that generated the housing market bubble evaporated, new buyers disappeared. And as housing prices then declined, subprime and ARM delinquencies rose.

Goldman, acting on the belief that the housing market was headed for trouble, now bought more insurance on mortgage-backed securities. This raised the price of insurance on these securities, which decreased the flow of capital to lenders and of mortgages to households, and hastened the trouble that Goldman anticipated.[9] Many firms had major exposures to subprime and ARM RMBSs, but failed to notice the weakness in the housing market—or noticed developing signs of weakness but failed to balance their exposure to it.[10] They were drawn into the undertow from the collapsing housing market. Bear Stearns, Lehman Brothers, Merrill Lynch, AIG, Citigroup, Washington Mutual, and Wachovia all collapsed, in one way or another, as a result of their exposure to the mortgage crisis.[11]

As of February 2007, the mortgage market was not yet in free fall: insurance on the AAA tranches of RMBSs remained inexpensive. At the end of February, the cost of $10 million of insurance on the AAA-rated portion of an index of RMBSs issued in the first half of 2006 was only $68,000 (plus a $9,000 annual premium). It is true that significant concerns had emerged about the viability of the BBB_ tranches, so that investment banks were reluctant to buy new subprime and ARM mortgages issued by lenders with poor risk-management practices (such as Countrywide, Ameriquest, and Option One). Still, no large players were yet concerned about the AAA tranches, which would face losses only after all the subordinate tranches had been wiped out. That soon changed. By July 2007, prices of the cheapest homes in San Francisco were down almost 13 percent from their peak; in San Diego they were down by 10 percent. Serious delinquency on subprime ARM loans, which had reached 9.16 percent by the fourth quarter of 2006, increased to 12.40 percent by the second quarter of 2007.

Between July 9 and August 3, 2007, the cost of insuring $10 million of AAA tranches of mortgage-backed securities went from $50,000 (plus a $9,000 annual premium) to more than $900,000 (plus the premium). Since the cost of insuring mortgage-backed securities provides a measure of the estimated losses on them, the rising insurance cost left many of the bad assets stranded in the hands of the subprime lenders. Worse, it also signaled to the market that assets

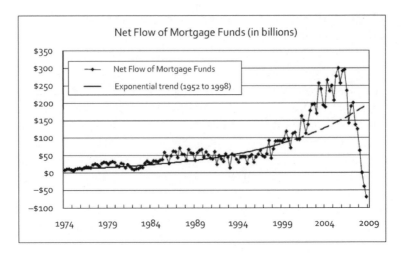

Figure 3.3. The mortgage-finance bubble pops. Federal Reserve Flow of
Funds historical data table F.218 (Home Mortgages); http://
www.federalreserve.gov/releases/z1/current/data.htm in the file utabs.zip.
Table F.218 is in the file utab218d.prn; net flow of mortgage funds is in the
third column.

that had already been acquired by banks and other financial institutions were at risk of substantial losses. By this time, expected losses at
the bottom tier of the investment grade (i.e., BBB_) subprime RMBS
tranches had reached 40 to 60 percent, depending on the issue date
of the securities. Expected losses on the investment-grade (e.g., AAA)
portions of the securities were in the 5 to 10 percent range. Since
about two-thirds of each RMBS was rated AAA, the expected losses
had surged between January and July 2007 from under 2 percent to
over 20 percent. Meanwhile, the market for mortgages issued by subprime lenders was completely frozen by August 3, and Countrywide
was considered a bankruptcy risk by August 10.

Figure 3.3 displays the quarterly net flow of mortgage funds
through the fourth quarter of 2008.[12] The data show clearly that the
final, and sudden, collapse of the market began in the third quarter
of 2007, when fears about subprime mortgage delinquencies and
defaults became acute.

In one local market after another, the housing bubble followed

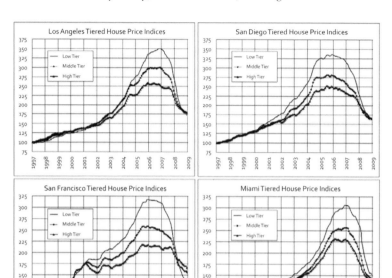

Figure 3.4. The cheaper the house, the bigger the bubble. See note 3 for details. Case-Shiller tiered price indices.

the same pattern. Prices of homes in the low-price tier appreciated the most and then fell the most; prices in the high-price tier appreciated the least and fell the least; house-price appreciation in the middle-price tier came between that of the other two tiers (Figure 3.4).

In Figure 3.4, the price-index graphs for Los Angeles, San Francisco, San Diego, and Miami show that, in all of these cities, prices in the low-price tier had fallen between 50 and 57 percent from 1997 to 2009. When the bubble burst it wiped out the slender equity of those households who were least able to sustain a decline in the value of their asset, and the financial system suffered a self-inflicted blow arising from the high-risk leverage game it had played. By the end of 2008, 1.9 million mortgages in California—29.5 percent of that state's outstanding mortgages—had negative equity; it was even worse in Arizona (31.8 percent), Florida (30.3 percent), Michigan (40 percent), and Nevada (55.1 percent).[13] When housing prices turned down, many borrowers with low incomes and few assets other than their home—which was often purchased with an adjustable-rate mortgage and no down payment—lost their occupancy rights. These were the households that public policies encouraging subprime lending had been intended most specifically to help (see Wallison 2009).

The Subprime Crisis Becomes a Financial Crisis

When housing prices began to plummet, many homeowners with low incomes and few assets became delinquent on their mortgage payments or defaulted entirely.[14] This sparked fear among banks as to the creditworthiness of their peer institutions, which were very often heavily invested in structured securities containing subprime mortgages. Consequently, banks became unwilling to lend to each other, as reflected in an unprecedented jump in the spread between short-term U.S. Treasury debt (which is considered secure) and the London Interbank Offered Rate (LIBOR)—from 0.44 to 2.40 percent between August 8 and August 20, 2007.

Banks, unable to get loans from other banks—and, by the same token, banks holding their own fearsome subprime RMBSs—began hoarding cash to protect themselves from further exposure to declining asset values. Lending quickly contracted. Figure 3.3 shows the rapid decline in net mortgage flow, from $291.5 billion in the first quarter of 2006 to $63.5 billion two years later.

As credit became more difficult to obtain, durable-goods sectors unrelated to housing began to suffer collateral damage. Lending for automobile purchases, for instance, contracted sharply: auto sales fell 36 percent between December 2007 and December 2008. Ultimately, the broader economy and labor market became victims of the collapse of the subprime mortgage market.

For comparison purposes, during the dot-com crash between December 1999 and September 2002, approximately $10 trillion of equity was erased,[15] but a measure of financial-system performance, the Keefe, Bruyette, & Woods BKX index of financial firms, fell less than 6 percent in real terms during that period.[16] In the more recent downturn, the value of residential real estate had fallen approximately $3 trillion by the third quarter of 2008,[17] while the BKX index had fallen 45 percent between its peak in January 2007 and September 2008, as the financial crisis gathered force. The financial sector had been devastated in this crisis, whereas it was almost completely unaffected by the downturn in the equities market early in the decade. This raises the question of how a crash that wipes out $10 trillion in assets can cause no damage to the financial system, while another that causes $3 trillion in losses undermines the financial system worldwide.

In the earlier market downturn, equities with declining prices were held by institutional and individual investors, pension funds, and retirement funds that either owned the assets outright or held only a small fraction on margin. The losses on these assets were immediately absorbed by their owners and did not cascade into the foundation of the financial system. But in the 2008 crisis, declining housing assets in many cases were, in effect, purchased by households between 90 and 100 percent on margin. In some of the cities hit hardest, borrowers who purchased in the low-price tier at the peak of the bubble have seen their home value decline 50 percent or more. Borrowers without equity who are unable to make payments on their loan can be forced out (through foreclosure) or may choose to move from the homes they occupy. As housing prices have fallen, more and more homes became worth less than the loans on them, and more and more losses have been transmitted to lending institutions, investment banks, investors in mortgage-backed securities, sellers of credit-default swaps, and the insurers of last resort, the U.S. Treasury and the Federal Reserve system.

Subprime and adjustable-rate mortgage originators, such as Ameriquest, Indymac, and Countrywide, were caught with inadequately secured assets in inventory when the market for their loans froze in mid-summer 2007. Similarly, investment banks got caught with many mortgages in the pipeline extending from the time that they acquired them (from mortgage originators) until they had been securitized, rated, registered with the SEC, and marketed to investors. In addition, commercial banks and other financial institutions that held the securities as investments also faced large losses. Credit-default swaps on RMBSs were the primary form of insurance on these securities, so they were essential to maintain the flow of funds to the subprime and ARM lenders. The market for these swaps evaporated in the summer of 2007.

The Role of Derivatives in the Collapse

We have argued that derivatives—specifically, credit-default swaps—were the linchpin of the housing-finance market. The collapse in the ABX index for AAA-rated securities in July 2007 led soon afterward to the collapse in the market for the loans written by many subprime lenders, and also to a collapse in the market for the structured securities into which these loans were gathered by investment banks. The vast regulation-exempt and publicly unregistered market for these derivatives was at the core of the mortgage-market expansion and its collapse.

The credit-default-swap (CDS) market grew from $631.5 billion in notional value in the first half of 2001 to over $62.1 trillion in notional value in the second half of 2007.[18] How did such a large market, with so much risk accumulated in it, remain so opaque? If these securities had been registered and summary exposures had been disclosed, the Fed and investors might have been able to better assess the risks from the mortgage-market bubble. Summary disclosures of the exposures that AIG, Ambac, and MBIA had accumulated on RMBS credit-default swaps would have alerted informed investors to the risks that these firms had undertaken.

Ten years before the crisis reached a critical stage, the Treasury, the Federal Reserve, and the SEC had gone to great lengths to make sure that neither they nor the one federal agency that considered revisiting the exempt unregistered status of the CDS market—the Commodity Futures Trading Commission (CFTC)—would have the information that they needed to assess the risks of derivatives. On May 7, 1998, the CFTC issued a Concept Release to solicit input regarding potential prospective regulatory oversight of the derivatives markets, including markets for credit-default swaps. In its press release accompanying the Concept Release, the CFTC explained its rationale for a regulatory review:[19]

> The goal of this reexamination is to assist [CFTC] in determining how best to maintain adequate regulatory safeguards

without impairing the ability of the OTC derivatives market to grow and the ability of U.S. entities to remain competitive in the global financial marketplace.

In that context, the Commission is open both to evidence in support of broadening its existing exemptions and to evidence of the need for additional safeguards. Thus, the concept release identifies a broad range of issues in order to stimulate public discussion and elicit informed analysis. The Commission seeks to draw on the knowledge and expertise of a broad spectrum of interested parties, including OTC derivatives dealers, end-users of derivatives, other industry participants, other regulatory authorities, and academicians.

The concept release seeks comment on a number of areas where potential changes to current CFTC exemptions might be possible, including eligible transactions, eligible participants, clearing, transaction execution facilities, registration, capital, internal controls, sales practices, recordkeeping and reporting. The release also asks for the views of commenters as to whether issues described in the release might be addressed through industry bodies or self-regulatory organizations.

It is hard not to be impressed by the benign and unthreatening tone of this release; here was an agency seeking knowledge with an open mind and a willingness to reduce as well as increase regulation. Remarkably, Treasury Secretary Robert Rubin, SEC Chairman Arthur Levitt, and Federal Reserve Board Chairman Alan Greenspan issued a terse statement on the same day questioning the authority of the CFTC to review the markets, and stating that the Fed, the SEC, and the Treasury had "grave concerns about this [CFTC] action and its possible consequences."[20]

In his July 30, 1998, congressional testimony on the CFTC concept release, Deputy Secretary of the Treasury Lawrence Summers argued that "the parties to these kinds of contract are largely sophisticated financial institutions that would appear to be eminently capable of protecting themselves from fraud and counterparty insolvencies." Summers, like others who opposed the concept release, offered no proof for the soundness of his position. Instead, he suggested that "to date there has been no clear evidence of a need for additional regulation of the institutional OTC derivatives market, and we would submit that proponents of such regulation must bear the burden of demonstrating that need" (Summers 1998).

Many of the issues raised in the concept release ultimately proved to be at the heart of the problems with the derivatives market, which contributed to the spread of the riskiest subprime and ARM lending practices. AIG and many other insurers of mortgage-backed securities had inadequate capital to meet the obligations they had undertaken with credit-default swaps; regulators had an inadequate understanding of these risks due to the lack of registration of the securities; and investors (in AIG, Ambac, MBIA, etc.) had an inadequate understanding of the risks they faced due to the lack of disclosure.[21] The derivatives they used differed in substance from other derivatives in that they were not exchange traded under standard private-exchange transparency rules; and in that the lack of standardization, registration, rating, disclosure, and capital-reserve requirements made them more complex and—as we have now learned—inherently more unstable than futures and options markets for commodities and equities.

Reassessing the Great Depression

In an important scholarly paper, Ben Bernanke (1983) argued that, during the Great Depression, severe damage to the financial system impeded its ability to lend to households for durable goods consumption and to firms for production and trade. The same process played out after the collapse of the financial system in 2008. The housing market peaked at the end of 2006; losses from the mortgage market subsequently began to infect the financial system; asset prices in that sector began to decline early in 2007, and then lending declined and affected the broader economy, as reflected in equities markets—which had been performing quite well into 2007. The sequential footprints of these three turning points are clearly visible in Figure 3.5.

Bernanke takes a weakened financial system in the Great Depres-

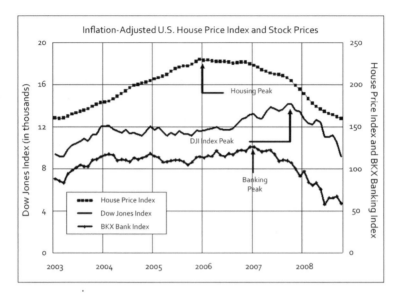

Figure 3.5. The housing, financial, and equities markets decline. Dow Jones Index; housing: Case-Shiller 10-city composite; banking: KBW BKX index.

sion—not its antecedents—as his starting point. But there are parallels between the fundamental causes of that crisis and our own.

The standard explanation of the precipitating factor in the crash of 1929 has been excessive speculation on Wall Street. Speculation does appear to have been a factor, but then, as now, we believe that mortgage and consumer finance growth were also at the core of the problem.

Many aspects of the Crash of 1929 suggest that it was not the primary cause of the subsequent deterioration of the financial system. John Kenneth Galbraith (1972, 37) notes that "margins were not low in 1929; a residue of caution had caused most brokers to require customers to put up 45 to 50 percent of the value of the stocks they were buying in cash." Barrie Wigmore (1985, 161) notes that banks' "earnings per share declined only 25–30 percent in 1930, and four of the top ten paid higher dividends in 1930" than in 1929. He also points out that brokerages survived the crash intact (31–32). In many ways, the stock-market crash of 1929 caused only slightly more damage than the downturn in the stock market between 2000 and 2002, which raises the question, what was the source of the storm that overtook the financial system between late fall 1930 and spring 1933, dragging the country into the Great Depression?

As long ago as 1950, Ernest M. Fisher pointed to the growth of the housing sector and of mortgage finance from 1920 until the early postwar era:

> The general economic expansion of that period found no more dramatic expression in any area than in that of mortgage lending. The expansion of mortgage lending was, in turn, a manifestation of a rapid expansion of our urban real estate inventory. During the decade 1920 to 1929, according to the best evidence available, new construction accounted for about 5.7 million dwelling units, reflected in an increase in inventory from an estimated 17.6 million dwelling units in 1920 to nearly 23.3 million in 1930, an increase of over 32 per cent.
>
> There was also a rapid increase in home ownership during the decade. The number of owner-occupants increased by about 50 per cent, from a little over 7 million to about 10.5 million. The expansion of real estate facilities occurred largely on the basis of extension of credit secured by mortgage liens. All [residential and commercial] real estate mortgage indebtedness is estimated to have increased from $12.1 billion to $33.1 billion, or 174 per cent.
>
> Included in this total is the large volume of mortgage bond issues, estimates of the amount of which vary between $5 billion and $10 billion in 1935, rising to this sum from an estimated $300 million outstanding around 1920. (1950, 307–9)

Similarly, Charles E. Persons (1930, 104) estimated total residential real-estate mortgages outstanding of $11.1 billion as of 1920—and $27.1 billion as of 1929. In the same paper, Persons (126) provides monthly figures on residential construction contracts for 1927 through 1929. On a year-over-year basis, construction contracts increased in every month from January 1928 until September 1928 and then declined (also on a year-over-year basis) in every month

Figure 3.6. New housing expenditures during the Roaring Twenties. Grebler, Blank, and Winnick 1956, table B-3.

from September 1928 until December 1929.[22] By September 1929, one month before the crash, construction contracts were 40 percent lower than they had been in September 1928. Problems were appearing in the automobile industry as well, but with a lag, as in the 2008 crisis. Automobile production was increasing on a year-over-year basis from January 1928 until August 1929, but the increases were dropping off rapidly:[23] 76 percent more cars were produced in January 1929 than in January 1928; 24 percent more in July 1929 than in July 1928; 2 percent fewer in September 1929, the month before the crash, than in September 1928.[24] The crash of October 1929 resulted from a sudden recognition that the credit system had been stretched to its limit: new houses and consumer durables could be produced, but creditworthy borrowers were scarce.

The data provided by Fisher, by Persons, and especially by Leo Grebler, David M. Blank, and Louis Winnick (1956) indicate a rapid rate of residential expansion and a commensurate build up of debt. Figures 3.6 and 3.7 provide graphical representations of how precisely commensurate they were. Between 1922 and 1928, average real residential construction expenditures exceeded the average annual figure

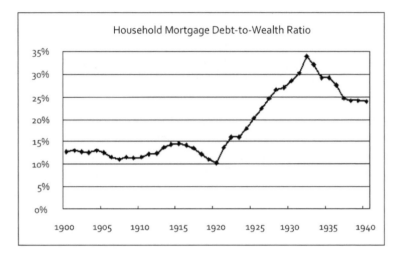

Figure 3.7. Household mortgage debt-to-wealth ratio during Roaring Twenties. Grebler, Blank, and Winnick 1956, table L-6.

from 1889 to 1916 by 138 percent. Between 1921 and 1929, household debt as a percentage of household wealth increased from 10.2 percent to 27.2 percent. A huge boom in residential housing construction was financed by an equally rapid increase in household indebtedness.

When the collapse came, between 1929 and 1932, the net flow of funds into mortgages fell dramatically. Net mortgage originations fell from $2.202 billion in 1929 to $736 million in 1930, and turned sharply negative from 1931 to 1933. Note the similarity between the pattern of net residential mortgage lending between 1900 and 1931, shown in Figure 3.8, and the pattern observed for 1974–2008, shown in Figure 3.3. The prolonged increase above the trend in mortgage growth from the second quarter of 2001 through the second quarter of 2006 has a striking parallel in the escalation in mortgage lending from 1923 through 1928. The sudden reduction in the net flow of mortgage funds from $2.88 billion in 1928 to $736 million in 1930 is remarkably similar to the rapid decline from $201 billion in the second quarter of 2007 to $5 billion a year later.

The two precipitous declines that began in 1930 and 2007 are also notable for standing out from the historical experience of the previ-

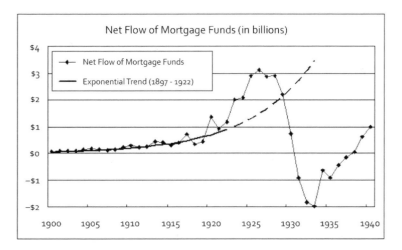

Figure 3.8. Housing finance collapse in the Great Depression. Authors' calculations based on Grebler, Blank, and Winnick 1956, table L-3.

ous 120 years. Net mortgage issuance remained negative from 1931 to 1937; but thereafter, with the exception of 1942–1944 (when financing and production were diverted to military requirements), the net flow of mortgage funds has been positive every year—until it turned negative in the third quarter of 2008.

The problem in modern economies is not what can be produced. The technology and resources available for production in the 1930s were the same as, or better than, they had been in the 1920s. The real problem is how markets allocate output so that those who acquire it have the capacity to pay for it. Since so much production, trade, and durable-goods consumption depends on credit, the real issue is market effectiveness in the assessment of credit risk.

The Milton Friedman-Anna Schwartz argument, which is also standard now, concerned the monetary policies that turned the crash into a depression—after the crash had been precipitated. Schwartz summarized the view she and Friedman developed:

Our main theme was that the effect of whatever economic forces produced the contraction was magnified by the unprecedented decline in the quantity of money resulting from the banking crisis. Our ancillary judgment was that the Federal Reserve could have prevented the monetary consequences of the banking crisis but failed to do so. (Schwartz 1981, 7)

In the same paper Schwartz states that she and Friedman "continue to believe that had [Benjamin] Strong [president of the Federal Reserve Bank of New York] lived or had he been succeeded by someone of similar views and equal personal force, the same monetary growth policies followed in 1924 and 1927 would have been followed in 1930, hence the decline in high-powered money either would not have occurred or would have been promptly reversed, and the economy would have been spared its prolonged ordeal" (42).

It is true that, as Friedman and Schwartz argued, the Fed should have expanded the money supply in 1929 and 1930—once the crash had occurred. This is a lesson that Bernanke, a specialist in the field, learned all too well. As a result, the Fed aggressively expanded the money supply beginning in August 2007—even before the financial crash was fully underway—but to little effect. The monetarist view, including Bernanke's version of it, begs the question of what causes collapses of the financial system in the first place and how this should affect public policy. Aggressive monetary policy designed to increase liquidity did not resolve the crisis. It also seems likely that it would not have resolved the crisis that overtook the financial system between late 1930 and the spring of 1933. Both crises appear to have originated in widespread household insolvencies that then infected the financial system. Liquidity alone could not make banks and households whole again.

Consider again that the massive loss of shareholder equity between 2000 and 2002 caused almost no damage to the financial system. Similarly, when the Dow Jones Industrial Average declined from 362 in September 1929 to 225 in September 1930, the banking system had not yet suffered any serious damage. Surely another factor must have been present in that case, and in the present one. Arguably, this factor was, in both cases, excessive debt among borrowers with especially limited assets and income—hence with an especially constrained ability to repay. The mortgages made to these borrowers turned on poor credit assessment.

Blindsided Experts

As the 2008 crisis reached one critical stage after another, the Federal Open Market Committee (FOMC) reacted with evident surprise to the developments in the financial markets. Until 7 August 2007, the FOMC maintained the federal funds rate at 5.25 percent. In statements on March 21, May 9, June 28, and August 7, the FOMC reiterated verbatim that "the Committee's predominant policy concern remains the risk that inflation will fail to moderate." The August 7 statement also recognized an ongoing housing correction, but as we have seen in Figures 3.3 and 3.5, the net flow of mortgage funds had by then declined dramatically from its peak in the second quarter of 2006, and housing prices had been picking up much downward momentum in 2007.

On August 10, 2007 the FOMC announced that

> the Federal Reserve will provide reserves as necessary through open market operations to promote trading in the federal funds market at rates close to the Federal Open Market Committee's target rate of 5 1/4 percent. In current circumstances, depository institutions may experience unusual funding needs because of dislocations in money and credit markets. As always, the discount window is available as a source of funding.[25]

The Fed appears to have been misled by its monetarist (proliquidity) preconceptions. Depository institutions were encountering much stress because banks were reluctant to lend to each other (or to signal distress by borrowing from the Fed).[26] LIBOR was spiking, and Countrywide was going down the drain. This was not the familiar world in which the financial system merely needed a shot of short-term liquidity—as the Fed treated it. It was a crisis of confidence in the banks' own assets (Taylor 2010; Taylor and Williams 2009), based on the realization that subprime borrowers might not be able to pay back their loans.

Seven days later, the FOMC announced that "financial market conditions have deteriorated." A month after that, the FOMC reacted to the deterioration by lowering the target funds rate to 4.75 percent—even as it cautioned that "some inflation risks remain." The rate continued to be lowered into 2008, and numerous open-market operations in 2008 continued to facilitate short-term liquidity. These actions were explained on August 5, 2008: "Over time, the substantial easing of monetary policy, combined with ongoing measures to foster market liquidity, should help to promote moderate economic growth." In the view of the Fed, liquidity, not solvency, was the problem, and the standard tools were being used. Moreover, the inflation—which on August 5 was still named a "concern"—had occurred years earlier. The massive bubble in housing prices (driven by self-reinforcing price expectations) and the supporting expansion of credit (undisciplined by traditional equity requirements), as well as the tiered internal structure of the housing market, had all depended on further unsustainable housing-price growth, premised on unfathomably easy mortgage credit—fueled by easy money. Once that momentum turned negative, buyers of homes, mortgages, and bank obligations reined in their activity, the stock market plummeted, and monetary policy was impotent to stem the collapse. Monetary policy was "pushing on a string" that only absent buyers could have pulled.

The Second Crisis of the Fourth Capitalist Era

N. S. B. Gras (1938) identified three stages in the history of capitalism: the petty capitalism of itinerant merchants in the period before the commercial revolution of the thirteenth century; the mercantile capitalism characteristic of international trade from about 1300 until shortly after the financial revolution of the seventeenth century; and industrial capitalism. Transitions between stages created new economic opportunities but also produced new financial stresses. New institutional responses were essential for the effective management of the new conditions, and these responses typically developed only after many decades of false starts and iterative steps toward a solution. For example, mercantile capitalism required deployment of capital at the time scale of international trade in raw materials and finished goods (i.e., many months). Industrial capitalism required capital deployment at a much longer time scale, and the risks were of an entirely new sort. The profitability of a railroad would depend on population growth, demand for the products from a developing region, and general market conditions over a period of a decade or more. It is unsurprising that nineteenth-century economic history was punctuated by numerous financial crises given changes in the scale, the duration, and the novelty of many industrial enterprises—relative to the business requirements of the mercantile era.

The past century has grafted a new form of capitalism onto the mercantile capitalism of large-scale trade and the industrial capitalism of large-scale production. Consumer capitalism uses capital markets to support widespread purchases of consumer durable goods. It seems that we are now witnessing the second major crisis of consumer capitalism (the first having begun in 1929). Just as industrial capitalism involved greater risks than mercantile capitalism due to the longer time span of credit and debt, consumer capitalism poses new problems in credit-risk assessment and in structural characteristics of consumer-durables markets.

One of the most important messages of this debacle, however, is that even the best-informed scholars did not recognize the historical changes in the function of credit and debt, and accordingly were unable to guide public policy well—in large part, because we have so little experience with consumer-debt crises.

During Alan Greenspan's tenure at the Fed, many scholars knew that we were in a housing bubble. But this did not translate into corrective policies that would have commanded agreement. Ben Bernanke had as thorough an understanding of the Great Depression as anyone; however, that expertise was retrospective—as has been our own attempt to analogize the crashes of 1929 and 2008. In contrast, when one encounters a new situation in the present moment, one cannot know which historical analogies apply. We are reminded of the distinction that F. A. Hayek (1967, 43–44) borrowed from Michael Polanyi: the distinction between "knowing how" to do something—knowledge that may be gained through the long experience of a craftsman; and "knowing that" something is true (or so one believes)—knowledge that may be gained through long years of study. Perhaps fortunately— because of their infrequency of occurrence—none of our policy makers have a craftsman's experience with Great Depression-like events.

It may be that new precautionary institutional controls are required at this advanced stage in the development of consumer capitalism in order to effectively manage its risks and harness its opportunities—just as our predecessors developed institutions to manage the risks of industrial capitalism. But it is important first to recognize that the crisis of 2008 differed in many ways from the crises that have punctuated the development of industrial capitalism over the past two centuries.

PART II

What Went Wrong (and What Didn't)?

Chapter 4

The Anatomy of a Murder:
Who Killed America's Economy?

JOSEPH E. STIGLITZ

The search is on for whom to blame for the global economic crisis. It is not just a matter of vindictiveness; it is important to know who or what caused the crisis if one is to prevent another, or perhaps even to fix this one.

The notion of causation is, however, complex. Presumably, it means something like, "If only the guilty party had taken another course of action, the crisis would not have occurred." But the consequences of one party changing its actions depend on the behavior of others; presumably the actions of other parties, too, may have changed.

Consider a murder. We can identify who pulled the trigger. But somebody had to sell that person the gun. Somebody may have paid the gunman. Somebody may have provided inside information about the whereabouts of the victim. All these people are party to the crime. If the person who paid the gunman was determined to have the victim shot, then even if the particular gunman who ended up pulling the trigger had refused the job, the victim would have been shot: someone else would have been found to pull the trigger.

There are many parties to this crime—both people and institutions. Any discussion of "who is to blame" conjures up names like Robert Rubin, co-conspirator in deregulation and a senior official in one of the two financial institutions into which the American government has poured the most money. Then there was Alan Greenspan, who also pushed the deregulatory philosophy, who failed to use the regulatory authority that he had, who encouraged homeowners to take out highly risky adjustable mortgages, and who supported President George W. Bush's tax cut for the rich,[1]—making lower interest rates, which fed the bubble, necessary to stimulate the economy. But if these people hadn't been there, others would have occupied their seats, arguably doing similar things. There were others equally willing and able to perpetrate the crimes. Moreover, the fact that similar problems arose in other countries—with different people playing the parts of the protagonists—suggests that there were more fundamental economic forces at play.

The list of institutions that must assume considerable responsibility for the crisis includes the investment banks and the investors; the credit-rating agencies; the regulators, including the SEC and the Federal Reserve; the mortgage brokers; and a string of administrations, from Bush to Reagan, that pushed financial-sector deregulation. Some of these institutions contributed to the crisis in multiple roles—most notably the Federal Reserve, which failed in its role as regulator, but which also may have contributed to the crisis by mishandling interest rates and credit availability. All of these—and some others discussed below—share some culpability.

The Main Protagonists

But I would argue that blame should be centrally placed on the banks (and the financial sector more broadly) and the investors.

The banks were supposed to be the experts in risk management. They not only didn't manage risk, they created it. They engaged in excessive leverage. At a 30-to-1 leverage ratio, a mere 3 percent change in asset values wipes out one's net worth. (To put matters in perspective, as of March 2009, real-estate prices had fallen some 20 percent and were expected to fall at least another 10–15 percent.) The banks adopted incentive structures designed to induce short-sighted and excessively risky behavior. The stock options that they used to pay some of their senior executives, moreover, provided incentives for bad accounting, including incentives to engage in extensive off-balance-sheet accounting.

The bankers seemingly didn't understand the risks being created by securitization—including those arising from information asymmetries. The originators of the mortgages did not end up holding onto them, so the originators didn't bear the consequences of any failure at due diligence. The bankers also misestimated the extent of correlation among default rates in different parts of the country—not realizing that a rise in the interest rate or an increase in unemployment might have adverse effects in many parts of the country—and they underestimated the risk of real-estate price declines. Nor did the banks assess with any degree of accuracy the risks associated with some of the new financial products, such as low- or no-documentation loans.

The only defense that the bankers have—and it's admittedly a weak defense—is that their investors made them do it. Their investors didn't understand risk. They confused high returns brought on by excessive leverage in an up market with "smart" investment. Banks that didn't engage in excessive leverage, and so had lower returns, were "punished" by having their stock values beaten down. The reality, however, is that the banks exploited this investor ignorance to push their stock prices up, getting higher short-term returns at the expense of higher risk.

Accessories to the Crime

If the banks were the main perpetrators of the crime, they had many accomplices.

Rating agencies played a central role. They believed in financial alchemy, and converted F-rated subprime mortgages into A-rated securities that were safe enough to be held by pension funds. This was important, because it allowed a steady flow of cash into the housing market, which in turn provided the fuel for the housing bubble. The rating agencies' behavior may have been affected by the perverse incentive of being paid by those that they rated, but I suspect that even without these incentive problems, their models would have been badly flawed. Competition, in this case, had a perverse effect: it caused a race to the bottom—a race to provide ratings that were most favorable to those being rated.

Mortgage brokers played a key role: they were less interested in originating good mortgages—after all, they didn't hold the mortgages for long—than in originating many mortgages. Some of the mortgage brokers were so enthusiastic that they invented new forms of mortgages. The low- or no-documentation loans to which I referred earlier were an invitation to deception, and came to be called liar loans. This was an "innovation," but there was a good reason that such innovations hadn't occurred before.

Other new mortgage products—low- or no-amortization, variable-rate loans—snared unwary borrowers. Home-equity loans, too, encouraged Americans to borrow against the equity in their homes, increasing the (total) loan-to-value ratios and thereby making the mortgages riskier.

The mortgage originators didn't focus on risk, but rather on transactions costs. But they weren't trying to minimize transactions costs; they were trying to maximize them—devising ways that they could increase them, and thereby their revenues. Short-term loans that had to be refinanced—and left open the risk of not being able to be refinanced—were particularly useful in this respect.

The transactions costs generated by writing mortgages provided a strong incentive to prey on innocent and inexperienced borrowers— for instance, by encouraging more short-term lending and borrowing, entailing repeated loan restructurings, which helped generate high transactions costs.

The regulators, too, were accomplices in crime. They should have recognized the inherent risks in the new products; they should have done their own risk assessments, rather than relying on self-regulation or on the credit-rating agencies. They should have realized the risks associated with high leverage, with over-the-counter derivatives, and especially the risks that were compounding as these were not netted out.

The regulators deceived themselves into thinking that if only they ensured that each bank managed its own risk (which it had every incentive, presumably, to do), then the system would work. Amazingly, they did not pay any attention to *systemic* risk, though concerns about systemic risk constitute one of the primary rationales for regulation in the first place. Even if every bank were, "on average," sound, they could act in a correlated way that generated risks to the economy as a whole.

In some cases, the regulators had a defense: they had no legal basis for acting, even had they discovered something was wrong. They had not been given the power to regulate derivatives. But that defense is somewhat disingenuous, because some of the regulators—most notably Greenspan—had worked hard to make sure that appropriate regulations were not adopted.

The repeal of the Glass-Steagall Act played an especial role, not just because of the conflicts of interest that it exposed (made so evident in the Enron and WorldCom scandals), but also because it transmitted the risk-taking culture of investment banking to commercial banks, which should have acted in a far more prudential manner.

It was not just *financial* regulation and regulators that were at fault. There should have been tougher enforcement of antitrust laws. Banks were allowed to grow to be too big to fail—or too big to be managed. And such banks have perverse incentives. When it's heads I win, tails you lose, too-big-to-fail banks have incentives to engage in excessive risk taking.

Corporate governance laws, too, are partly to blame. Regulators and investors should have been aware of the risks that the peculiar incentive structures engendered. These did not even serve shareholder interests well. In the aftermath of the Enron and WorldCom scandals, there was much discussion of the need for reform, and the Sarbanes-Oxley Act represented a beginning. But it didn't attack perhaps the most fundamental problem: stock options.

The capital-gains tax cuts, enacted under George W. Bush and Bill Clinton, in conjunction with the deductibility of interest, provided enhanced incentives for leverage—for homeowners to take out, for instance, as large a mortgage as possible.

Credentialed Accomplices

There is one other set of accomplices—the economists who provided the arguments that those in the financial markets found so convenient and self-serving. These economists provided models—based on unrealistic assumptions of perfect information, perfect competition, and perfect markets—in which regulation was unnecessary.

Modern economic theories, particularly those focusing on imperfect and asymmetric information and on systematic irrationalities, especially with respect to risk judgments, had explained how flawed those earlier "neoclassical" models were. They had shown that those models were not robust—even slight deviations from the extreme assumptions destroyed the conclusions. But these insights were simply ignored.

Some important strands in recent economic theory, moreover, encouraged central bankers to focus solely on fighting inflation. They seemed to argue that low inflation was necessary, and almost sufficient, for stable and robust growth. The result was that central bankers (including the Fed) played little attention to the financial structure.

In short, many of the most popular micro- and macro-economic theories aided and abetted regulators, investors, bankers, and policy makers—they provided the "rationale" for their policies and actions. They made the bankers believe that, in pursuing individual self-interest, they were, in fact, advancing the well-being of society; they made the regulators believe that in pursuing policies of benign neglect, they were allowing the private sector to flourish, from which all would benefit.

Rebutting the Defense

Alan Greenspan (2009) has tried to shift the blame for low interest rates to China, because of its high savings rate. Clearly, Greenspan's defense is unpersuasive. The Fed had enough control, at least in the short run, to have raised interest rates in spite of China's willingness to lend to America at a relatively low interest rate. Indeed, the Fed did just that in the middle of the decade, which contributed—predictably—to the popping of the housing bubble.

Low interest rates did feed the bubble. But that is not the necessary consequence of low interest rates. Many countries yearn for low interest rates to help finance needed investment. The funds could have been channeled into more productive uses. Our financial markets failed to do that. Our regulatory authorities allowed the financial markets (including the banks) to use the abundance of funds in ways that were not socially productive. They allowed the low interest rates to feed a housing bubble. They had the tools to stop this. They didn't use the tools they had.

If we are to blame low interest rates for "feeding" the frenzy, then we have to ask what induced the Fed to pursue low interest rates. It did so, in part, to maintain the strength of the economy, which was suffering from inadequate aggregate demand as a result of the collapse of the tech bubble.

In that regard, Bush's tax cut for the rich was perhaps pivotal. It was not designed to stimulate the economy and did so only to a limited extent. His war in Iraq, too, played an important role. In its aftermath, oil prices rose from $20 a barrel to $140 a barrel. (We don't have to parse out here what fraction of this increase is due to the war; but there is little doubt that it played a role. See Stiglitz and Bilmes 2008.) Americans were now spending hundreds of billions of dollars a year more to import oil, money no longer available to be spent at home.

In the 1970s, when oil prices soared, most countries faced recessions because of the transfer of purchasing power abroad to finance the purchase of oil. There was one exception: Latin America, which used debt finance to continue its consumption unabated. But its borrowing was unsustainable. Over the decade prior to 2008, America took the Latin American route. To offset the negative effect of higher spending on oil, the Fed kept interest rates *lower than they otherwise would have been*, and this fed the housing bubble more than it otherwise would have. The American economy, like the Latin American economies of the 1970s, seemed to be doing well, because the housing bubble fed a consumption boom, as household savings fell all the way down to zero.

Given the war and the consequent soaring oil prices and given Bush's poorly designed tax cuts, the burden of maintaining economic strength fell to the Fed. The Fed could have exercised its authority as a regulator to do what it could do to direct the resources into more productive uses. Here, the Fed and its chairman have a double culpability. Not only did they fail in their regulatory role, they became cheerleaders for the bubble that eventually consumed America. When asked about a possible bubble, Greenspan suggested there was none—only a little froth. That was clearly wrong. The Fed argued that you could not tell a bubble until after it broke. That, too, was not fully correct. You can't be sure there is a bubble until after it breaks, but one can make strong probabilistic statements.

All policy is made in the context of uncertainty. House prices, especially at the lower end, soared, yet the real incomes of most Americans stagnated. There was a clear problem, and it was clear that the problem would get worse once interest rates rose. Greenspan had encouraged people to take out variable-rate mortgages when interest rates were at historically low levels. And he allowed them to borrow up to the hilt—assuming interest rates would remain at the same low level. But because interest rates were so low—real interest rates were negative—it was unreasonable to expect them to remain at that level for long. When they rose, it was clear that many Americans would be in trouble—and so would the lenders who had lent to them.

Apologists for the Fed sometimes try to defend this irresponsible and short-sighted policy by saying they had no choice: raising interest rates would have killed the bubble, but also would have killed the economy. But the Fed has more tools than just the interest rate. There were, for instance, a number of regulatory actions that would have dampened the bubble. It chose not to employ these tools. It could have reduced maximum loan-to-value ratios as the likelihood of a bubble increased; it could have lowered the maximum house payment-to-income ratios allowed. If it believed it did not have the requisite tools, it could have gone to Congress and requested them.

This doesn't provide a *fully* satisfactory counterfactual. True, perhaps the money could have been deployed by financial markets more productively to support, for instance, more innovation or important projects in developing countries. But perhaps the financial markets would have found another scam to support irresponsible borrowing—for instance, a new credit-card boom.

Defending the Innocent

Just as all the accomplices are not equally culpable, some suspects should be acquitted.

In the long list of possible culprits, there are two that many Republicans often name. They find it difficult to accept that markets fail, that market participants could act in such an irresponsible manner, that the wizards of finance didn't understand risk, that capitalism has serious flaws. It is government, they are sure, which is to blame.

I have suggested government is indeed to blame, but for doing too little. The conservative critics believe that government is to blame for doing too much. They criticize the Community Reinvestment Act (CRA) requirements imposed on banks, which required them to lend a certain fraction of their portfolio to underserved minority communities. They also blame Fannie Mae and Freddie Mac, the peculiar government-sponsored enterprises, which, though privatized in 1968, play a very large role in mortgage markets. Fannie and Freddie were, according to conservatives, "under pressure" from Congress and the president to expand home ownership (President Bush often talked about the "ownership society").

This is clearly just an attempt to shift blame. A recent Fed study showed that the default rate among CRA mortgagors is actually below average (Kroszner 2008). The problems in America's mortgage markets began with the subprime market, while Fannie Mae and Freddie Mac primarily financed "conforming" (prime) mortgages.

It is America's fully private financial markets that invented all the bad practices that played a central role in this crisis. When government encouraged home ownership, it meant permanent home ownership. It didn't intend for people to buy homes beyond their ability to afford them. That would generate ephemeral gains and contribute to impoverishment: the poor would lose their life savings as they lost their home.

There is always a home that is of an appropriate cost to an individual's budget. The irony is that because of the bubble, many of the impoverished wound up owning a home no bigger than they would have if more prudent lending policies had been enforced—which would have dampened the bubble. To be sure, Fannie Mae and Freddie Mac did get into the high-risk high-leverage "games" that were the fad in the private sector, though rather late and rather ineptly. Here, too, there was regulatory failure; the government-sponsored enterprises have a special regulator which should have constrained them, but evidently, amid the deregulatory philosophy of the Bush administration, did not. Once they entered the game, they had an advantage, because they could borrow somewhat more cheaply because of their (ambiguous at the time) government guarantee. They could arbitrage that guarantee to generate bonuses comparable to those that they saw were being "earned" by their counterparts in the fully private sector.

Politics and Economics

There is one more important culprit that, in fact, has played a key behind-the-scenes role in many various parts of this story: America's political system, and especially its dependence on campaign contributions. This allowed Wall Street to exercise the enormous influence that it has had, to push for the stripping of regulations and to the appointment of regulators who didn't believe in regulations—with the predictable and predicted consequences (Stiglitz 2003) that we have seen. Even today, that influence is playing a role in the design of effective means of addressing the financial crisis.

Any economy needs rules and referees. Our rules and referees were shaped by special interests; ironically, it is not even clear whether those rules and referees served those special interests well. It is clear that they did not serve the national interests well.

In the end, this is a crisis of our economic and political system. Each of the players was, to a large extent, doing what they thought they should do. The bankers were maximizing their incomes, given the rules of the game. The rules of the game said that they should use their political influence to get regulations and regulators that allowed them, and the corporations they headed, to walk away with as much money as they could. The politicians responded to the rules of the game: they had to raise money to get elected, and to do that, they had to please powerful and wealthy constituents. There were economists who provided the politicians, the bankers, and the regulators with a convenient ideology. According to this ideology, the policies and practices they were pursuing would supposedly benefit all.

There are those who now would like to reconstruct the system as it was prior to 2008. They will push for regulatory reform, but it will be more cosmetic than real. Banks that are too big to fail will be allowed to continue little changed. There will be "oversight," whatever that means. But the banks will continue to be able to gamble, and they will continue to be too big to fail. Accounting standards will be relaxed, to give them greater leeway. Little will be done about incentive structures or even risky practices. If so, then, another crisis is sure to follow.

Chapter 5

Monetary Policy, Economic Policy and the Financial Crisis: An Empirical Analysis of What Went Wrong

JOHN B. TAYLOR

What caused the financial crisis? What prolonged it? Why did it worsen so dramatically more than a year after it began? Rarely in economics is there a single answer to such questions, but the empirical research presented in this chapter strongly suggests that specific government actions and interventions should be first on the list of answers to all three. The period from the start of the crisis through October 2008, when market conditions deteriorated precipitously and rapidly, is the focus.

What Caused the Financial Crisis?

The classic explanation of financial crises, going back hundreds of years, is that they are caused by excesses—frequently monetary excesses—which lead to a boom and an inevitable bust. In the 2008 crisis, we had a housing boom and bust, which in turn led to financial turmoil in the United States and other countries. I begin by showing that monetary excesses were the main cause of that boom and the resulting bust.

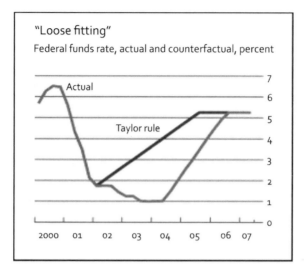

Figure 5.1. Loose-fitting monetary policy. *Economist*, October 18, 2007. Reproduced by permission of the author.

Loose-Fitting Monetary Policy

Figure 5.1 is a simple way to illustrate the story of monetary excesses. The figure is based on Taylor (2007), presented at the annual Jackson Hole conference in August 2007.[1] It examines Federal Reserve policy decisions—in terms of the federal funds interest rate—from 2000 to 2006. The line that dips to 1 percent in 2003, stays there into 2004, and then rises steadily until 2006 shows the actual interest rate decisions of the Federal Reserve. The other line shows what the interest rate would have been if the Fed had followed the type of policy followed fairly regularly during the previous twenty-year period of good economic performance. The *Economist* labels that line the Taylor rule, because it is a smoothed version of the interest rate one obtains by plugging actual inflation and GDP into a policy rule that I proposed in 1992.[2] But the important point is that this line shows what the interest rate would have been if the Fed had followed the kind of policy that had worked well during the historical experience of the "Great Moderation" that began in the early 1980s.

Figure 5.1 shows that the actual interest rate decisions fell well below what historical experience would suggest policy should be and thus provides an empirical measure that monetary policy was too easy during this period, or too "loose fitting," as the *Economist* put it. This was an unusually big deviation from the Taylor rule. There has been no greater or more persistent deviation of actual Fed policy since the turbulent days of the 1970s. So there is clearly evidence of monetary excesses during the period leading up to the housing boom.

The unusually low interest rate decisions were, of course, made with careful consideration by monetary policy makers. One can interpret them as purposeful deviations from the "regular" rate settings based on the usual macroeconomic variables. The Fed used transparent language to describe the decisions, saying, for example, that interest rates would be low for "a considerable period" and that they would rise slowly at a "measured pace," which were ways of clarifying that the decisions were deviations from the rule in some sense. These actions were thus effectively discretionary government interventions in that they deviated from the regular way of conducting policy in order to address a specific problem—in particular, fear of deflation, as had occurred in Japan in the 1990s.

The Counterfactual: No Boom, No Bust

In presenting Figure 5.1 in 2007, I argued that this extra-easy policy was responsible for accelerating the housing boom and thereby ultimately leading to the housing bust. To support such an argument empirically, I provided statistical evidence that the interest rate deviation shown in the figure could plausibly bring about a housing boom. I did this by using regression techniques to estimate a model of the empirical relationship between the interest rate and housing starts; I then simulated that model to see what would have happened in the counterfactual event that policy had followed the rule shown in Figure 5.1. In this way, an empirical proof was provided that monetary policy was a key cause of the boom and hence the bust and the crisis.

Figure 5.2 summarizes the results of this empirical approach. It is a picture of housing starts in the United States during the same period as Figure 5.1, drawn from that same 2007 paper. The jagged line shows actual housing starts in thousands of units. Both the housing

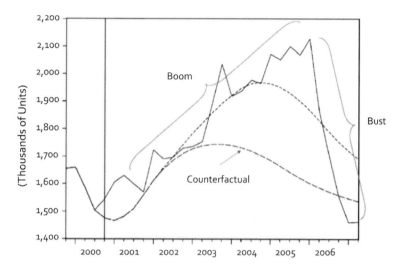

Figure 5.2. The boom and bust in housing starts compared with the counterfactual. The line with shorter dashes shows model simulations using the actual interest rate. Author's calculations based on Taylor 2007.

boom and the bust are very clear. The line labeled "counterfactual" is what a statistically estimated model of housing starts suggests would have happened had interest rates followed along the rule in Figure 5.1; clearly, there would not have been such a big boom and bust. Hence, Figure 5.2 provides empirical evidence that the unusually low interest rate policy was a factor in the housing boom. One can challenge this conclusion, of course, by challenging the model, but an advantage of using a model and an empirical counterfactual is that one has a formal framework for debating the issue.

Not shown in Figure 5.2 is the associated boom and bust in housing prices in the United States. The boom-bust was evident throughout most of the country, and was worst in California, Florida, Arizona, and Nevada. The only exceptions were in states such as Texas and Michigan, where local factors offset the monetary excess stressed here.

Though the housing boom was the most noticeable effect of the monetary excesses, effects also could be seen in more gradually rising overall prices: CPI inflation, for example, averaged 3.2 percent at an annual rate during 2003–2008, well above the 2 percent target suggested by many policy makers and implicit in the policy rule in Figure 5.1. It is always difficult to predict the exact initial impacts of monetary shocks, but housing was also a volatile part of GDP in the 1970s, a period of monetary instability before the onset of the Great Moderation. The monetary policy followed during the Great Moderation had the advantages of keeping both the overall economy stable and the inflation rate low.

A Competing Explanation: A Global Savings Glut

Some argue that the low interest rates in 2002–2004 were caused by global factors beyond the control of the monetary authorities. If so, then the interest rate decisions by the authorities were not the major factor causing the boom. This explanation is potentially appealing, because long-term interest rates remained low for a while, even after the short-term federal funds rate started increasing.

An alternative explanation is that there was an excess of world savings—a global savings glut—which pushed interest rates down in the United States and other countries. The main problem with this explanation is that there is no evidence for a global savings glut. On the contrary, as Figure 5.3 shows in very simple terms, there seems to have been a savings shortage. This figure, produced by staff at the International Monetary Fund (IMF) in 2005, shows that the global savings rate—world savings as a fraction of world GDP—was very low in 2002–2004, especially compared with the 1970s and 1980s. So this alternative explanation does not stand up to empirical testing using data that have long been available.

To be sure, there was a gap of saving over investment in the world outside the United States during that period, and this may be the source of the term "savings glut." But the United States was saving less than it was investing; it was running a current account deficit, which implies that saving was less than investment. Thus, the positive savings gap outside the United States was offset by an equal negative savings gap in the United States. No extra impact on world interest rates would be expected. As implied by simple global accounting, there is no global gap between savings and investment.

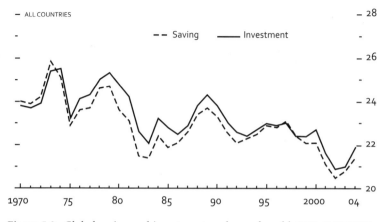

Figure 5.3. Global saving and investment as share of world GDP. IMF 2005, ch. 2, p. 92.

Monetary Policy in Other Countries: Central Banks Looking at Each Other?

Nevertheless, there are possible global connections to remember when assessing the root cause of the crisis. Most important is the evidence that interest rates at several other central banks also deviated from what historical regularities, as described by a Taylor rule, would predict. Even more striking is that housing booms were largest where the deviations from the rule were largest.[3] Within Europe, for example, the deviations from the Taylor rule vary in size because inflation and output data vary from country to country. The country with the largest deviation from the rule was Spain, and it had the biggest housing boom, measured by the change in housing investment as a share of GDP. The country with the smallest deviation was Austria; it had the smallest change in housing investment as a share of GDP. The very close correlation is shown in Figure 5.4, which plots the sum of deviations from the policy rule on the horizontal axis and the change in housing investment as a share of GDP on the vertical axis.

An important question, with implications for reform of the international financial system, is whether the low interest rates at

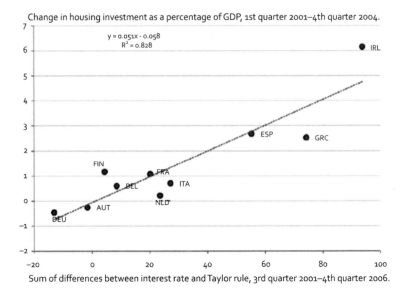

Figure 5.4. Housing investment versus deviations from the Taylor rule in Europe. Ahrend, Cournède, and Price 2008.

other central banks were influenced by the decisions in the United States, or whether they represented an interaction among central banks that caused global short interest rates to be lower than they otherwise would have been. To test this hypothesis, I examined the decisions at the European Central Bank (ECB) (Taylor 2009b),[4] I studied the deviations (or the residuals) of the ECB interest-rate decisions from the same type of policy rule used in Figure 5.1 but using euro zone inflation and GDP data. The interest rate set by the ECB was also below the rule; in other words, there were negative residuals. To determine whether those residuals were influenced by the Federal Reserve's interest-rate decisions, I ran a regression of them for 2000–2006 on the federal funds rate shown in Figure 5.1. I found that the estimated coefficient was .21 and that it was statistically significant.

Figure 5.5 gives a visual sense of how much the ECB interest rate decisions can be explained by the influence of the Fed's interest-rate decisions. It appears that a good fraction can be explained in this way.

Percent

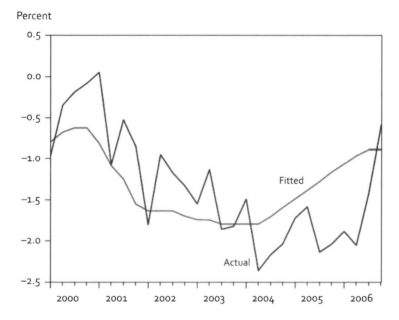

Figure 5.5. Actual deviations from a Euro policy rule and the predicted (fitted) values based on the federal funds rate. Author's calculations based on Taylor 2009b.

The jagged-looking line in Figure 5.5 shows the deviations of the actual interest rates set by the ECB from the policy rule. (The high-frequency jagged movements have not been smoothed out as in Figure 5.1.) By this measure, the ECB interest rate was as much as 2 percentage points too low during this period. The smoother line shows that a good fraction of the deviation can be "explained" by the federal funds rate in the United States.

The reasons for this connection are not clear from this statistical analysis and, in my view, are a fruitful subject for future research. Indeed, it is difficult to distinguish statistically between the ECB following the Fed and the Fed following the ECB; similar regressions show that there is a connection the other way as well. Concerns about the exchange rate, or the influence of the exchange rate on inflation, could generate such a relationship. So could a third factor, such as changes in the global real interest rate.

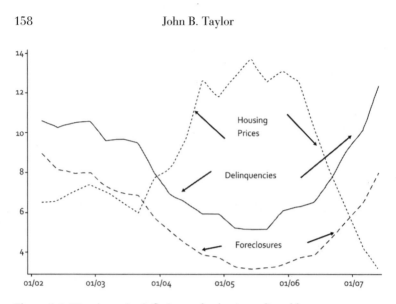

Figure 5.6. Housing price inflation and subprime adjustable-rate mortgage delinquencies and foreclosures. Taylor 2007.

Monetary Interaction with the Subprime Mortgage Problem

A sharp boom and bust in the housing markets would be expected to have had impacts on the financial markets as falling house prices led to delinquencies and foreclosures. These effects were amplified by several complicating factors, including the use of subprime mortgages, especially the adjustable-rate variety, which led to excessive risk taking. In the United States, this was encouraged by government programs designed to promote home ownership, a worthwhile goal but, in retrospect, overdone.

It is important to note, however, that the excessive risk taking and the low-interest monetary policy decisions are connected. Evidence for this connection is shown in Figure 5.6, which plots housing price inflation along with foreclosure and delinquency rates on adjustable-rate subprime mortgages. The figure shows the sharp increase in housing price inflation from mid-2003 to early 2006 and the subsequent decline. Observe how delinquency rates and foreclosure rates were inversely related to housing price inflation in this period. During the years of the rapidly rising housing prices, delinquency and foreclosure rates declined rapidly. The benefits of holding onto a house, perhaps working longer hours to make the payments, are higher when the price of the house is rising rapidly. When prices are falling, the incentives to do so are fewer and turn negative if the price of the house falls below the value of the mortgage. Hence, delinquencies and foreclosures rise.

Mortgage-underwriting procedures are supposed to take account of the actual realizations of foreclosure rates and delinquency rates in cross-section data. The procedures would therefore have been overly optimistic during the period when prices were rising, unless they took account of the time-series correlation in Figure 5.6. Thus, there is an interaction between the monetary excesses and the risk-taking excesses. It is an illustration of how unintended things can happen when policy deviates from the norm. In this case, the rapidly rising housing prices and the resulting low delinquency rates likely threw the underwriting programs off track and misled many people.

More Complications: Complex Securitization, Fannie, and Freddie

A significant amplification of these problems occurred because the adjustable-rate subprime and other mortgages were packed into mortgage-backed securities of great complexity. The risk was underestimated by the rating agencies because of lack of competition, poor accountability, or, most likely, an inherent difficulty in assessing risk owing to the complexity. It led to what might be called the "queen of spades" problem corresponding to the game of hearts. In hearts, you don't know where the queen of spades is, and you don't want to find yourself holding it. Well, the queens of spades—and there are many of them in this game—were the securities with the bad mortgages in them, and people didn't know where they were. We didn't know which banks were holding them in July 2007, and as of 2009 we still didn't know where they are. This risk in the balance sheets of financial institutions has been at the core of the financial crisis from the beginning.

In the United States, other government actions were at play. The government-sponsored enterprises Fannie Mae and Freddie Mac were

Percent

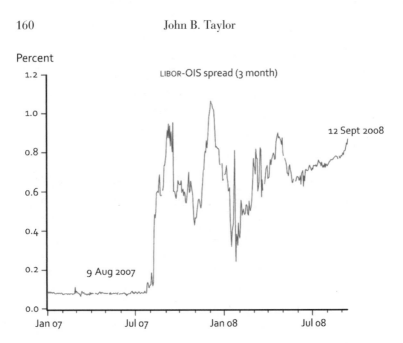

Figure 5.7. LIBOR-OIS spread during the first year of the crisis. Taylor and Williams 2009.

encouraged to expand and buy mortgage-backed securities, including those formed with the risky subprime mortgages. While legislation such as the Federal Housing Enterprise Regulatory Reform Act of 2005 was proposed to control these excesses, it was not passed into law. The actions of these agencies should be added to the list of government interventions that were part of the problem.

What Prolonged the Crisis?

The financial crisis became acute on 9 and 10 August 2007, when the money-market interest rates rose dramatically. Figure 5.7 illustrates this, using a measure that has since become the focus of many studies. The measure is the spread between 3-month LIBOR and the 3-month Overnight Index Swap (OIS). The OIS is a measure of what the markets expect the federal funds rate to be over the 3-month period comparable to 3-month LIBOR. Subtracting OIS from LIBOR effectively controls for expectations effects, which are a factor in all term loans, including 3-month LIBOR. The difference between LIBOR and OIS is thus due to things other than interest-rate expectations, such as risk and liquidity effects.

The lower left of Figure 5.7 shows a spread of about 10 basis points. If it were extended farther to the left, one would see a similarly steady level of about 10 basis points. On 9 and 10 August 2007, this spread jumped to unusually high levels and remained high for months afterwards. In our research on this episode, John Williams and I called the event "a black swan in the money market," because it appeared to be so unusual (Taylor and Williams 2009).[5] Observe that Figure 5.7 focuses on the first year of the crisis. The worsening situation in September and October 2008 is covered in the next section.

In addition to being a measure of financial stress, the LIBOR-OIS spread affects the transmission mechanism of monetary policy to the economy, because trillions of dollars of loans and securities are indexed to LIBOR. An increase in the spread, holding the OIS constant, will increase the cost of such loans and have a contractionary effect on the economy. Bringing this spread down, therefore, became a major objective of monetary policy as well as a measure of its success in dealing with the market turmoil.

Diagnosing the Problem: Liquidity or Counterparty Risk?

Diagnosing the reason for the increased spreads was essential, of course, for determining what type of policy response was necessary. If it was a liquidity problem, then providing more liquidity by making discount-window borrowing easier or opening new windows or facilities would be appropriate. But if the issue was counterparty risk, then a direct focus on the quality and transparency of the banks' balance sheets would be appropriate, either by requiring more transparency, dealing directly with the increasing number of mortgage defaults as housing prices fell, or looking for ways to bring more capital into the banks and other financial institutions.

In autumn 2007, Williams and I embarked on what we thought would be an interesting and possibly policy-relevant research project

(Taylor and Williams 2009) to examine the issue. We interviewed traders who deal in the interbank market and we looked for measures of counterparty risk. The idea that counterparty risk was the reason for the increased spreads made sense because it corresponded to the queen of spades theory and other reasons for uncertainty about banks' balance sheets. At the time, however, many traders and monetary officials thought it was mainly a liquidity problem.

To assess the issue empirically, we looked for measures of risk in these markets to see if they were correlated with the spread. One good measure of risk is the difference between interest rates on unsecured and secured interbank loans of the same maturity. Examples of secured loans are government-backed repurchase agreements (repos) between banks. By subtracting the interest rate on repos from LIBOR, you could get a measure of risk. Using regression methods, we then looked for the impact of this measure of risk on the LIBOR spread and showed that it could explain much of the variation in the spread. Other measures of risk gave the same results.

The results are illustrated in Figure 5.8, which shows the high correlation between the unsecured-secured spread and the LIBOR-OIS spread. There seems to be little role for liquidity. These results suggested, therefore, that the market turmoil in the interbank market was not a liquidity problem of the kind that could be alleviated simply by central bank liquidity tools. Rather, it was inherently an issue of counterparty risk, which linked back to the underlying cause of the financial crisis. This was not a situation like the Great Depression, where simply printing money or providing liquidity was the solution; rather, it was due to fundamental problems in the financial sector relating to risk.

But this was not the diagnosis that drove economic policy during this period. While it is difficult to determine the diagnosis of policy makers because their rationales for the decisions are not always explained clearly, it certainly appears that the increased spreads in the money markets were seen by the authorities as liquidity problems rather than problems of risk. Thus, their early interventions focused mainly on policies other than those that would deal with the fundamental sources of the heightened risk. As a result, in my view, the crisis continued.

Percent

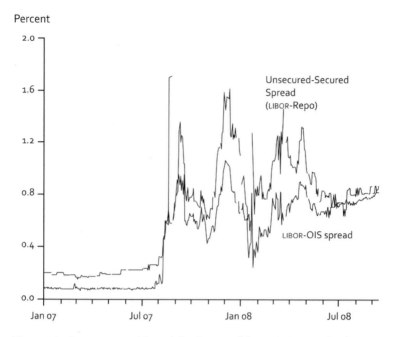

Figure 5.8 Counterparty risk explained most of the variation. Author's calculations based on Taylor and Williams 2009.

As evidence, what follows are three specific examples of interventions that prolonged the crisis either because they did not address the problem or because they had unintended consequences.

The Term Auction Facility

To make it easier for banks to borrow from the Fed, the term auction facility (TAF) was introduced in December 2007. With this new facility, banks could avoid going to the discount window; they could instead bid directly for funds from the Fed. Similar facilities were set up simultaneously at other central banks. The main objective of the TAF was to reduce the spreads in the money markets and thereby increase the flow of credit and reduce interest rates. Figure 5.9, which is drawn from Taylor and Williams (2009), shows the amount of funds taken up (on the right scale) along with the LIBOR and OIS

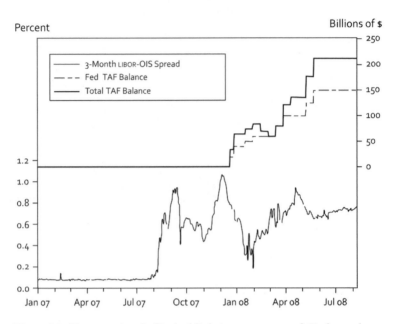

Figure 5.9. Term auction facility had little impact on spread. Taylor and Williams 2009.

spread (on the left scale). Note that this figure does not go beyond mid-September 2008.

Soon after the introduction of the TAF in December 2007, the spread came down a bit and some policy makers suggested that it was working. But soon the spread rose again, and when looking at Figure 5.9, it is difficult to see any effect on the spread during the entire period. This visual impression is confirmed with detailed regression analysis. The TAF did not appear to make much difference. If one considers the reason for the spread as counterparty risk, as distinct from liquidity, this is not surprising.

Temporary Cash Infusions

Another early policy response was the Economic Stimulus Act of 2008, passed in February 2008. The prime goal of this package was to

Billions of dollars

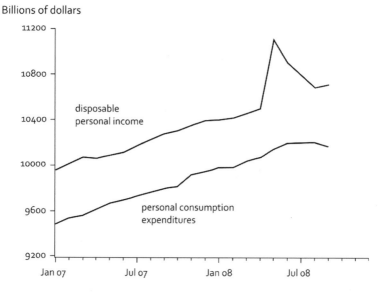

Figure 5.10. Rebates increased income, but not consumption. Monthly data, seasonally adjusted, annual rates. Author's calculations based on Taylor 2008c.

send cash totaling over $100 billion to individuals and families in the United States so they would have more to spend and thus jump-start consumption and the economy. Most checks were sent in May, June, and July. While not a purely monetary action—because the rebate was financed by borrowing rather than by money creation—the stimulus, like the liquidity facilities, was not focused on the underlying causes of the crisis.

Moreover, as would be predicted by the permanent-income theory of consumption, people spent little if anything of the temporary rebate, and consumption was not jump-started as had been hoped. The evidence is in Figure 5.10. The top line shows how personal disposable income spiked at the time of the rebate. The lower line shows that personal consumption expenditures did not increase in a noticeable way. As with the earlier figures, formal statistical work shows that the rebates resulted in no statistically significant increase in consumption.[6]

The Initial Cuts in Interest Rates Through April 2008

A third policy response to the financial crisis was the sharp reduction in the federal funds rate in the first half-year of the crisis. The target for the federal funds rate went from 5.25 percent when the crisis began in August 2007 to 2 percent in April 2008. The Taylor rule also called for a reduction in the interest rate during this early period, but not a reduction as sharp as that. Thus, the reduction was more than would be called for using the historical relation stressed at the beginning of this chapter, even adjusting for the LIBOR-OIS spread, as suggested in February 2008 (Taylor 2008a, b).

It is difficult to assess the full impact of this extra-sharp easing, and more research is needed. The lower interest rates reduced the size of the re-set of adjustable-rate mortgages and thereby were addressed to some of the fundamentals causing the crisis. Some of these effects would have occurred if the interest rate cuts were less aggressive.

The most noticeable effects at the time of the cut in the federal funds rate, however, were the sharp depreciation of the dollar and the very large rise in oil prices. During the first year of the financial crisis, oil prices doubled from about $70 per barrel in August 2007 to over $140 in July 2008, before plummeting as expectations of world economic growth declined sharply. Figure 5.11 shows the close correlation between the federal funds rate and the price of oil during this period using monthly average data. The figure ends before the global slump in demand became evident and oil prices fell back.

When the federal funds rate was cut, oil prices broke out of the $60 to $70 per barrel range and then rose rapidly throughout the first year of the financial crisis. Clearly, this bout of high oil prices hit the economy hard, as gasoline prices skyrocketed and automobile sales plunged in the spring and summer of 2008. In my view, this interest-rate cut helped raise oil and other commodity prices and thereby prolonged the crisis. Taylor 2008e discusses the impact of the sharp monetary easing on oil and other commodity prices and proposes the idea of a global inflation target as a means of preventing the spread of central-bank interest-rate decisions to other central banks.

Econometric evidence of the connection between interest rates and oil prices is found in existing empirical studies. For example, in

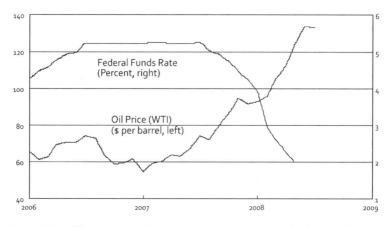

Figure 5.11. The sharp cut in interest rates was accompanied by rapid increase in oil prices through first year of the crisis. Last observation is July 2008. Taylor 2009a.

early May 2008, the First Deputy Managing Director of the IMF, John Lipsky (2008), said: "Preliminary evidence suggests that low interest rates have a statistically significant impact on commodity prices, above and beyond the typical effect of increased demand. Exchange rate shifts also appear to influence commodity prices. For example, IMF estimates suggest that if the U.S. dollar had remained at its 2002 peak through end-2007, oil prices would have been $25 a barrel lower and non-fuel commodity prices 12 percent lower."

When it became clear in autumn 2008 that the world economy was declining sharply, oil prices returned to the $60 to $70 range. But, by this time the damage of high prices had been done.

Why Did the Crisis Worsen So Dramatically More Than a Year After It Began?

Figure 5.12 shows—using the same LIBOR-OIS measure of tension in the financial markets as in Figure 5.7—how dramatically the financial crisis worsened in October 2008, an even more unusual occurrence than the August 2007 "black swan in the money market."

Percent

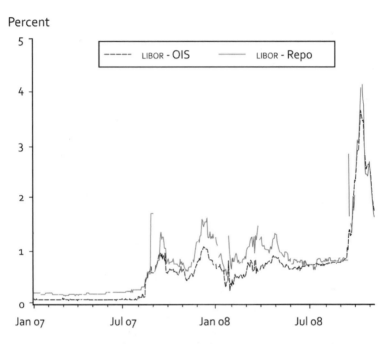

Figure 5.12. Evidence of crisis worsening dramatically 14 months after it began. Taylor 2009a.

Suddenly, a year after the crisis began, the LIBOR-OIS spread worsened by a factor of four and became a significant credit crunch with large spillovers, seriously weakening an economy already suffering from the lingering impacts of the oil-price bout and the housing bust. Notice the close correlation between our measure of counterparty risk and the LIBOR-OIS spread, which demonstrates convincingly that, all along, the problems in the market were related to risk rather than to liquidity.

An Event Study

Many commentators have argued that the reason for the worsening of the crisis was the decision by the U.S. government (more specifically, the Treasury and the Federal Reserve) not to intervene to prevent the bankruptcy of Lehman Brothers over the weekend of 13 and

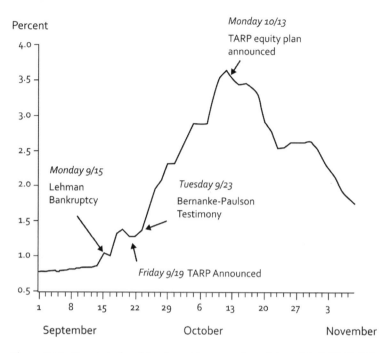

Figure 5.13. Event study of the dramatic worsening of the crisis. LIBOR-OIS spread. Taylor 2009a.

14 September. It is difficult to bring rigorous empirical analysis to this question, but it is important that researchers do so, because future policy actions depend on the answer. Perhaps the best empirical analyses we can hope for at this time are "event studies" that look carefully at reactions in the financial markets to various decisions and events. Such an event study, summarized below, suggests that the answer is more complicated than the decision not to intervene to prevent the Lehman bankruptcy and, in my view, lies elsewhere.

Figure 5.13 focuses on a few key events from 1 September through mid-October 2008—the last few observations in Figure 5.12. Recall that for the year previous to the events represented in Figure 5.13, the LIBOR-OIS spread had been fluctuating in the 50 to 100 basis point range, where it remained through the first half of September 2008. It is evident that the spread moved a bit on 15 September, the Monday after the weekend decision not to intervene in Lehman Brothers. It then bounced back down a little on September 16, around the time of the AIG (American International Group) intervention. While the spread did rise during the week following the Lehman Brothers decision, it was not far out of line with the range of the previous year.

On Friday of that week, the Treasury announced it was going to propose a large rescue package, although the size and details hadn't yet been determined. Over the weekend the package was put together and on Tuesday, September 23, Federal Reserve Board Chairman Ben Bernanke and Treasury Secretary Henry Paulson testified at the Senate Banking Committee that TARP would be $700 billion in size. They provided a two-and-one-half-page draft of legislation with no mention of oversight and few restrictions on the funds' use. They were questioned intensely in this hearing; and the reaction was quite negative, judging by the large volume of critical mail received by many members of Congress. As shown in Figure 5.13, it was following this testimony that one really begins to see the crisis deepening, as measured by the relentless upward movement in the LIBOR-OIS spread for the next three weeks. The situation steadily deteriorated, and the spread went through the roof to 3.5 percent.

The Lack of a Predictable Framework for Intervention

The main message of Figure 5.13 is that identifying the decisions over the weekend of September 13 and 14 as the cause of the increased severity of the crisis is questionable. It was not until more than a week later that conditions deteriorated severely. Moreover, it is plausible that events around September 23 actually drove the market, including the realization by the public that the intervention plan had not been fully thought through and that conditions were much worse than many had been led to believe. At a minimum, a great deal of uncertainty about what the government would do to aid financial institutions, and under what circumstances, was revealed and thereby had to be factored into investment decisions at that time. Such uncertainty would have driven up risk spreads in the interbank market and elsewhere. Some evidence of the uncertainty is found in a survey taken later (November 5) by the Securities Industry and Financial

Markets Association; it showed that 94 percent of securities firms and banks found that TARP lacked clarity about its operations.

The problem of uncertainty about the procedures or criteria for government intervention to prevent financial institutions from failing had existed since the time of the Bear Stearns intervention in March. The implication of that decision for future interventions was not made clear by policy makers. This lack of predictability about Treasury-Fed intervention policy and recognition of the harm it could do to markets likely increased in autumn 2008, when the underlying uncertainty was revealed for all to see. What was the rationale for intervening with Bear Stearns, and then not with Lehman, and then again with AIG? What would guide the operations of TARP?

Concerns about the lack of clarity were raised in many quarters. I have argued elsewhere (Taylor 2008d) that the U.S. Treasury and the Fed urgently needed to develop a new framework for exceptional access to government support for financial institutions.[7]

This chapter provides empirical evidence that government actions and interventions caused, prolonged, and worsened the 2008 financial crisis. They caused it by deviating from historical precedents and principles for setting interest rates that had worked well for twenty years. They prolonged it by misdiagnosing the problems in the bank credit markets and thereby responding inappropriately by focusing on liquidity rather than risk. They made it worse by providing support for certain financial institutions and their creditors but not others in an ad hoc fashion, without a clear and understandable framework. While other factors were certainly at play, these government actions should be first on the list of answers to the question of what went wrong.

Chapter 6

Housing Initiatives and Other Policy Factors

PETER J. WALLISON

The current financial crisis is not—as many have said—a crisis of capitalism. It is in fact the opposite: a demonstration that well-intentioned government intervention in the private economy can have devastating consequences.

The crisis has its roots in the U.S. government's efforts to increase home ownership, especially among minority, low-income, and other underserved groups, through hidden financial subsidies rather than through direct government expenditures. Instead of a government subsidy, say, for down-payment assistance to low-income families, the government used regulatory and political pressure to force banks and other government-regulated or -controlled private entities to reduce lending standards, so more applicants would have access to mortgage financing.

The two key instances of this policy are the Community Reinvestment Act (CRA), adopted in 1977, and the affordable-housing "mission" adopted by Congress in the 1990s as a responsibility of the government-sponsored enterprises (GSEs), Fannie Mae and Freddie Mac. Amendments to the CRA in the early 1990s pressured banks into making loans they would not otherwise have made. Together, the tighter CRA requirements and the affordable-housing regulations imposed on the GSEs substantially reduced the standards that had to be met to qualify for a mortgage. The number of CRA loans was not large, but they required banks to devise ways of lending to people who would not previously have qualified for a mortgage. Once Fannie and Freddie began accepting loans with low down payments and other liberalized terms, the same unsound standards were extended to borrowers who could have qualified under the traditional underwriting standards. In addition, federal regulations encouraged bank lending for housing in preference to other lending, and tax policy favored borrowing against (and thus reducing) the equity in a house.

These policies were effective in the sense that they achieved some of the intended results. Between 1995—when lending quotas based on the CRA became effective—and 2005, the proportion of American households that owned their own home rose from 64 percent, where it had been for about twenty-five years, to 69 percent (Vlasenko 2008). A measure of the unintended results of federal policy, however, is that home prices doubled between 1995 and 2007; and that the housing bubble was composed—to an unprecedented degree—of subprime and other nonprime and risky loans. Banking-capital regulations and the deductibility of interest on home-equity loans made a crisis inevitable once this housing bubble collapsed.

The Community Reinvestment Act

As originally enacted in 1977, the CRA was a vague mandate for regulators to "consider" whether a federally insured bank was serving the needs of its entire community. The "community" was not defined, and the act stated only that it was intended to "encourage" banks to meet community needs. This encouragement included the denial of applications for mergers and acquisitions to banks judged to be in violation of the Act. The Act also stated, however, that serving community needs had to be done within the context of safe and sound lending practices. Although the Act was adopted to prevent "redlining"—the practice of refusing loans to otherwise-qualified borrowers in low-income areas—it also contained language that included small business, agriculture, and similar groups among the community interests that banks had to serve. With all its ambiguities, the CRA was invoked relatively infrequently when banks applied for permission to merge or needed other regulatory approvals, until the Clinton administration decided to strengthen the Act.[1]

This decision was probably due to the substantial amount of media and political attention that had been paid to the Boston Federal Reserve Bank 1992 study (Munnell et al. 1992) of discrimination in home mortgage lending. The study concluded that while there was no overt discrimination in the allocation of mortgage funds, more subtle forms of discrimination led to better treatment of white applicants by loan officers as compared to minority-group applicants. The methodology of the study has since been questioned (e.g., McKinley 1994), but at the time of its publication, it seems to have been highly influential with regulators and members of the incoming Clinton administration.

In 1993, bank regulators initiated a major effort to reform the CRA regulations. Some of the context in which this was occurring can be gleaned from the following statement by Attorney General Janet Reno in January 1994:

> We will tackle lending discrimination wherever and in whatever form it appears. No loan is exempt, no bank is immune. For those who thumb their nose at us, I promise vigorous enforcement. (quoted in McKinley 1994, 30)

New rules were adopted in May 1995 that were phased in fully by July 1997. These rules attempted to establish objective criteria for determining whether a bank was meeting the standards of the CRA, taking much of the discretion out of the hands of bank examiners. "The emphasis on performance-based evaluation," writes A. K. M. Rezaul Hossain (2004, 54), "can be thought of as a shift of emphasis from procedural equity to equity in outcome," according to which it was no longer "sufficient for lenders to prove elaborate community lending efforts directed towards borrowers in the community"; instead, they had to prove "an evenhanded distribution of loans across LMI [low and moderate income] and non-LMI areas and borrowers."

In other words, it was now necessary for banks to show that they had actually made the requisite loans, not just that they were trying to find qualified borrowers. To help achieve this result, one of the standards in the new regulations required the use of "innovative or flexible" lending practices to address credit needs of LMI borrowers and neighborhoods (Hossain 2004, 57). This clearly meant the relaxation of lending standards, despite the original language about safe and sound practices.

Before the increases in housing prices that began in 2001, reviews of the CRA were generally unfavorable. The Act increased costs for banks, and there was an inverse relationship between their CRA lending and their regulatory ratings (see Benston 1999). One of the very few studies of CRA lending compared to normal lending was done by the Federal Reserve Bank of Cleveland, which reported in 2000 that "respondents who did report differences [between regular and CRA housing loans] most often said they had lower prices or higher costs or credit losses for CRA-related home purchase and refinance loans than for others" (Avery et al. 2000).

After 2000, however, and until housing prices stopped rising in late 2006 and early 2007, CRA lending occurred during a period of enormous growth in housing values, which tended to suppress the number of defaults and reduce loss rates. In this light, a recently released Fed Study (Kroszner 2008) arguing that CRA loans in 2005–6 performed comparably to other loans is irrelevant, at best. The real question, moreover, is not the default rates on the mortgages made under the CRA, which could not have been sufficient to cause a worldwide financial crisis. The most important fact about the CRA is the associated effort to reduce underwriting standards so that more low-income people could purchase homes. Once these standards were relaxed—particularly by allowing loan-to-value (LTV) ratios higher than the 80 percent that had previously been the norm—they spread rapidly to the prime market and to subprime markets, where loans were made by lenders other than insured banks.

The effort to reduce mortgage underwriting standards was led by the Department of Housing and Urban Development's enforcement of the National Homeownership Strategy, which was published in 1994 in response to a request by President Clinton. Among other things, it called for "financing strategies, fueled by the creativity and resources of the private and public sectors, to help homeowners that lack cash to buy a home or to make the payments."[2] After this effort began, and the new regulations of 1997 were issued, LTV ratios and other indicators of loosened lending standards rose (see Demyanyk and Hemert 2008; England 2002). The era of subprime lending had begun.

There is no universally accepted definition of either "subprime" or "Alt-A" loans, except that neither of them is considered a prime mortgage (fifteen- or thirty-year amortization, fixed interest rate, good credit history). Thus, both represent enhanced risk. The Federal Reserve Bank of New York defines a subprime loan as one made to a borrower with blemished credit, or who provides only limited documentation. The federal bank regulators define a loan to a borrower with less than a 660 FICO score as subprime. Alt-A loans generally have a higher balance than subprime loans, and one or more elements of added risk, such as a high LTV ratio (often as a result of a piggy-back second mortgage), interest-only payments, little or no income documentation, or an investor rather than a homeowner as the borrower. The term *subprime*, accordingly, generally refers to the financial capabilities of the borrower, while *Alt-A* generally refers to the quality of the loan terms.

The growth in housing demand doubled home prices between 1995 and 2007.[3] According to data published by the Joint Center for Housing Studies at Harvard University (2008), the share of all mortgage originations that were made up of conventional/conforming mortgages (that is, the 20 percent down, thirty-year fixed-rate mortgage that had been the mainstay of the U.S. mortgage market) fell from 57.1 percent in 2001 to 33.1 percent in 2006. Correspondingly, subprime loans (defined here as loans made to borrowers with blemished credit) rose from 7.2 percent to 18.8 percent, and Alt-A loans (defined as those made to speculative buyers or to buyers without the usual underwriting standards) rose from 2.5 to 13.9 percent.

The Role of Fannie Mae and Freddie Mac

Fannie Mae and Freddie Mac were two key mechanisms for transmitting relaxed lending standards to the prime market. The two big GSEs repurchased mortgages from originators of all types, and they were both key implementers of the new HUD policies.

In 1994, HUD had required that 30 percent of GSE mortgage purchases consist of affordable-housing mortgages. In 1997, apparently doubting that Fannie and Freddie were doing all they could for affordable housing, HUD commissioned the Urban Institute to study the GSE underwriting guidelines. The report concluded that the GSE guidelines, designed to identify creditworthy applicants, are more likely to disqualify borrowers with low incomes, limited wealth, and poor credit histories; applicants with these characteristics are disproportionately minorities. Informants said that some local and regional lenders serve a greater number of creditworthy low-to-moderate income and minority borrowers than the GSEs, using loan products with more flexible underwriting guidelines than those allowed by Fannie and Freddie (Temkin et al. 1999).

Following this report, Fannie and Freddie modified their automated underwriting systems to accept loans with characteristics that they had previously rejected. This opened the door to the acquisition of large numbers of nontraditional and subprime mortgages.

By 1997, Fannie was purchasing 97 percent LTV mortgages (meaning those with a 3 percent down payment), and by 2001, it was buying mortgages with no down payment at all. By 2007, Fannie and Freddie were required to show that 55 percent of their mortgage purchases were LMI. Moreover, 38 percent of all purchases had to be from underserved areas (usually in inner cities), and 25 percent had to be purchases of loans that had been made to low-income and very-low-income borrowers (Federal National Mortgage Association 2008a, 5).

The decline in underwriting standards is clear in the financial disclosures of Fannie and Freddie. From 2005 to 2007, Fannie and Freddie bought approximately $1 trillion in subprime and Alt-A loans, amounting to about 40 percent of their mortgage purchases. This was only the end of the process: Freddie acquired 6 percent of its Alt-A loans in 2004; this jumped to 17 percent in 2005, 29 percent in 2006, and 32 percent in 2007. Fannie purchased 73 percent of its Alt-A loans during the latter three years. Similarly, in 2004, Freddie purchased 10 percent of the loans in its portfolio that had FICO scores

of less than 620 (well under the 660 FICO score that federal bank
regulators consider subprime); it increased these purchases to 14 percent in 2005, 17 percent in 2006, and 30 percent in 2007, while Fannie
purchased 57.5 percent of its loans in this category during the same
period (Federal Home Loan Mortgage Corporation 2008; Federal
National Mortgage Association 2008b, 29–30). All told, by 2007 Fannie and Freddie probably held or guaranteed $1.6 trillion in subprime
and Alt-A mortgages, or roughly 40 percent of the total outstanding.

The GSE purchases of subprime and Alt-A loans affected the rest
of the market for these mortgages in two ways. First, it increased the
competition for these loans with private-label issuers. Prior to 2004,
the financial advantages of the GSEs, including their access to cheaper
financing, enabled them to monopolize the conventional/conforming
market. When the GSEs ramped up their purchases of subprime and
Alt-A loans, however, they not only took market share from the private-label issuers, but also created greater demand for subprime and
Alt-A loans from mortgage originators and brokers. This drove up
the value of subprime and Alt-A mortgages, reducing the risk premium that had previously suppressed subprime origination and
securitization. As a result, many more marginally qualified or unqual-
ified applicants for mortgages were accepted by private originators,
including banks and other lenders (such as Countrywide), and then
purchased for securitization by GSEs and private firms (such as Bear
Stearns). During this period, conventional loans (including jumbo
loans) declined from 78.8 percent of all mortgages in 2003 to 50.1
percent at the end of 2006. From 2003 to 2006, subprime and Alt-A
loans increased from 10.1 percent to 32.7 percent of all mortgages
issued. (The remainder of nonconventional mortgages consisted of
home-equity loans and FHA/VA loans; Joint Center for Housing
Studies 2008, 39.)

The GSE regulation-induced competition with private-label issuers almost certainly had the same effect on the quality of the mortgages the private-label issuers were securitizing. Since these mortgages
aggregate to more than $2 trillion, this accounts for the weakness in
bank assets that was the principal underlying cause of the financial
crisis. In a very real sense, then, competition from Fannie and Freddie
beginning in late 2004 caused both groups to scrape the bottom of

the barrel—Fannie and Freddie to demonstrate to Congress their ability to increase support for affordable housing, and the private-label issuers trying to maintain their market share against the GSEs' increased demand for subprime and Alt-A products.

Thus, the gradual decline in lending standards that began with the revised CRA regulations in 1993, and continued with the GSE attempts to show Congress that they were meeting their affordable-housing mission, had come to dominate mortgage lending in the United States.

Homeowner Options Under U.S. Law

State-based residential finance laws, accommodated by the national mortgage system, give American homeowners two options that contributed substantially to the financial crisis.

First, any homeowner may, without penalty, refinance a mortgage whenever interest rates fall, or whenever home prices rise to a point where there is significant equity in the home.

The right to refinance without penalty is very rare in the commercial world, because it increases the difficulty of matching assets and liabilities and thus places significant risks on financial intermediaries. Because home mortgages can be refinanced at any time, banks and others must engage in sophisticated and expensive hedging transactions to protect themselves against the disappearance of their mortgage assets if interest rates decline. Moreover, the ability of homeowners to refinance their mortgages whenever they want to enables them to extract any equity that has accumulated in the home between the original purchase and any subsequent refinancing.

"Cash-out refinancing" permitted homeowners to obtain in cash, at the time of refinancing, a significant portion of the equity that had accumulated in the home up to that point. That equity, of course, could have been the result of a general increase in home prices rather than a homeowner's gradual amortization of principal under the mortgage loan. Once the housing bubble drove up the value of the equity in homes, cash-out refinancing became widespread: home-owners treated their homes like savings accounts, drawing out funds through refinancing to buy cars, boats, or second homes, or to pay for other family expenditures. By the end of 2006, 86 percent of all home-mortgage refinancings were cash-out refinancings, and amounted to $327 billion in that year (Joint Center for Housing Studies 2008, 37). Unfortunately, this meant that when the bubble burst, there was little equity in many homes, and therefore little reason to continue making payments on the mortgage. With subprime and Alt-A loans, where it is likelier that the homeowner will find it difficult or unprofitable to keep making payments, the default risk has proven to be much greater.

Second, walking away from an "underwater" mortgage is, de facto, legal.

In most states, mortgages are either "without recourse"— meaning that defaulting homeowners are not personally responsible for paying any difference between the value of the home and the principal amount of the mortgage obligation—or else the process for enforcing this obligation is so burdensome and time-consuming that lenders simply cannot afford to pursue it. The homeowner's opportunity to walk away from a home that is no longer more valuable than the mortgage it carries exacerbates the effect of the cash-out refinancing that occurred throughout the bubble period.

With the bursting of a housing bubble, cash-out refinancing and the ability to default on a mortgage without penalty would normally have led to concerns about how many prime loans will default. To this uncertainty was added the greater worry about the much higher default prospects of subprime and Alt-A loans. The resulting fears about the value of securitized mortgage holdings triggered the financial crisis.

Tax Policies

Taxation policy also aggravated both the housing bubble and the problem of homeowners extracting equity from their homes.

The deductibility of mortgage interest is, of course, very well known, and it substantially tilts the decision about whether to rent or buy a home in favor of ownership. This involves more people in a given housing bubble, widening the scale of defaults when the bubble bursts. In this case, however, the default risk applies to high-end borrowers, not the poor. Only people who are well enough off to (1) pay income tax and (2) itemize their deductions get the mortgage-interest deduction.

The deductibility of interest on home-equity loans has a similar effect, but it is less widely appreciated, even though its magnitude is greater. Interest on consumer loans of all other kinds—for cars, credit cards, and so on—is not deductible, but interest on home-equity loans is deductible no matter what the purpose of the loan or the use of the funds. As a result, homeowners are encouraged to take out home-equity loans to pay off their credit-card or auto loans, or to make the purchases that would ordinarily be made with credit cards, auto loans, or ordinary consumer loans. The resulting reduction in home equity enhances the likelihood that defaults and foreclosures will rise precipitously as housing prices fall, or as the economy contracts.

Bank-Capital Regulations

Under the 1988 international protocol known as Basel I (still in effect in the United States, but replaced in the rest of the world by Basel II in 2006), the bank regulators in most of the world's developed countries adopted a uniform system of assigning bank assets to different risk categories. The purpose of the system was to permit some flexibility in the allocation of capital, based on the perceived riskiness of various types of assets. Capital is viewed as a shock absorber, and thus more capital should be held against the possibility of losses from riskier assets.

The general rule under Basel I is that banks are required to hold 8 percent risk-weighted capital in order to be adequately capitalized, and 10 percent in order to be well capitalized. Sovereign debt is assigned a risk weight of zero, while commercial loans receive a risk weight of 100 percent, meaning that to be adequately capitalized, a bank must have capital equal to 8 percent of the value of its commercial loans. Because residential mortgages are considered to be half as risky as commercial loans, they are assigned a 50 percent risk weight, so banks are required to hold only 4 percent capital against the value of a residential mortgage. In addition, asset-backed securities rated AAA or issued by a GSE are assigned a 20 percent risk weight, so only 1.6 percent capital (.08 × .20) is necessary for a bank to hold AAA-rated securities, including residential mortgage-backed securities.

The 50 percent risk weight placed on mortgages by the Basel rules provides an incentive for banks to hold mortgages in preference to commercial loans. Even more important, by purchasing a portfolio of GSE or AAA-rated residential mortgage-backed securities (MBSs), or by converting their portfolios of originated mortgages into an MBS portfolio rated AAA, banks can reduce their capital requirement to 1.6 percent, enabling them to lend more (and to make more money on these loans).

The 1.6 percent capital reserve might have been sufficient if the mortgages were of high quality, or if the AAA rating correctly predicted the risk of default, but the gradual decline in underwriting standards meant that even the prime mortgages in a given MBS pool often had high loan-to-value ratios, low FICO scores, or other indicators of low quality. This is all the more true of subprime and Alt-A loans, which were mixed in to MBSs containing prime loans, yet still received an AAA rating. Thus, the combination of the Basel rules with the subprime-lending boom, and its associated reduction in underwriting standards, left an indeterminate proportion of the world's financial institutions with deteriorating assets. It is these continuing and indeterminate losses that caused the financial crisis, and thus the global recession.

The policies I have reviewed here sparked the subprime-lending boom, helped inflate the housing bubble, and magnified the effects of its bursting. The financial crisis should thus be attributed to public policies—not to any "failure of capitalism."

Chapter 7

How Securitization Concentrated
Risk in the Financial Sector

VIRAL V. ACHARYA AND MATTHEW RICHARDSON

There is almost universal agreement that the fundamental cause of the crisis was the combination of a credit boom and a housing bubble.

In the five-year period covering 2002–2007, the ratio of debt to national income increased from 3.75:1 to 4.75:1. It had taken the prior full decade to accomplish an increase in debt of this magnitude, and it had taken fifteen years to do the same thing prior to that. Moreover, from 2002 to 2007, house prices grew at an unprecedented rate of 11 percent per year.

When the "bubble" burst, a severe economic crisis was bound to come. The median family, whose house was highly leveraged and whose equity represented 35 percent of its wealth, would not be able to continue to consume as much as it did through 2007. The economy was going to feel the brunt of it.

It is much less clear, however, why this combination of events led to such a severe financial crisis: that is, why we had widespread failures of financial institutions and freezing up of capital markets. The systemic crisis that ensued reduced the supply of capital to creditworthy institutions and individuals, amplifying the effects on the real economy.

There is no shortage of proximate causes of the financial crisis. There were mortgages granted to people with little ability to pay them back, and mortgages designed to systemically default or refinance in just a few years, depending on the path of house prices. There was the securitization of these mortgages, which allowed credit markets to grow rapidly, but at the cost of some lenders having little "skin in the game"—contributing to the deterioration in loan quality (Berndt and Gupta 2008; Dell'Ariccia, Igan, and Laeven 2008; Keys et al. 2008; Mian and Sufi 2009). Finally, opaquely structured securitized mortgages were rubber-stamped AAA by rating agencies due to modeling failures and, possibly, conflicts of interest, as the rating agencies may have been more interested in generating fees than doing careful risk assessment.

Somewhat surprisingly, however, these are not the ultimate reasons for the collapse of the financial system. If bad mortgages sold to investors hoodwinked by AAA ratings had been all there was to it, those investors would have absorbed their losses and the financial system would have moved forward. The crash would have been no different, in principle, from the bursting of the tech bubble in 2000.

In our view, what made the 2008 crisis so much worse than the crash of 2000 was the behavior of many of the large, complex financial institutions (LCFIs)—the commercial banks, investment banks, insurance companies, and (in rare cases) even hedge funds—that dominate the financial industry. These LCFIs ignored their own business model of securitization and chose not to transfer the credit risk of securitized assets to other investors.

The legitimate and worthy purpose of securitization is to spread risk. It does so by removing large concentrations of risk from the balance sheets of financial institutions and placing many small concentrations into the hands of large numbers of investors. But especially from 2003 to 2007, the main purpose of securitization was not to share risks with investors, but to make an end run around capital-adequacy regulations. The net result was to keep the risk concentrated in the financial institutions—and, indeed, at a greatly magnified level, because of the overleveraging it allowed.

Banking: The Old Model and the New

The simple theory of banking is that banks act as financial intermediaries between depositors and borrowers (Diamond 1984). Depositors provide funds to make loans, and banks provide expertise in assessing the creditworthiness of borrowers. Historically, then, the asset side of a commercial bank's balance sheet would consist of loans funded by deposits (as well as loans funded by non-deposit debt and equity).

A bank's loans, such as its mortgages, are considered assets because they are owed back to the bank. Deposits are considered liabilities because, upon demand, they must be returned by the bank to its depositors. In the meantime, however, most deposits have been lent out to borrowers, such as mortgagors; the interest on these loans is the main source of the bank's profits. Most deposits, therefore, are unavailable at any given time to be reclaimed by the depositors.

To avoid the possibility that all the depositors will demand the return of their deposits at the same time—as occurred during the several panics between 1850 and 1914 and during the Great Depression—deposits are generally insured up to a certain amount by the government. In return for this guarantee, and to ensure that banks have a stake in the process, banks are required to hold a minimum amount of "capital" as a buffer against losses. (While there are other complementary explanations of bank-capital regulation, this simple one suffices for exposition of our main point.)

For these purposes, "capital" must be defined by regulators. In the run-up to the crisis, the regulations in most Western countries equated capital with funds obtained either by raising equity (selling stock or certain forms of "hybrid" debt that has equity-like features); or by retaining earnings. We argue below that banks' efforts to circumvent these capital-adequacy requirements caused the financial crisis.

In a world without deposit insurance, capital-adequacy regulations might be unnecessary. The creditors of financial institutions (depositors, uninsured bondholders, and other counterparties) might curb excessive risk taking. Uninsured bondholders and other counterparties could do so by charging higher interest rates to banks that took what seemed to be excessive risks. Similarly, depositors could demand higher interest rates on their deposits in exchange for the higher risk involved in using these banks; and if unanticipated risks seemed to arise, they would participate in bank runs (akin to the run of unsecured creditors on banks during the ongoing crisis). But the creation of deposit insurance carried with it a risk of moral hazard for traditional banks, and implicit government bailout guarantees for institutions considered too big to fail did the same for today's LCFIs.

The bank-capital regulations of most Western countries follow the terms recommended by the Bank for International Settlements Basel Committee on Banking Supervision. Under the Basel accords, banks must maintain at least an 8 percent capital buffer against a risk-adjusted measure of their assets. In the United States, the FDIC has interpreted "at least" 8 percent to mean 10 percent, if a bank is to be designated "well capitalized" (a designation that brings certain privileges, such as a lower deposit-insurance premium). Maintaining this capital buffer is inherently costly. The two main forms of "capital," according to the Basel rules, are equity and retained earnings. If a bank's capital must be boosted through issuing equity shares, it generally signals to investors the adverse news that retained earnings are unlikely to be enough to meet capital needs (Myers and Majluf 1984). Moreover, the new equity injections will dilute the value of existing shares (Myers 1977), which hurts the bank's existing shareholders.

Securitization, however, allowed banks to use less capital by essentially turning them into underwriters that still originate loans, but then sell them off to others. Once a commercial bank's loans (such as mortgages) are sold to a securitizer (such as Fannie Mae, Freddie Mac, or an investment bank—including, in some cases, the investment-bank arm of the LCFI that is the parent company of the commercial bank)—capital is freed up for other purposes. Among these purposes might be the repurchase of the original bundle of loans, or other commercial banks' or mortgage originators' loans, in the form of an asset-backed security (ABS)—such as a mortgage-backed security (MBS). According to the Basel I rules, adopted in America in 1991 but amended in 2001, a "well-capitalized" U.S. commercial bank, which had a minimum capital level of 10 percent, would have had to fund 5 percent of its mortgages with capital (as opposed to borrowed funds, such as deposits). But it would have had to use capital amounting to just 2 percent of the face value of mortgage-backed securities issued by Fannie or Freddie, or issued by an investment bank that had obtained an AA or AAA rating for the security.

How Securitization Backfired

Securitization explains the fact that there are far fewer deposits in the modern financial system than there are loans. The U.S. banking system currently holds approximately $7 trillion in deposits, but the credit market includes $2.7 trillion in bank and leveraged loans, $3.3 trillion of commercial mortgages, $1.3 trillion of subprime mortgages, $5.8 trillion of non-agency (not Fannie Mae or Freddie Mac) prime residential mortgages, and $2.6 trillion of consumer loans, among others. The riskier credit, such as high-yield corporate loans, non-prime mortgages, commercial mortgages, and consumer credit, is generally securitized.

Securitization altered the original idea of banking: banks now became intermediaries between *investors* (rather than just depositors) and borrowers.

To understand how this worked, consider the evolution of securitized prime mortgages. At first this involved pooling *prime* mortgages into mortgage-backed securities that pay their owners fractional streams of the interest and principal payments collectively made by the mortgage holders. The principal and interest of these mortgages were guaranteed by Fannie Mae and Freddie Mac, the two biggest "government-sponsored enterprises" (GSEs). The U.S. residential mortgage market is worth more than $10 trillion; over 55 percent of it is securitized; and 64 percent of these securities were ultimately backed by Fannie and Freddie.

In the period beginning around the end of 2002, as credit markets began to recover from the preceding recession, investment banks extended the prime-mortgage securitization model pioneered by the GSEs to other, riskier asset classes. This allowed banks to transfer these risks from their balance sheets to the broader capital market, including pension funds, hedge funds, mutual funds, insurance companies, and foreign-based institutions. The new asset-backed securities, issued by banks rather than by a GSE, were called "private-label" ABSs.

These were "structured" securities, meaning that (for example) mortgage pools were divided into "tranches" according to the predicted riskiness of the loans in the entire pool. Holders of shares in the riskier tranches received higher premium payments, but in exchange, they were subject to losses before the holders of shares in the less-risky tranches. Thus, the holders of the least-risky tranches, as determined by the three rating agencies—Moody's, Standard and Poor's, and Fitch—got a lower risk payment, but these investors received the principal and interest payments of the mortgagors in the pool before anyone else did. They were therefore first in "seniority" to the other investors in the MBS, and consequently they would feel the effect of any delinquencies or defaults in the mortgage pool only after investments in the "junior" tranches had stopped performing (through delinquency or default). The relatively low risk level of an AAA-rated tranche, however, did not necessarily mean that it was backed by prime loans. It might only mean that, of the thousands of nonprime loans in a given mortgage-backed security, this tranche was designated as the one that would continue to yield income from performing debts throughout the entire security until all the other tranches had been wiped out.

The growth in structured securities across Wall Street from 2002 to 2007 was staggering. While residential mortgage-related securities were certainly a large component, so, too, were securities backed by such assets as commercial mortgages, leveraged loans, corporate bonds, and student loans. Figure 7.1 graphs the new issuance of various asset-backed securities during this period. Note that there is an almost threefold increase in new issuance from 2002 through 2006. In the aggregate, securitization worldwide went from roughly $2 trillion at the end of 2001 to $3 trillion in 2004 to nearly $5 trillion at the peak of the "bubble," in December 2006 (IMF 2009, 84, Fig. 2.2). By late October 2008, the market had effectively collapsed.

The greatest demand was for the AAA-rated tranches of these products, which appealed to a host of potential investors. Since the AAA ratings indicated to investors that these tranches of asset-backed investments—including collateralized debt obligations (CDOs) and collateralized loan obligations (CLOs)—were as safe as the safest corporate bonds, the role of the rating agencies in this process was important (see Chapter 9).

Nevertheless, we believe that the rating agencies' role in marketing asset-backed securities *to investors* can be overestimated as a factor in the crisis, because, in fact, investors were not the most important purchasers of these securities, in terms of trying to analyze the causes

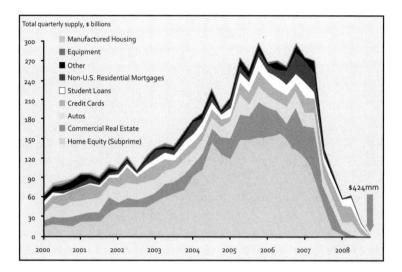

Figure 7.1. Asset-backed security issuance, 2000–2008. CDO: collateralized debt obligation; ABS: asset-backed security (excluding mortgage-backed); CMBS: commercial mortgage-backed security; RMBS: residential mortgage-backed security. Reprinted with permission from Mark Zandi.

of the crisis. Investors lost many hundreds of billions of dollars when the tech bubble burst in 2000, but that did not cause a financial crisis; what was different this time is that *banks* were important buyers of asset-backed securities, particularly MBSs rated AA or AAA by the rating agencies. Instead of acting as intermediaries between borrowers and investors by transferring the risk from mortgage lenders to the capital market, the banks themselves became primary investors. Since—unlike a typical pension fund, fixed-income mutual fund, or sovereign-wealth fund—banks are highly leveraged, this investment strategy was very risky. The goal, however, was logical: namely, to avoid minimum-capital regulations.

Capital Regulation of Off-Balance-Sheet Assets

One of the two primary means for this "regulatory arbitrage" was the creation of off-balance-sheet entities (OBSEs), which held onto many of the asset-backed securities. These vehicles were generically called "conduits." Structured investment vehicles (SIVs), which have received the most public attention, were one type of conduit.

With loans placed in conduits rather than on a bank's balance sheet, the bank did not need to devote any capital to them. However, the conduits funded the asset-backed securities through asset-backed commercial paper (ABCP)—bonds sold in short-term capital markets. To be able to sell the ABCP, a bank would have to provide the buyers, that is, the banks' "counterparties," with *guarantees* of the underlying credit—essentially bringing the risk back onto itself, even if it was not shown on its balance sheet.

These guarantees had two important effects, however.

First, guaranteeing the risk to banks' counterparties was essential to moving these assets off the banks' balance sheets. Designing the guarantees as "liquidity enhancements" of less than one year maturity (to be rolled over each year) allowed banks to exploit a loophole in Basel capital requirements: Basel I assigned a zero risk weight to short-term exposures (BCBS 1998, 20), which meant that they required no bank capital. Using ABCP to fund conduits effectively eliminated the usual 10-percent "capital charge" for well-capitalized commercial banks, which could therefore achieve a tenfold increase in leverage for a given pool of loans.

Second, the guarantees ensured the highest ratings for the vehicles from the rating agencies. AAA-equivalent ratings made it possible for banks to sell ABCP to money-market funds, which are required by law to invest mainly in the highest-rated securities. This allowed banks to fund the ABCP at low interest rates, similar to that paid on deposit accounts.

Figure 7.2 graphs the growth and collapse of the ABCP market over the years 2001–2009. The issuance peaked from 2004 until the second quarter of 2007. When the collapse occurred in the next quarter, the ABCP could not be rolled over, and the banks had to return the loans to their balance sheets. Acharya and Schnabl 2009a show that of the $1.25 trillion in asset-backed securitized vehicles when the crisis hit, a loss of only 4.3 percent was structured to remain with investors. The remaining loss wiped out significant bank capital and threatened banks' solvency.

Figure 7.2. Rise and fall of asset-backed commercial paper, 2001–2008.
Federal Reserve Board.

Capital Regulation of On-Balance-Sheet Assets

Not all banks used off-balance-sheet assets financed by ABCP. Some
chose an alternative route that had a similar effect. A bank would still
make loans and move them off its balance sheet by securitizing them.
But the bank then turned around and reinvested in AAA-rated
tranches of the very securitized products that they (or other banks)
had created.

Because of their AAA ratings, these securities had a significantly
lower capital requirement. For commercial banks, the Basel accords
weighted the risk of AAA-rated securities at less than half the risk of
ordinary commercial or mortgage loans, and thus required a propor-
tionately lower capital reserve for them. In 2004, the SEC granted
stand-alone American investment banks the ability to employ internal
models to assess credit risk and corresponding capital charges. This
allowed investment banks to use even higher leverage than commercial banks.

As Table 7.1 shows, banks, government-sponsored entities such as Fannie and Freddie, and broker/dealers held $789 billion worth of the AAA-rated CDO tranches that were backed by nonprime loans, or approximately 50 percent of the market. Moreover, the majority of the subordinated tranches of the CDOs was also held by banks, broker/dealers, and monoline insurers (which insure only one type of bonds—e.g., municipal bonds or, in this case, purchasers of CDOs), which collectively owned $320 billion of the $476 billion total.

Thus, while the assets on banks' balance sheets doubled between 2004 and the middle of 2007, the regulatory assessment of the risk of these assets grew at a far more sluggish pace. Regulators deemed banks to be relatively safely invested, because the assets were rated AAA. This enabled banks to increase their leverage, and thus the quantity of profitable loans they could make. Figure 7.3 shows this trend succinctly: in the top ten publicly traded banks, the magnitude of total assets doubled even though the size of the banks' *risk-weighted* assets increased by less than 50 percent.

Why did the banks retain the risks of assets such as subprime mortgages?

Take the AAA-rated tranches of subprime CDOs. True, they were risky if the underlying mortgage pools consisted of subprime or nonprime (nondocumented, low-down payment, etc.) loans. But banks that held these tranches had it both ways. On the up side, they reduced their capital requirements, and they (or other investors) earned the higher premium commanded by the risky nature of subprime assets. (For example, at the peak of the housing bubble, in June 2006, even the relatively low-paying AAA-rated tranches of subprime CDOs offered twice the premium of the typical AAA credit-default swap of a corporation.) On the down side, they would incur losses only in the rare event that a large number of subprime mortgages defaulted at once, such that even the AAA tranche of a CDO got hit. Such a scenario, however, would almost surely result from an economic catastrophe—a systemic shock that would affect all markets.[1] The banks were betting that this would not happen—or perhaps the bank decision makers' time horizons were too short for them to care if it did happen. But, of course, it did.

Table 7.1. Dollar Value of Mortgage Debt (billions), April 2008

	Nonsecuritized mortgages	HELOC*	Fannie Freddie, & Ginnie** MBS	Privately issued AAA MBS tranches	Privately issued AAA CDO tranches	Privately issued subordinate tranches	Total	
Banks & Thifts	2,020	869	852	383	90		4,212	39%
GSEs & FHLB***	444		741	308			1,493	14%
Brokers/dealers			49	100	130	24	303	3%
Financial Guarantors					100		162	2%
Insurance Companies		62	856	125	65	24	1,070	10%
Overseas			689	413	45	24	1,172	11%
Other	461	185	1,175	307	46	49	2,268	21%
Total	2,925	1,116	4,362	1,636	476	121	10,680	
	27%	10%	41%	15%	4%	1%		

*home equity line of credit; **Fannie Mae, Freddie Mac, and Ginnie Mae; ***Federal Home Loan Bank.
Source: Krishnamurthy

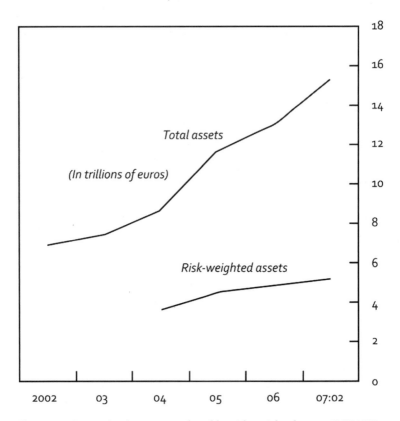

Figure 7.3. Increasing leverage produced by risk-weighted assets. IMF 2008.

To see how hard the systemic shock hit the AAA tranches, Figure 7.4 graphs various AAA-rated ABX index series from their initiation until the end of 2008. ABX creates indices of 20 representative CDOs of subprime mortgages. These indices are initially priced at par, and one can see that the 2006 series stayed around that level until late July 2007, when the crisis started. Depending on the series, the AAA tranches were, as of March 2009, selling from 40 cents to 80 cents on the dollar. Putting aside issues specific to the pricing of the ABX, at the prices in Figure 7.4, and given the aforementioned $789 billion worth of loans, losses to the financial sector ranged from $158 to $473

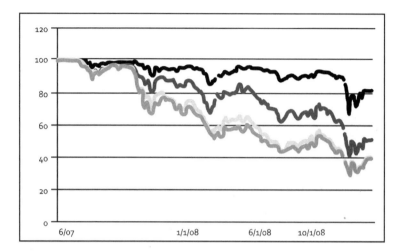

Figure 7.4. Prices of ABX indexes of AAA tranches of subprime mortgage-backed securities, June 1, 2007–December 31, 2008. Top line: issued in first half of 2006; second line: issued in second half of 2006; third line: issued in first half of 2007; bottom line issued in second half of 2007. ABX index reflects the prices of insuring twenty representative tranches. Markit.com.

billion on their holdings of the AAA tranches of mortgage-backed securities alone.

Similarly, the financial firms that used off-balance-sheet entities had, through the guarantees they issued on the ABCP, written huge quantities of insurance against a systemic decline in the overall economy, especially in the housing market. With both conduits and, especially, AAA tranches, the guarantees were often provided by third-party insurers such as monolines and the infamous AIG, which also had it both ways. They collected insurance premia when times were good, and would have to honor their promises only when there was a systemic decline of markets and the economy.

The problem with writing huge amounts of such insurance, however, is that it guaranteed that the very problem being insured against—a systemic decline—would prevent the underwriters of the insurance from making good when the problem materialized. Hence the financial crisis.

Why Did the Banks Bet the House on Housing?

The reason banks took this highly leveraged bet can be found in the risk-taking incentives of employees within financial firms.

In the period leading up to the crisis, bankers were increasingly paid through short-term cash bonuses based on volume and on marked-to-market profits, rather than on the long-term profitability of their "bets."[2] Thus, they had no incentive to discount for the liquidity risk of asset-backed securities if their bets were wrong and nobody wanted to buy these securities. Nor was there an incentive to discount for the "maturity mismatch" inherent in structured investment vehicles—which funded long-term assets through short-term debt that had to be rolled over frequently, generally overnight. Nor, apparently, did their managers assess the true skills of the employees who were generating these large "profits." Thus, regulatory arbitrage became the primary business of the financial sector because of the short-term profits it was generating.

A case in point.[3] In the summer of 2005, UBS, the Swiss-based LCFI, became a major player in subprime mortgage CDOs. It would purchase pools of subprime mortgages from mortgage originators and slice and dice them, so that the "super senior" tranches would receive the highest designation from the rating agencies. The resulting AAA securities would then be sold off to investors. UBS was paid handsomely for structuring these deals. This business usually worked as intended. The credit risk that would normally be held by UBS, or by other banks or mortgage lenders, was transferred to the better-capitalized investment community.

Starting in 2006, however, the CDO group at UBS noticed that their risk-management systems treated the AAA securities as essentially riskless, even though they yielded a risk premium: the proverbial free lunch. So they decided to hold onto them rather than sell them. They held less than $5 billion of these securities in February 2006, but by September 2007 the figured had multiplied tenfold, reaching a staggering $50 billion. Incredibly, this happened even though the housing market had turned south in June 2006; even though subprime lenders had begun to go belly-up in December 2006; and even though UBS itself had shut down its in-house hedge fund, Dillon

Read Capital Management, in May 2007—due to subprime investment losses. None of this mattered to the UBS CDO group. For every
$1 of super-senior securities held, it booked the premium as immedi-
ate profit; and for every dollar of current "profit" booked, the members of the CDO group received correspondingly higher bonuses. The
members of the group had every incentive to increase the quantity of
CDOs on the balance sheet as much as possible, since their own
bonuses were tied to instant profits with no recognition of any risk.
In similar fashion, by the late summer of 2007, Citigroup had accumulated over $55 billion of AAA-rated CDOs.

The Crisis Spreads

The collapse of the ABCP market in the third quarter of 2007 forced
commercial banks to bring the assets held in their conduits back onto
their balance sheets. This affected Citigroup adversely, and consumed
the Royal Bank of Scotland (which inherited the conduits of ABN
AMRO in January 2009), to take just two examples. Investment
banks, which are not subject to the same capital requirements as commercial banks, held their CDOs on their books, but since investment
banks, too, are typically funded overnight, they suffered the same
maturity mismatch as did commercial banks' off-balance-sheet entities. By September 2008, investment banking operations that had
loaded up on AAA tranches of subprime mortgages had effectively
brought down UBS, Bear Stearns, and Lehman Brothers.

While the post-Lehman phase was the "crisis" period of the
financial crisis, the first signs of the impending calamity can now be
traced back to nearly two years earlier, with the bankruptcy of Ownit
Solutions, a non-bank specialist in subprime and Alt-A (not-quite-
prime) mortgages. From then on, there was a slow run on other non-
bank, non-prime mortgage lenders. Most of their loans were hybrid
"2/28" or "3/27" adjustable-rate mortgages. These loans offered a
fixed "teaser" rate for the first two or three years, and then adjustable
rates for the remaining 28 or 27 years respectively. After the first two
or three years, the adjustment of rates would be substantial enough
as to be unaffordable for the subprime borrowers; thus, the mortgages

were designed to be refinanced. But for the most part this would be possible for subprime borrowers only if the collateral on the loan (the price of the house) had increased in value. Otherwise, they would default.

Because these mortgages were all originated around the same time, mortgage lenders had inadvertently created an environment that could lead to a systemic wave of defaults if the price of housing declined two or three years later, when the mortgages reset (Ashcraft and Schuermann 2008; Gorton 2008). Once the failure of lenders such as Ownit Solutions signaled that this had begun to happen, the short-term finance available to nonprime lenders dried up, and hundreds of such specialists failed. The next wave of the crisis began on August 9, 2007, when three investment funds that were part of BNP Paribas, the French LCFI, could not assess the mark-to-market values of their securitized investments backed by subprime mortgages. This led to a suspension of redemptions by Paribas, which, in turn, caused the asset-backed commercial paper market for OBSEs to "freeze": purchasers of ABCP suddenly realized that assets backing the conduits were of such dubious quality that they might have little to no resale value, especially if they were all hit at once with delinquencies and defaults (cf. Acharya, Gale, and Yorulmazer 2008).

A year later, most of the assets funded by banks through securitized markets were subjected to the same doubts, which brought down the investment banks that repackaged subprime and other mortgages into structured securities. The failure of the likes of Fannie Mae, Freddie Mac, and Lehman Brothers, which invested in the securities created out of these mortgages, led to severe counterparty risk concerns that paralyzed capital markets and thus caused the worldwide recession.

Standing behind the collapse of the investment banks and the GSEs was the systemic failure of the securitization market; which had, in turn, been triggered by the popping of the overall housing bubble; which had, in turn, had been fueled by the ability of these firms, as well as commercial banks, to finance so many mortgages in the first place. The severity of the resulting recession and its worldwide scope has been magnified by the huge decline in lending by commercial banks, including not just BNP Paribas, Citibank, Royal Bank of Scotland, and UBS, but Bank of America, JPMorgan Chase, and others, such as Wachovia, that no longer exist. These banks had been huge buyers of subprime mortgages.

The genesis of it all was the desire of employees at highly leveraged LCFIs to take even higher risks, generating even higher short-term "profits." They managed to do so by getting around the capital requirements imposed by regulators—who, in turn, were hoping to diminish the chance that deposit insurance, and the doctrine of "too big to fail," might cause LCFIs to take just such risks.

Chapter 8

A Regulated Meltdown: The Basel Rules and Banks' Leverage

JULIUSZ JABŁECKI AND MATEUSZ MACHAJ

In trying to identify the immense cluster of bankers' and investors' errors that caused the financial crisis, some writers (e.g., the authors of Chapters 3 and 5) have emphasized the role of artificially low interest rates; others have blamed "animal spirits" (e.g., Akerlof and Shiller 2009, chap. 14); still others have identified the deregulation of the financial system, or at least the failure to impose regulations on new financial instruments, as the major cause (e.g., the authors of Chapters 2 and 4; Posner 2009). While we generally find ourselves in agreement with the first explanation, we are somewhat skeptical about the third, as we think it was a particular set of regulations, rather than deregulation per se, that helped sow the seeds of the crisis. In what follows, we shall focus on how the primary weapon in the banking supervisors' arsenal—capital regulation—created incentives for banks to securitize assets and then shift them off of financial institutions' balance sheets.

Roots of Capital Regulation

In their classic study, Sudipto Bhattacharya and his colleagues (1998, 756, 760) provide a rigorous explanation of how "deposit insurance, intended to solve a liquidity problem, creates moral hazard of its own" as it "invites insured banks to seek excessive portfolio risk and keep lower liquid reserves relative to the social optimum." Deposit insurance has this perverse effect because it shields banks from one of the worst possible consequences of imprudent risk management: a run on the bank, which can drain liquidity and produce insolvency in even an initially solvent bank. By eliminating the risk of such disasters for individual banks, deposit insurance encourages systemically imprudent lending: for example, lending to the riskiest borrowers, who carry higher repayment obligations.[1]

To guard against systemic imprudence, banking regulators everywhere have turned to minimum-capital regulations. Capital regulations are designed to cushion banks against unexpected losses —caused, for instance, by excessively risky lending. But that is not the effect that capital regulations achieved in the present case. Instead, the regulations encouraged banks to hide their loans in the vast "shadow banking system," where capital minima do not apply.

One of the tools that enabled banks to get around capital regulations was the sale of their assets to be securitized—that is, turned into bonds, such as mortgage-backed securities.

Prior to the crisis, economists generally believed that securitization would disperse the risks that are inherent in making loans, so that they would be less likely to be concentrated, in potentially disastrous fashion, within a particular bank, region, or country. And while securitization might (and in most cases does) achieve this desirable risk sharing, in the case at hand it did the opposite. According to the IMF 2008 report on global financial stability, roughly 75 percent of the losses experienced during the crisis were concentrated in the leveraged financial system (investment and commercial banks; hedge funds; and finance companies). By contrast, mutual funds and pension funds, to which the risk of subprime assets might have been spread if banks had not held onto them, suffered only 2.7 percent of the losses (IMF 2008, 78).

It was not just economists who were caught off guard by the failure of securitization in this case. The regulatory authorities remained largely satisfied with the situation until it dissolved beneath their feet. Alan Greenspan—by now the favorite scapegoat—famously admitted that he really did not quite get what was going on until very late

("Greenspan Says" 2007). This underscores one reason to doubt that lack of regulation was at fault. Banking is one of the most tightly regulated economic sectors in all Western countries, including the United States. If regulators had had even more power, there is no reason to think that they would have foreseen and prevented the coming crisis, since they tended to endorse the securitization that was at the heart of the problem.

Once the full regulatory context is taken into account, however, the surprising results of securitization are perfectly understandable: banks responded to capital regulations by practicing "regulatory arbitrage." This involved securitizing their assets; obtaining high ratings for the "asset-backed securities" (ABSs)—including mortgage-backed securities (MBSs)—that the capital regulations equated with safety; and then either keeping the ABSs on their balance sheets, where their putatively lower risk enabled the banks to lend out more money; or moving them into "off-balance-sheet entities" (OBSEs), including SIVs (structured investment vehicles), which were unconstrained by capital minima.

Why the Basel Rules Regulate Bank Capital

The regulations with which banks practiced arbitrage fall under the heading of the "Basel rules." At the end of the 1980s, the G-10 countries decided to coordinate their banking regulation, including the capital minima they set for banks, through the Basel Committee on Banking Supervision (located in Basel, Switzerland) of the Bank for International Settlements (BIS). According to the Basel accords, all commercial (i.e., deposit-taking) banks in the countries that adhered to the accords must maintain a certain minimum fixed relation between their capital and their assets.

The "capital" held by a bank is typically referred to as a "buffer against losses" (Heffernan 2005, 109, 144). This usage, however, might create the impression that capital is cash that banks set aside in case their loans turn out badly. It is true that capital is intended to cushion the effects of unexpected losses. However, "capital" is the portion of a bank's funds that does not have to be ultimately repaid

Assets		Liabilities	
cash	$10	capital	$5
loans	$90	deposits	$95
Total	$100	Total	$100

Figure 8.1. Simplified bank balance sheet.

to creditors—such as depositors, who are, after all, merely lending their funds to a bank. Capital funds can be used by a bank to make mortgage loans, commercial loans, or investments—just as can the funds that *do* ultimately have to be repaid to creditors. So "capital" is not sitting in a vault, waiting for disaster to strike. It is employed by banks, along with borrowed funds, to make loans and investments that earn interest for the bank.

However, since capital is not owed to anyone, it provides a margin of safety. For instance, what is considered the highest-quality form of capital is equity capital: funds from issuing shares of common stock in the bank. These funds do not have to be repaid to anyone; stock-holders who buy their shares from the bank itself (rather than from other investors)—such as when a bank's stock is initially offered to the public—part with their money and hope that their "equity shares" will rise in value (and perhaps generate dividends), but the money with which they have parted is now owned by the bank, free and clear. (Even in the event of bankruptcy, the bank's equity capital is not owed back to the shareholders until after the bank's creditors and bond holders have been paid.)

To see why capital should offer protection against unexpected losses, consider the following simple example of a bank's balance sheet (Figure 8.1). The balance sheet consists of the bank's sources of funds (liabilities plus capital) and the uses to which these funds are put (assets). By definition, the two must be equal at all times. We can see that our bank has collected $100 of funds: $95 in deposits from retail customers, representing liabilities, and $5 in capital. Of the $100 total, 90 percent is then turned into credit by being lent out, while 10 percent is held as cash in the bank's vault; the sum of loans and cash (plus any investments) equals the bank's assets. The cash in the vault is a reserve against potential withdrawals from depositors of a portion of the $95 they have lent to the bank. This reserve fund is *not* the bank's capital, however. In principle, the bank could lend or invest all $100 in assets, including the $5 in capital, leaving nothing in the vault.

Now imagine that some of those to whom the bank has lent money unexpectedly default on their loans, rendering $2 of loaned assets worthless. The bank has to write off these losses, diminishing the total value of assets to $98. But while the value of the bank's assets has declined by $2, the amount that it owes to depositors remains exactly the same ($95). Thus, for assets ($98) to continue to equal liabilities, capital must fall to $3. Suppose, by contrast, that the bank didn't initially have any capital, and that its assets ($90 in loans plus $10 in cash) were financed fully by the collection of $100 in deposits. Any unexpected (and unaccounted for) loss would then render the bank immediately insolvent, as the $98 in assets—all the bank has—would not suffice to pay off all that it owes.

It is only due to the fact that a portion of its financing does not have to be repaid (e.g., the portion obtained from issuing stock) that the bank has the capacity to withstand unexpected losses on the investments it makes with the funds entrusted to it. That is the primary reason that bank regulators believe it necessary to control the amount of capital financial institutions hold.

On the other hand, holding capital constrains risk taking (and thus, potentially, profitability); that is the purpose of the capital regulations. To the extent that bank managers view regulatory capital as a tax imposed on them, they will tend to see capital regulations as obstacles to be gotten around.

The Basel Capital Formulae

There are, in principle, many ways in which capital requirements could be devised, but the general standard worked out by the Basel Committee required banks to hold certain minimum ratios of clearly

$$\text{Basel capital ratio} = \frac{\text{capital}}{\text{risk-weighted assets}} = \frac{\text{capital (tier 1 + tier 2)}}{\text{assets (weighted by credit risk)} + \text{credit risk equivalents}}$$

Figure 8.2. Basel I capital requirements.

defined capital (calculated at book values) against assets that were adjusted by clearly defined risk weights, as depicted in Figure 8.2.

Under the Accord, "adequately capitalized" banks were required to hold, against total risk-weighted assets, no less than 8 percent capital, of which at least half was supposed to be tier-1, or "core," capital. For the sake of simplicity we can continue to think of core capital as common stock, that is, the strongest possible variant of capital, which doesn't have to be repaid; but in reality tier-1 capital also includes other similarly unencumbered wealth, such as retained earnings. The other component of the Basel numerator, supplementary capital (tier 2), consists of all the funds that are less like common stock and more like regular debt.[2] Banks typically find it easier to secure debt rather than equity, but the regulators insist that at least half of a bank's capital be equity and retained earnings.

The other side of the equation, the denominator, serves to balance regulatory capital against various assets, which are supposed to require more capital as the risk level rises. Thus, the Basel Committee was compelled to assign risk weights to various asset classes, and these were supplemented by various national banking regulators. In the United States, the Recourse Rule, an amendment to Basel I adopted by the American financial regulators that became effective on January 1, 2002, set the risk weightings as follows:

- No risk (0 percent weight) was attributed to cash, gold, and bonds issued by OECD governments.
- 20 percent risk weight was attributed to AAA- and AA-rated ABSs; claims on OECD banks; claims on local public-sector entities; and agencies of OECD governments, such as the now infamous government-sponsored enterprises (GSEs)—the Federal National Mortgage Association (Fannie Mae) and the Federal Home Loan Mortgage Corporation (Freddie Mac).

- 50 percent risk weight was attributed to mortgage loans and to A-rated ABSs.
- 100 percent risk weight was attributed to claims on non-OECD governments; investments in real estate, such as commercial real-estate loans; claims on the private sector, such as other commercial loans, equities, and corporate bonds; and BBB-rated ABSs.
- 200 percent risk weight was attributed to BB-rated ABSs. (ABSs rated lower than BB were not eligible for capital relief.)

Even though the division between tier 1 and tier 2, like the specification of assets and weights, was hardly unambiguous, the standards were immediately adopted by the G-10 governments, and by the late 1990s the Accord had spread to over 100 countries worldwide (Jackson et al. 1999, 1). In the United States, the Basel framework was extended by the FDIC to require additionally that banks aspiring to be deemed "well capitalized"—and thus to enjoy valuable privileges, such as securities underwriting[3]—must hold their capital in a configuration that meets three additional ratios: capital to risk-weighted assets, 10 percent; tier-1 capital to risk-weighted assets, 6 percent; and tier-1 capital to total assets, 5 percent.

Figure 8.3 plots the evolution of the three main ratios for American FDIC-insured banks over the six years leading up to the financial crisis. One thing seems striking: the values of the ratios are 2–3 percentage points higher than those mandated by the FDIC for being "well capitalized" (and higher still than those recommended by the Basel Committee for being "adequately capitalized")—which might at first seem hard to square with the expansion of indebtedness that took place in the years 2000–2007, graphically displayed in Figure 8.4.

How could total debt grow by more than 80 percent, to close to $50 trillion (with household indebtedness increasing almost twofold, from $7 trillion to $13.8 trillion), without leading to a deterioration of banks' capital adequacy?

In some part, this may have been achieved by building up capital stocks. But clearly, as a matter of pure arithmetic, regulatory ratios can be attained not only by increasing the numerator but also by decreasing the denominator, which entails cutting back on lending or

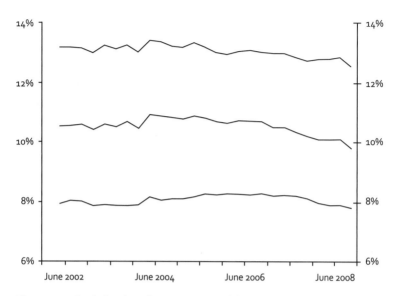

Figure 8.3. Capital ratios of U.S. commercial banks, 2002–2008. Top line: tier-1 plus tier-2 capital divided by risk-weighted assets; middle line: tier-1 capital divided by risk-weighted assets; bottom line: tier-1 capital divided by total assets. FDIC Quarterly Banking Profile.

reducing the riskiness of the balance sheet, as measured by the Basel risk weights. With credit expansion underway, neither might seem feasible. But in fact, both methods were used, which led to the impression of a financial system that was safer than it really was.

Playing by the Basel Rules

Note, first, that with capital requirements based not directly on the portfolio's underlying risk, but based instead on the risk weight assigned by regulators to a broad class of asset categories, regulatory arbitrage could take the form of restructuring a bank's portfolio so that it had the same or even greater risk as before, yet produced a lower capital requirement.

To illustrate the extensive possibilities for this type of arbitrage, Robert C. Merton (1995, 468–69) offered the following example:

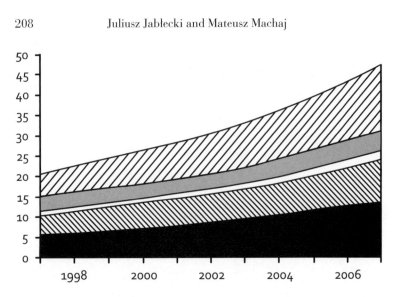

Figure 8.4. Debt outstanding by sector, 1997–2007 (trillions of dollars). Top segment: financial sectors; second segment: federal government; third segment: state and local governments; fourth segment: businesses; bottom segment: households. U.S. Federal Reserve, Flow of Funds.

If a bank were managing and holding mortgages on houses, it would have to maintain a capital requirement of 4 percent. If, instead, it were to continue to operate in the mortgage market in terms of origination and servicing, but sells the mortgages and uses the proceeds to buy U.S. government bonds, then under the BIS rules, U.S. government bonds produce no capital requirement and the bank would thus have no capital maintenance. However, the bank could receive the economic equivalent of holding mortgages by entering into an amortizing swap in which the bank receives the total return on mortgages, including the amortization features and prepayments, and pays the returns on U.S. Treasury bonds to the swap counterparty. The net of that series of transactions is that the bank receives the return on mortgages as if it had invested in them directly. However, the BIS capital calculation, instead of being 4 percent, appears to produce a capital requirement using the swap route of about 0.5 percent.

Benchmark scenario		Securitization scenario	
Assets	Liabilities	Assets	Liabilities
mortgages $100	deposits $95 equity $5	mortgages $80	deposits $75 equity $5

Figure 8.5. Securitization from an accounting point of view.

Central to Merton's example is the active management of a bank's balance sheet by selling and swapping assets through their securitization. The idea is quite simple.

It is costly to maintain capital, which must be done for any asset with a risk weight other than zero—such as a mortgage, risk-weighted at 50 percent. Thus, if a bank can pool assets such as mortgages and sell them to another entity, which can repackage them as an asset-backed security (ABS),[4] the bank receives cash in payment, which it can use either to pay down its debt (diminishing its balance sheet) or to make even more loans (expanding its balance sheet by creating more assets).[5] In either case, however, the bank's balance sheet will no longer reflect the true amount of credit in the economy.

How would such a sale of assets look from an accounting point of view? Consider the very simple example presented in Figure 8.5. On the left-hand side of the figure—the "benchmark scenario"—the bank holds all its mortgages on its balance sheet, whereas on the right-hand side—the "securitization scenario"—the bank has decided to sell a $20 package of its mortgages to a securitizer, such as Fannie Mae or Bear Stearns, leaving $80 of mortgage assets on its books.[6] In the benchmark scenario, with all $100 of its mortgages retained on its books, the bank's total risk-weighted assets equal $50 (because mortgage loans have a 50 percent risk weight), and its total tier-1 capital ("equity") is $5. Thus, the Basel capital ratio equals $5 divided by $50, or 10 percent—exactly what the FDIC requires for the bank to be considered "well capitalized," and 25 percent more than the 8 percent that makes banks "adequately capitalized" under the Basel rules. But on the right-hand side of the figure, where $20 of the bank's mortgages have been sold for securitization, its total risk-weighted assets decline to $40, so the ratio produced by the same $5 of equity capital increases to 12.5 percent ($5 divided by $40). Thus, the transfer of loans allows the bank to extend $20 worth of further mortgage loans, if it chooses.

Even better, if the bank uses the $20 to buy securities rated AA or AAA, or issued by a government-sponsored enterprise such as Fannie Mae or Freddie Mac, it has exchanged a bundle of mortgages with a risk weight of 50 percent for an asset with a risk weight of 20 percent, against which much less capital needs to be maintained. Therefore, paradoxically, a bank would benefit by originating mortgages, selling them to a securitizer, and then buying them back in the form of an asset-backed security, as long as it was rated AA or AAA or was issued by a GSE.

The GSEs, whose purpose was to facilitate home ownership, were among the most eager buyers of securitized home mortgages and had already, by 1989, surpassed commercial banks and savings institutions in the amount of mortgages held, as indicated by Figure 8.6. (Ginnie Mae is different from Fannie Mae and Freddie Mac in that, rather than merely being implicitly backed by the full faith and credit of the U.S. government, it is officially a branch of the U.S. government.)

A bank that securitized its mortgages and bought them back would retain the size and essential composition of its balance sheet, yet with a higher capital ratio. Its $5 of capital would remain in the numerator, while the denominator would now consist of $40 (the $80 in unsecuritized mortgages that remain on the balance sheet × .50, their risk weight) + $4 (the $20 in securitized mortgages × their risk weight, .20), yielding a Basel capital ratio of 11.36 percent: 13.6 percent greater than the minimum of 10 percent to qualify a bank as "well capitalized," and 15.6 percent higher than the level needed to be "adequately capitalized." This is obviously advantageous to the bank, since it can now take on more debt, with which it can grant further income-generating mortgage loans.

Subprime Lending as a Product of the Basel Rules

This quirk in the Basel rules encouraged banks to relax their credit standards and originate mortgages from the "subprime" niche of borrowers. The same logic of capital reduction applied, after all, to mort-

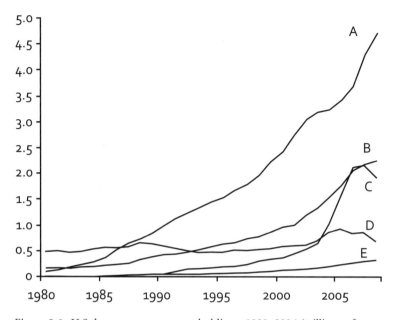

Figure 8.6. U.S. home mortgage asset holdings, 1980–2006 (trillions of dollars). Line A: GSE- and other agency-backed residential mortgage pools; line B: assets or privately issued RMBSs held by commercial banks; line C: assets held by private RMBS securitizers; line D: assets held by savings institutions; line E: assets held by credit unions. U.S. Federal Reserve, Flow of Funds.

gages of any quality, prime or subprime. As long as the securitizer was either a GSE or a private firm that managed to get a double- or triple-A rating for tranches of the security, a commercial bank that bought back the security received the same reduction in its capital risk weight, from 50 percent to 20 percent. Thus, Demyanyk and van Hemert (2007) observe that the quality of loans deteriorated for the six consecutive years leading up to the crisis.

However, securitizers had devised a way for bond-rating agencies to confer the AAA or AA designation on a portion of a security backed by assets consisting even of risky, subprime mortgages. The mechanism was to divide the ABS into "tranches" and pay those who invested in them interest rates that corresponded to various levels of default within the *entire* ABS. Thus, in principle, an ABS consisting of home-mortgage loans—a residential mortgage-backed security (RMBS)—that had been made entirely to subprime borrowers could have an AAA tranche, because the investors in that tranche were secure against any losses from delinquency or default among any of the mortgages pooled into the RMBS, until investments in all the "junior" tranches in the RMBS had been wiped out by such losses.

Investors in the AAA "senior" or "super-senior" tranches of an RMBS are akin to the preferred shareholders in a publicly held corporation, and the RMBS is like the company itself. If the company goes bankrupt, the preferred shareholders get any proceeds before the common shareholders—who, in this case, correspond to investors in the junior tranches of the RMBS. However, investors in the senior tranches also receive lower interest payments due to their lower risk exposure. The greater degree of security from loss enjoyed by investors in the senior tranches is what justified the AAA rating for those tranches. Conversely, someone who invested in a junior tranche would suffer losses from defaulting mortgages before anyone invested in the AAA tranches would. But the subordinate-tranche investors would, in exchange, receive a higher stream of income from the investment (absent defaults and delinquencies).

Off-Balance-Sheet Entities, the Concentration of Risk, and Leveraging

The mainstream opinion among economists is—or used to be, before the crisis—that securitization would follow an "originate-and-distribute" model that, by spreading risks, would benefit everyone:

> First, being capital costly, the ability to sustain a given level of credit supply with a lower volume of capital enables the banking sector to reduce the costs of financing for borrowers and favours financial development, which is ultimately associated with economic growth.
> . . . In addition, the securitisation of loans in principle could reduce a secular source of vulnerability of the economies, by taking risk concentrations associated with loan port-

folios away from the balance sheets of the banking sector and spreading them more broadly across other sectors. As a result, the "originate to distribute" model may potentially diminish the likelihood of the credit busts and banking crises that have historically been a major source of macroeconomic and financial instability in many countries. (González-Páramo 2008, 2–3)

In reality, it is true that by boosting capital adequacy according to the Basel rules, the securitization of loans allowed for the expansion of lending. But it did not—in this case—reduce risk by distributing it to other sectors of the economy, thus rendering the financial system more stable and resilient. Quite the contrary. One study (Greenlaw et al. 2008) persuasively argues that roughly 49 percent of U.S. subprime exposure remained in the "leveraged sector" of the financial system: American commercial banks, investment banks, and hedge funds. Adding foreign investment banks and foreign hedge funds increases to more than two thirds the exposure of the leveraged sector to subprime-related losses.

One reason this happened is that banks were prime purchasers of asset-backed securities, allowing them to take advantage of imperfections in the Basel regulations to economize on capital. Another reason, however, is that banks often sold subprime mortgages for securitization to an "off-balance-sheet entity" (OBSE) such as a structured investment vehicle (SIV).

The purpose of setting up off-balance-sheet entities was also to take advantage of low capital requirements, as explained in the International Monetary Fund 2008 report on global financial stability:

> SIVs and commercial paper conduits . . . are entities that allow financial institutions to transfer risk off their balance sheet and permit exposures to remain mostly undisclosed to regulators and investors; to improve the liquidity of loans through securitization; to generate fee income; and to achieve relief from regulatory capital requirements. (IMF 2008, 69).[7]

Typically, a bank had to provide some sort of credit or liquidity enhancement for the underlying assets of a SIV it sponsored. However, the capital requirement for such enhancements was enticingly lower than for assets kept on the balance sheet. The liquidity enhancement for an asset pool placed off the balance sheet was equal to at most 0.8 percent of the asset's value.

Possibly the most important reason that the banking system turned out to be so significantly exposed to subprime-related losses is that SIVs, after buying, say, subprime mortgage-backed securities from sponsoring banks, failed to "distribute" these assets to more distant investors. This is because of the way SIVs financed their purchases of the securities. Like mortgages themselves, an ABS consisting of mortgages is a long-term, fixed-income asset. The SIV pays for them, however, with short-term liabilities, such as asset-backed commercial paper (ABCP). ABCP was popular among money-market investors, not least because of the safety that the investors supposed was conferred by the assets backing the paper. And in contrast to the 50 percent risk weight that Basel I assigned to "formal standby facilities and credit lines . . . with an original maturity of over one year," Basel regulators reasoned that "similar commitments with an original maturity of up to one year, or which can be unconditionally cancelled at any time," deserved a zero risk weight, because they "generally carry only a low risk" (BCBS 1998, 20, 12).

In principle, the use of short-term funding to buy long-term assets is consistent with the nature of banking itself (Diamond and Dybvig 1983). Even on their balance sheets, banks borrow short and lend long, profiting from the fact that short-term, liquid liabilities (deposits) are generally preferable to, and cheaper than, long-term, illiquid assets. This is called "maturity mismatching," and it is the main source of a bank's profits. What makes it possible is that by the law of large numbers, most of a bank's short-term lenders (depositors) are unlikely to withdraw their money at the same time. The exceptional case is, of course, a run on the bank. But deposit insurance has largely rendered that possibility a dead letter for commercial banks.

Maturity mismatching was transferred from banks' balance sheets to those of the banks' SIVs. SIVs paid for long-term securitized assets by issuing ABCP in the money market. The SIV profited from the difference between the low rate of interest it had to pay on the ABCP and the higher rate generated by the fixed-income securities it bought.

Assets	Liabilities
securities $100	short-term debt $95 equity $5

Figure 8.7. Leveraging at 20:1.

Assets	Liabilities
securities $110	short-term debt $95 equity $15

Figure 8.8. Leverage after asset value rises by $10.

However, like depositors in a conventional bank, short-term lenders who doubt the prospect of getting repaid may also produce a run on the bank by refusing to buy the ABCP when it is due to "roll over"—typically, the next month. And there was no deposit insurance to dissuade them. The BIS apparently did not think about this prospect.

Crucially, SIVs were "marked to market." That is, their assets were valued daily or weekly by reference to the most recent market prices for similar securities. This value determined SIVs' credit rating (assigned by the rating agencies), which affected the rates at which they could borrow. It also determined the leverage on which they could operate. For example, suppose that a SIV targets a leverage ratio of 20:1.[8] The SIV's asset, an ABS with a market value of $100, is financed by issuing debt and equity (usually capital notes provided by the sponsoring bank) equaling $100. Leverage is the ratio of assets to capital, so to reach leverage of 20:1, the SIV needs $5 in equity, along with $95 in short-term paper (ABCP), as shown in Figure 8.7.

Assume now that the market price of the ABS increases from $100 to $110 (Figure 8.8). If the value of the short-term debt remains constant, the SIV's net worth (assets minus liabilities) increases by 10 percent as well, to accommodate the rising value of assets. Now, however, the SIV finds that its leverage has declined substantially, from 20:1 to about 7:1 ($110 in assets divided by $15 in equity). In other

Assets	Liabilities
securities $300	short-term debt $285 equity $15

Figure 8.9. Releveraging to 20:1 after $10 increase in asset value.

words, it has "excess capital" compared to its leverage target of 20, which it can reach again either by reducing the amount of equity (e.g., by buying back some of its capital notes) or by taking on more debt to buy more securities.

How much would its balance sheet have to grow for the SIV to keep its target leverage of 20? The answer is $(20 \times \$15) - \$110 = \$190$. Thus, the initial 10 percent increase in the value of the ABS would almost triple the SIV's balance sheet if the leverage target were to be maintained (Figure 8.9).

The method of active balance-sheet management presented here, and the underlying assumption of targeting a given level of leverage, are obviously rather simplistic, but they do illustrate under what set of circumstances SIVs—being leveraged and marked-to-market entities—would find it profitable to expand their balance sheets by issuing more ABCP to buy more securities.

Off-Balance-Sheet Banking with Low Interest Rates

The advantage of increasing leverage (setting aside the risk) is even greater if other means of making a profit are scarce—for instance, if interest rates, and thus returns on assets, are low.

Arguably, then, one of the most important factors in precipitating the financial crisis was the accommodative monetary policy of the Federal Reserve following the burst of the dot-com bubble. The Fed's major operational target, the so-called federal funds rate, went down to just 1 percent in 2002, which translated into *negative* real interest rates for longer maturities until well into 2004. As might be expected, this monetary easing exerted the strongest impact on the relatively capital-intensive sectors, most notably housing, producing what came

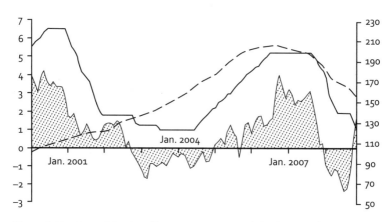

Figure 8.10. Central bank policy, easy money, and the housing bubble. Dotted line: Case-Shiller U.S. National Home Price Index (right scale). Solid line: federal funds rate (interest rates on left scale). Shaded area: inflation-adjusted 12-month LIBOR (interest rate on left scale). Federal funds rate and LIBOR: Reuters. Case-Shiller index: S&P.

to be a real-estate bubble—one measure of which is the Case-Shiller house-price index. It is represented by the dashed line in Figure 8.10, against which the reader may compare both the federal funds rate and the real (inflation-adjusted) long-term interbank interest rate, the twelve-month London Interbank Offered Rate (LIBOR).

In turn, Figure 8.11 shows that the strong growth in real-estate prices was coupled with a preference for fixed-income securities and a general perception of the demise of risk. This is evidenced by the declining differentials, or spreads, between yields on commercial paper and government securities. As government securities are considered the safest assets, declining spreads between the yield on U.S. Treasury bonds and corporate paper—in essence, the declining difference between the borrowing cost of the corporate sector and the government's borrowing cost—reflects the fact that the investors who were choosing between the two were less anxious about the general economic outlook, and thus more willing to lend money to private companies by buying their bonds, which paid higher interest rates—but which might, in times of economic trouble, be unable to pay that interest. The bottom line in the figure shows the spread between the

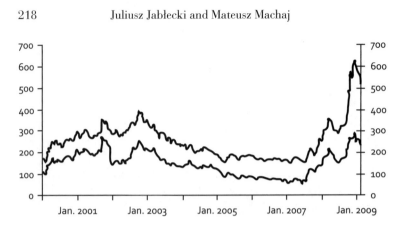

Figure 8.11. Declining perceptions of economic risk. Vertical axis: basis points. Top line: spread between yield on Baa-rated corporate bonds and 10-year Treasury bonds; bottom line: spread between yield on Aaa-rated corporate bonds and 10-year Treasury bonds. Reuters Ecowin.

yield on Treasuries and relatively risky—but higher-paying—Aaa-rated corporate bonds; the top line shows the spread between the yield on Treasuries and even riskier, higher-paying Baa-rated corporate bonds. (Moody's, whose corporate-bond ratings are shown here, uses a slightly different denotation for the riskiness of these securities from the more familiar AAA, BAA, etc. used by Standard and Poor's.)

When uncertainty about economic conditions and the state of global financial markets returned in mid-2007, spreads rose sharply, peaking—in the case of the Baa bonds—at over 600 basis points (6 percentage points), compared to just 200 basis points at the beginning of 2007. Had it not been for the Fed's efforts at that juncture to reduce borrowing costs, the spreads could have widened even more. Sudipto Bhattacharya et al. (1998, 754) note, for example, that over the first three years of the Great Depression (1929–32) the yield differential between Baa- equivalent bonds and U.S. government bonds increased from less than 200 to more than 750 basis points.

Easy money led to low interest rates, which not only contributed to a housing boom but depressed the return on assets, leading to a search for higher yields in the riskier niches of the market—as evidenced by the growth of subprime MBSs illustrated in Figure 8.12. Low interest rates and a preference for high-yield fixed-income

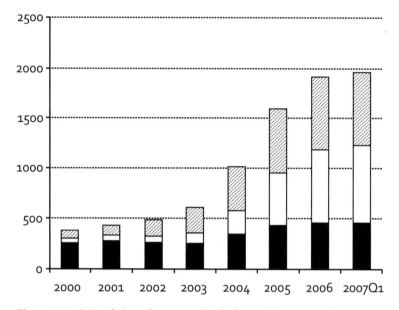

Figure 8.12. Privately issued mortgage-backed securities outstanding (trillions of dollars). Shaded: subprime; white: Alt-A (between prime and subprime); black: jumbo (loan amount above conventional limits). Adapted from Gorton 2008.

securities provided an excellent environment for the development of securitization, and particularly the securitization of subprime mortgages.

As seen in Figure 8.12, the total amount outstanding of privately issued mortgage-backed securities (i.e., not guaranteed by Fannie Mae, Freddie Mac, or Ginnie Mae) increased fivefold between 2000 and 2007, and 70 percent of the *rate* of growth occurred between 2003 and 2004—the two years over which, as is clear from Figure 8.10, longer-term interest rates were consistently negative. Thus, after all prime borrowers had been served, financial institutions were still desperate to fill up their books with assets, and they moved on to the subprime segment.

With the use of sophisticated methods of pooling and tranching, securitizers were usually able to gain very good ratings for securities backed by subprime mortgages, increasing the market value of securi-

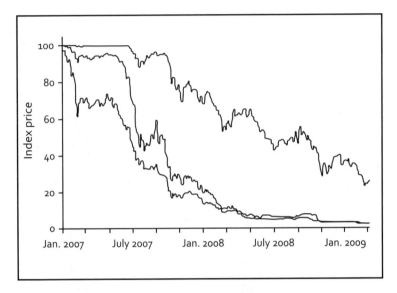

Figure 8.13. The rising cost of insuring an RMBS, January 2007–March 2009 (ABX.HE 07–1 index). Vertical axis: index price of mortgage loan insurance derivatives. Price is inversely related to cost of insuring a portfolio of RMBSs. Top line: AAA tranche; middle line: AA tranche; bottom line: BBB– tranche. Reuters.

tized products that—due to their higher risk, even in the senior tranches—commanded higher returns. Different RMBSs themselves could be combined into a pool to be tranched, to obtain diversification (it was thought): the result was a collateralized debt obligation (CDO). There were even "CDOs squared," which took the same idea a step further. At each step the triple-A rated tranches grew larger, and it is clear that investors took the high ratings very seriously. This is suggested by Figure 8.13, which shows the cost of RMBS (often CDO) insurance contracts, that is, credit-default swaps for them.

A credit-default swap (CDS) allows a buyer to insure against the default risk of a bond. The price of the CDS is typically treated as a proxy for the probability of default. To oversimplify a bit, if an investor wants to insure $10 million in bonds against default and the market's assessment of the probability of default is 4 percent, then the

CDS price for those bonds is 4 percent × $10 million, that is, $400,000 per year.

Suppose that the $10 million worth of bonds are in a triple-A-rated tranche of an RMBS consisting of subprime mortgages. The cost of insurance for such a tranche is measured by the now famous ABX.HE index. The technicalities of how the index is constructed are rather complicated, but the important thing to grasp is that the lower the current market price of the index, the greater the insurance cost for the RMBS. For example, upon the launch of the new roll of the index in January 2007, the market price of the sub-index tracking the AAA tranches of RMBS (the top line in Figure 8.13) stayed roughly at par value (100 on the index), implying that the insurance cost equaled approximately the fixed coupon payment of $9,000. $9,000 per year to insure $10,000,000 of subprime mortgages is cheap, reflecting the fact that those selling this insurance estimated the risk of default to be negligible. But as the economic situation began deteriorating in mid-2007, the index price fell below par. By April 2009, the market price had dropped to just about 23 percent of par, which in turn increased the insurance premium to 77 percent of the amount of the security (plus the $9,000 coupon). Thus, in just over two years, the cost of insurance for our $10 million tranche of a triple-A rated RMBS had gone from $9000 to $9000 + (.77 x $10 million) = $7,709,000.

The surge in the insurance cost of RMBS portfolios rated A and BBB-, shown by the remaining two lines in Figure 8.13, was even more pronounced. This is less than surprising, given that unexpected defaults in subprime mortgages were being reported as soon as the index opened, in January 2007; the subordinate tranches of a sub-prime security would be the first to suffer from these losses. The steadily rising cost of insuring a senior tranche, however, shown in the drop in the top line that begins in November 2007, reflected a growing recognition that no matter what sophisticated techniques were used in their tranching, and no matter what risk grades were assigned by the rating agencies, subprime mortgages had not actually become less risky. They had merely been subsidized by a temporarily cheap source of liquidity.

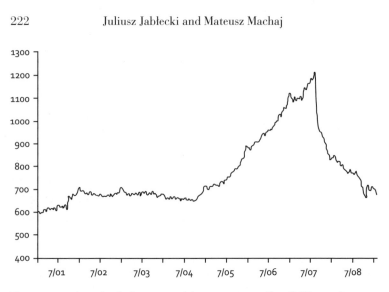

Figure 8.14. Asset-backed commercial paper outstanding (billions of dollars). U.S. Federal Reserve.

There seems to be at least some confirmation in these data for our hypothesis regarding the rationale for the expanding balance sheets of the leveraged financial institutions. Due to a particular set of circumstances—a prolonged period of accommodative monetary policy, rising house prices, and a preference for high-yield fixed-income securities—off-balance-sheet entities found it profitable to expand their own balance sheets by taking on more debt and using it to buy more asset-backed securities. It should come as little surprise, then, that the size of the SIV sector—which was only a subset of the entire sector of ABCP-funded off-balance-sheet entities—doubled from 2004 to 2007, reaching a peak of $400 billion.

The Run on the Off-Balance-Sheet Entities

We have presented a simple framework for understanding possible reasons behind the failure of the risk-dispersion process that had been promised by securitization. Off-balance-sheet entities—leveraged, marked to market, and relatively unconstrained by Basel capital regulations—found it profitable to react to the rising value of asset-backed

securities by filling their balance sheets with even more of them, contributing to a spiral of rising prices for them. These purchases, however, were financed by issuing liabilities maturing, usually, in 30 or
90 days at most; and the liabilities, in turn, were backed by the long-
term assets, such as mortgage-backed securities, which the short-term
paper was buying in a manner that to some extent resembled a Ponzi
scheme: SIVs and other conduits would typically apply the proceeds
of a new ABCP issuance to repay maturing ABCP (Moody's 2003).

There can be little doubt that these practices greatly enhanced the
lending capacity of the U.S. financial system, allowing the economy
to reap the benefits of credit expansion, while essentially sweeping all
the costs (embodied in credit risk) under an accounting carpet. The
costs, however, even if forgotten, were still there, and showed themselves as soon as the conditions in the housing market deteriorated,
instigating a run on the off-balance-sheet financial entities.

Figure 8.14 shows that, in mid-2007, the ABCP market began to
show signs of collapse, as indicated by the decline in the amount of
paper outstanding from roughly $1.2 trillion in August to $900 billion
in November. This suggests that SIVs must have had serious problems
with rolling over their short-term debt. According to a UBS report
(quoted in Gorton 2008, 208–9), the SIV sector contracted by over
$100 billion between August and December 2007, but in fact, even
the remaining $300 billion (of the initially $400 billion sector) was
completely illusory, since SIV ABCP was no longer held by investors;
it was now on the balance sheets of the sponsoring banks.

An instructive case in point is offered by investigating the crash
of Citigroup. The company sponsored seven SIVs—Beta, Centauri,
Dorada, Five, Sedna, Zela, and Vetra—whose assets totaled $87 billion
as of August 2007. As a result of unusual strains in the sector, Citigroup[9] later reported, "certain of the assets owned by the vehicles
have suffered significant declines in fair value, leading to an inability
to reissue maturing commercial paper and short-term notes." By the
end of 2007, Citigroup had had to take all the sponsored entities
back onto its balance sheet, offering the following explanation to the
Securities and Exchange Commission:

> In response to the ratings review of the outstanding senior
> debt of the SIVs, for a possible downgrade announced by two

ratings agencies and the continued reduction of liquidity in the SIV-related asset-backed commercial paper and medium-term note markets, on December 13, 2007, Citigroup announced its commitment to provide support facilities that would support the SIVs' senior debt ratings. As a result of this commitment, Citigroup became the SIVs' primary beneficiary and began consolidating these entities.[10]

The insertion of Citigroup's SIVs onto its balance sheet had significant effects—the most direct being a $212 million pretax loss reported for the first quarter of 2008. Moreover, Citigroup's capital adequacy—and thus its lending capacity—deteriorated after the balance sheet expanded by $59 billion in December 2007, with the addition of its SIVs' assets (marked to market). Thus, on the day of consolidation, the newly absorbed assets were estimated to worsen Citigroup's tier-1 capital ratio by 0.16 percent,[11] and the interim financial statement for the fourth quarter of 2007 indicates that the tier-1 capital ratio actually declined by 0.20 percent, reaching 7.12 percent (versus 8.6 percent in December 2006)—nearly a full point below the required level of capital adequacy. This still understates some of the effect of bringing the SIVs' assets onto Citigroup's balance sheet, since this calamity had been, to some extent, offset by raising $30 billion of new tier-1 capital in the fourth quarter of 2007. The case of Citigroup was by no means unique. In fact, Gorton (2008) reports that by early 2008, the SIV sector had essentially disappeared, as sponsors had transferred the off-balance-sheet entities back onto their balance sheets. This significantly helped to dry up liquidity in the interbank market.

Figure 8.15 shows two measures of declining liquidity and increasing default risk among banks: the average CDS price for American banks' debt, shown by the shaded area; and the differential between three-month LIBOR and repo rates, shown by the dark line. Repo rates are for secured interbank loans, while LIBOR rates are for unsecured interbank loans; the differential is the spread between interbank interest rates for loans that are backed by collateral and those that are not. Thus, while the shaded area reflects mainly the risk of default, the dark line reflects the liquidity conditions in the unsecured market, the

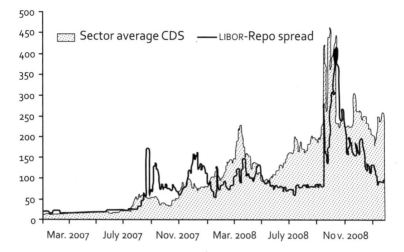

Figure 8.15. A problem of liquidity, not counterparty credit risk. Vertical axis: basis points; shaded area: simple average of five-year credit-default swap spreads on debt issued by Morgan Stanley, American Express, Citigroup, Goldman Sachs, Merrill Lynch, Bank of America, Wells Fargo, Wachovia, and JPMorgan Chase, a proxy for perceived counterparty risk. Dark line: Three-month LIBOR less 3-month repo rate, a proxy for low liquidity (see text). Bloomberg.

secured market, and the market for the underlying collateral, for example, subprime mortgage-backed securities (Michaud and Upper 2008).

The figure shows that the LIBOR-repo spread first increased much more than did the price of bank-debt CDSs, reaching 170 basis points in August 2007 versus 58 basis points for CDSs. Thus, tight liquidity in the interbank market seems to have occurred prior to the spike in default-risk worries. By the same token, in March 2008, once various central-bank liquidity programs were well under way, the average price for CDSs outstripped the LIBOR-repo spread, indicating that credit risk was now (given the collapse of Bear Stearns) a greater concern than lack of liquidity. In other words, the evidence suggests that banks initially stopped lending to each other not because they were concerned about their counterparties defaulting (due to their possession of undetermined amounts of subprime securities), but because they needed to come up with considerable amounts of liquidity to support the off-balance-sheet entities they had taken back onto their ledgers.

This was just the beginning of the meltdown. The liquidity squeeze was eventually cured by the central banks' innovative operations, but a much more significant problem emerged later. As the toxic-debt boom began unwinding, banks started to discover losses on the investments they had made, and accordingly had to mark down the value of their assets. This had a reverse-leveraging effect on the banks' capital, which not only threatened them with being taken over by the government for having falling beneath their capital requirement, but brought them closer to insolvency. What started as a liquidity problem soon morphed into a capital problem, forcing upon the financial system massive deleveraging and pushing the real economy into crisis—although that is a story that deserves separate treatment.

The Basel Rules with Players Too Big to Fail

The financial crisis is undoubtedly a complex event, the result of many factors that worked together and that may also have reinforced one another. However, we believe that to the extent that one wishes to focus on regulatory issues rather than psychological factors, the seeds of the crisis were sown by perversely designed policies, not by deregulation. Capital-adequacy rules based on fixed risk measurements—and designed (paradoxically) to protect the economy from excessive credit expansion—were used in unanticipated ways, hiding the risks from the sight of supervisors and investors alike and giving everyone an utterly false sense of security, confidence, and stability.

Unfortunately, obeying a rule designed to minimize risk is not the same thing as minimizing risk. It is adherence to a bureaucratic requirement, nothing more. And even if excessive risk could in fact be tamed by tighter regulations, the overall effect of regulation may be to diminish the regulated entity's incentive to regulate itself. This is especially true when it is widely expected that fiscal and monetary policy will be used to guarantee the stability of the financial system by rescuing from imprudence firms that are deemed too big to fail.

As the IMF April 2008 Global Financial Stability Report put it, financial firms became "more complacent about their liquidity risk management systems and 'underinsure[d]' against an adverse liquidity event, depending more heavily on central bank intervention for their liquidity problems" (IMF 2008, xi). In this light, it is naïve to blame bankers' "greed" or "delusion" for what happened. Even if a strong focus on short-term gains, or an uncritical approach to mathematical models of risk measurement, were necessary to produce the disaster that began to unfold in 2007, these preconditions were not sufficient. It is highly likely that, to the extent that the general political environment of modern social democracies allows for the privatization of profits and the socialization of losses, economic players whose losses are likely be socialized will strive to circumvent whatever restrictions are placed on them with the aim of minimizing these losses. But limiting their efforts to circumvent or arbitrage such restrictions is not an easy task, and in many cases has proved to be impossible (Stem and Feldman 2004).

Considered in a slightly different light, capital-adequacy regulations are just one example of how difficult it is to regulate risk-taking without redirecting it into other spheres of the financial system.[12] If the legal and economic system shifts the responsibility for risk onto taxpayers or, in the case of liquidity bailouts, onto holders of the central bank's currency, one should not be surprised that this leads to irresponsible risk-taking. The natural historical tendency is to deal with this problem, and the "moral hazard" posed by players who are "too big to fail," by piling new regulations atop old ones. So the worldwide reform of the financial system is sure to include the imposition of *higher and more tightly policed* capital-adequacy levels, with the pile of regulations eventually reaching such heights that bureaucratic controls increasingly substitute for market mechanisms; that is, government decrees replace the knowledge-discovery process of profit (when one has discovered a useful product that consumers are willing to buy) and loss (when one merely thinks one has done so). Moreover, since the alternative to new regulatory rules—namely, regulators' discretionary supervision over systemically risky actors—is likely to breed cartelization, it could actually aggravate the systemic risk that already pervades the financial markets.

The net result would be that the few huge remaining entities are indeed too big to fail—but too expensive to save.

Chapter 9

The Credit-Rating Agencies
and the Subprime Debacle

LAWRENCE J. WHITE

An insured state savings association . . . may
not acquire or retain any corporate debt
securities not of investment grade.
—12 Code of Federal Regulations §362.11

Any user of the information contained herein
should not rely on any credit rating or other
opinion contained herein in making an
investment decision.
—common S&P disclaimer

The three large U.S.-based bond-rating agencies—Moody's, Standard & Poor's (S&P), and Fitch—played a central role in the financial crisis that began in 2007. These three agencies' favorable ratings were essential for the sale of bonds that were securitized from subprime residential mortgages. The sale of these bonds, in turn, was an important underpinning of the U.S. housing boom of 1998–2006—a self-reinforcing price-rise bubble. When house prices stopped rising in mid-2006 and then began to decline, the default rates on the subprime mortgages underlying the bonds rose sharply, and bonds that the three rating agencies had proclaimed to be the safest possible investments (other than Treasury bonds) began to default—especially bonds that were based on mortgages that were originated in 2005 and 2006. These bonds were so widely held by banks that the decline in their value, combined with defaults on unsecuritized mortgages, ripped apart the financial system of the United States and many other Western countries.

How We Got Here

John Moody published the first publicly available bond ratings in 1909. In 1916, Moody's firm was joined by Poor's Publishing Company, and then in 1922 by the Standard Statistics Company. (In 1941 Standard and Poor's merged.) The Fitch Publishing Company established its rating business in 1924. These firms' bond ratings, contained in thick manuals, were sold to bond investors to help them assess the likelihood that the principal and interest of a bond would be repaid. In the language of modern corporate strategy, the original "business model" of these companies was "investor pays": investors were buying information. Prior to 1934, when the Securities and Exchange Commission (SEC) was created and began requiring corporations to issue standardized financial statements, Moody's, Poor's, Standard, and Fitch filled a similar role, but based on investor demand.

In 1936, in an attempt to ensure that banks invested only in safe bonds, U.S. bank regulators prohibited banks from investing in "speculative investment securities"—as determined by "recognized rating manuals." This prohibition is still in effect. "Speculative" securities are defined as bonds below "investment grade," meaning that since 1936, banks have been restricted to holding only bonds that are rated BBB − or higher (using the S&P grading system).[1]

As a result of this 1936 regulatory decision, banks were no longer free to act on information about bonds from any source they deemed reliable (with oversight by bank regulators). They were instead forced to use the judgments of the publishers of the "recognized rating manuals": Moody's, Poor's, Standard, and Fitch. The predictions of these third-party raters had attained the force of law. And since banks were important participants in the bond markets, other participants, too, now had to pay attention to these specific bond raters' predictions of default probability.

In the following decades, the insurance regulators of the 48 (and eventually 50) states took actions like those taken by the bank regulators in 1936. The state regulators wanted insurance companies to have capital (in essence, net worth) that was commensurate with the riskiness of the companies' investments. To achieve this goal, the regulators established minimum capital requirements that varied according to the ratings on the bonds in which the insurance companies invested—ratings issued by bond-rating firms. In the 1970s, federal pension regulators laid down similar rules.

The capstone of this process came in 1975, when the SEC decided to set minimum capital requirements for broker-dealers (i.e., securities firms). Following the pattern of the other financial regulators, it wanted its capital requirements to be sensitive to the riskiness of the broker-dealers' asset portfolios, so it again tied the requirements to the rating companies' judgments. But it worried that references to "recognized rating manuals" were too vague: a bogus rating firm might arise that would assign AAA ratings to companies that would pay for the privilege. So the SEC formalized the de facto status of Moody's, S&P, and Fitch by declaring that only the ratings of a "nationally recognized statistical rating organization" (NRSRO) would be acceptable, and by naming the three existing firms as the only NRSROs. The other financial regulators soon followed suit, so that these three firms' judgments of bonds' safety came to be *official* determinants of the bond portfolios of most major American financial institutions.[2]

The NRSRO category was a potentially fatal barrier to entry into the bond information business. Without the NRSRO designation, any new would-be bond rater would likely be ignored by most financial institutions; and since the financial institutions would ignore the rater, so would bond issuers, who needed to sell their bonds to institutions.

Over the next twenty-five years, the SEC made this potential into a reality, designating only four additional firms as NRSROs;[3] and mergers caused the number of NRSROs to fall back to the original three by the end of 2000. The SEC never established a formal application and review process, and never provided any explanation for why it anointed some firms with the NSRSRO designation and refused to do so for others. The SEC had created a very high (although not entirely impermeable) barrier to entry into the bond-rating business, making Moody's, S&P, and Fitch a de facto oligopoly. In the early 1970s, the business model of the rating firms also changed. In place of the "investor pays" model established by Moody's in 1909, the firms converted to an "issuer pays" model, according to which the entity that is issuing the bonds pays the rating firm to rate them.

The reasons for this change of business model have not been established definitively. Among the possibilities are these:

a. The high-speed photocopy machine was just entering widespread use, and the rating firms may have feared that many investors would use borrowed copies of the ratings manuals, depressing the agencies' sales of manuals.
b. The bankruptcy of the Penn Central Railroad in 1970 shocked the bond markets, which may have driven up the value of a low-risk rating to the point at which bond issuers were willing to pay for it. (However, the same shock should have made investors more willing to pay to find out which bonds were really safer and which were not.)
c. The bond-rating firms may have belatedly realized that their semi-official status compelled bond issuers to get their blessing, so that the issuers could be charged for it.
d. The bond-rating business, like many information industries, involves a "two-sided market," where payments can come from one or both sides of the market; in such markets, which side actually pays can be quite idiosyncratic.[4]

Regardless of the reason or reasons, the change to the "issuer pays" business model opened the door to potential conflicts of interest. A rating agency might shade its rating upward so as to command a higher fee or forestall the issuer from taking its business to a different rating firm. Moreover, Vasiliki Skreta and Laura Veldkamp (2008) point out that rating firms can make only *estimates* of the creditworthiness of a bond, so there will be errors. If the errors are distributed symmetrically but the issuers can choose which rating to purchase, the issuers will systematically choose the most optimistic estimate. As long as the raters are honest but less than perfect, the effect of the bond issuer's power to choose among them mimics the effect of bribing an agency to grant an optimistic rating.

In early 2003, the SEC designated a fourth NRSRO (Dominion Bond Rating Services, a Canadian credit rating firm), and in early 2005 a fifth (A.M. Best, which rates insurance companies). The SEC procedures remained opaque, however, and there were still no announced criteria for the designation of a NRSRO. In September 2006, the Credit Rating Agency Reform Act (CRARA) was enacted. The CRARA instructed the SEC to stop being a barrier to entry, specified the criteria it should use in designating new NRSROs, insisted on transparency and due process in SEC decisions about NRSRO designations, and provided it with limited powers to oversee the incumbent NRSROs—but specifically forbade it from influencing the ratings or the business models of the NRSROs.

In response to this legislation, the SEC designated three new NRS-ROs in 2007 (Japan Credit Rating Agency; Rating and Information, Inc. [of Japan]; and Egan-Jones) and another two in 2008 (Lace Financial and Realpoint). By early 2009, the total number of NRSROs had reached ten. The recent lowering of the barrier to entry, however, was too late to diminish the role of the "Big Three" NRSROs in the subprime debacle.

The Rating Agencies and the Subprime Debacle

It is not surprising that a tight, protected oligopoly might become lazy and complacent; and the "issuer pays" model had opened the door to more insidious abuses. Though these potential problems had existed since the early 1970s, the relative transparency of the corporations and governments whose debt was being rated apparently kept the problem in check. And there were thousands of corporate- and government-bond issuers, so the threat of any single issuer (if it was displeased by an agency's rating) to take its business to a different rating agency was not potent.

The complexity and opaqueness of the mortgage-related securities that were rated during the past decade, however, created new opportunities and apparently irresistible temptations (or, following the Skreta-Veldkamp model, new possibilities for error). The agencies' ratings of the various "tranches" (or slices) of these securities, based on their models of the creditworthiness of thousands of mortgages included in each security, were crucial in determining how profitable these securitizations would be. And unlike the market for rating corporate and government debt, the market for rating mortgage-related securities involved only a handful of investment banks as the entities whose bonds were being rated. An investment bank that was displeased with an agency's rating of any specific security had a more powerful threat—to move all of its securitization business to a different rating agency—than would any one corporate or government issuer. As a result, the rating agencies were not only compliant; they became involved in the very creation of these securities, specifying in negotiations the components that would allow a very high percentage of the securities that were issued from any bundle of subprime mortgages to garner AAA ratings.

The U.S. housing boom, which began in the late 1990s and ran through mid-2006, was fueled, to a substantial extent, by subprime mortgage lending (Chapter 7; Gorton 2008; Coval et al. 2009b; Mayer et al. 2009). In turn, the securitization of subprime mortgage loans, in collateralized debt obligations (CDOs) and other mortgage-related securities, provided an important incentive for subprime lending, which made such lending a source of profit, rather than of risk, for mortgage originators. And with securitization, we come to the ratings agencies. The favorable ratings that they bestowed on subprime-backed securities were indispensable to the securitization of subprime mortgages, for at least four reasons.

1. The generally favorable reputations that the ratings agencies had established through their lengthy history of integrity, and through the accuracy of their corporate- and government-bond ratings, meant that many bond purchasers were inclined

to trust the agencies' judgments about asset-backed bonds, including those backed by mortgages—even when (or, perhaps, especially when) the yields on *subprime* mortgage-backed bonds were higher than on comparably rated bonds issued by blue-chip corporations.

2. High ratings were legally important (and often mandatory) for most institutional investors to whom bonds might be marketed.

3. Banks, where half of the subprime securities ended up, could dramatically reduce the amount of capital that they were required to maintain if they traded a portfolio of mortgages, prime or subprime, for a portfolio of mortgage securities— even one backed by subprime mortgages—as long as the securities were rated AA or higher. Under the international Basel capital accords, an adequately capitalized bank was required to hold $4 in capital against every $100 in individual mortgages, but only $1.60 in capital against every $100 of AA- or AAA-rated mortgage-related securities. Therefore, by trading mortgages that it had originated for the AAA-rated (or even AA-rated) "senior tranches" of securitized mortgages, the bank could use the same $4 of capital to invest in $250 of these mortgage-related securities. Even though the yields on these senior tranches were somewhat less than the yields on the underlying mortgages, the higher leverage made the exchange worthwhile (Acharya and Schnabl 2009b).

4. The previous reason applied to high-rated securities that a bank held on its balance sheet. But a huge quantity of subprime mortgage-backed securities was held off-balance-sheet, in "structured investment vehicles" (SIVs): bank-sponsored entities that bought tranches of mortgage-backed securities (MBSs) or tranches of the tranches of different MBSs (CDOs) including tranches of tranches of subprime mortgage-backed securities. These purchases, which had a zero capital requirement, were financed through the issuance of short-term asset-backed commercial paper (ABCP). If the CDO tranches purchased by an SIV were highly rated, then the ABCP could also be highly rated. Interest-rate risk and liquidity risk were apparently

ignored in the ratings. But such ratings were essential if an SIV's ABCP were to be bought by money-market funds, which, as one might have guessed, were required by law[5] to hold almost entirely high-rated securities.

The pivotal role of these factors in causing the crisis can be gauged by the dominance of high-rated tranches in the origination and securitization of subprime mortgages. According to the IMF,

> About 75 percent of recent U.S. subprime mortgage originations have been securitized. Of these, about 80 percent have been funded by AAA-rated MBS "senior" tranches, and about 2 percent by noninvestment grade (BB + and lower) "junior" tranches. . . . Over 90 percent of a typical high-grade, structured-finance CDO liability structure is composed of AAA-rated senior tranches. (IMF 2008, 59)

There can be little question, then, that AAA ratings—from the Big Three rating agencies—were important in generating the subprime bubble that burst in 2007 and 2008. Nor is there much doubt about the incentives that animated the securitizers. An investment bank would make more money if it could obtain high ratings for more tranches of a given MBS. In addition, the senior tranches of an MBS, in exchange for being (apparently) more secure against default risk than subordinate tranches, yielded lower interest payments to senior-tranche investors—leaving a greater profit margin for the securitizers. It is not surprising, then, that the securitizers would be prepared to pressure the rating agencies, or threaten to choose a different agency, or simply shop among the three agencies until they got favorable ratings.

The Historical Counterfactual

Without the high credit ratings that were conferred on 80–90 percent of the tranches of mortgage-backed CDOs that had subprime mortgages as their collateral, such mortgages surely would not have been issued in the huge quantities seen during the runup to the crisis, since there would have been much less reason to securitize them. Subprime mortgages would not have been in such high demand if very high percentages of their derivative securities had not then been stamped AAA. Nor could they have been concentrated on the banks' balance sheets and in the banks' SIVs—which is what directly led to the financial crisis. It is safe to say, then, that without those high ratings, the financial crisis either would not have happened at all or would have been substantially less severe.

It is clear that the credit rating agencies were at the center of the subprime debacle. Consequently the *historical* counterfactual is well worth considering. What would have happened if financial regulators had not, for seventy years, given the rating agencies' judgments the force of law—and then compounded the error by giving three agencies a legally protected oligopoly?

The first question one might ask is whether, in this counterfactual world, the "issuer pays" business model would have survived—or how it might have operated if it arose. The answer rests on whether bond buyers would have been able to ascertain which bond raters provided reliable advice. If they could,[6] then they would have been willing to pay higher prices (and thus accept lower interest yields) on bonds rated by the reliable advisers. In turn, bond issuers—even in an "issuer pays" framework—would have sought to hire these advisers, since the issuers would thereby be able to pay lower interest rates on the bonds that were rated highly by these firms. And that, in turn, would have meant that the advisory firms would have had every incentive to do whatever they could do to remain reliable. This would not have guaranteed them against corruption or mistakes, but it might have improved the odds considerably.

That the "issuer pays" business model *might* have survived in the historical counterfactual is no guarantee that it would have survived. That outcome would have been determined by the competitive process.

In discussing the historical counterfactual thus far, I have used the term "advisory firm" rather than "rating agency" because, in the absence of the quasi-official status that regulators began to bestow on the rating agencies in 1936, banks and other financial institutions would have had a far wider choice in where they got advice about the safety of bonds they were considering for investments. Some institutional investors might have chosen to do the necessary research on bonds themselves, or to rely primarily on the information produced by the credit-default swap market that eventually emerged. Or they might have turned to outside advisory firms that they considered reliable—based on a firm's track record, business model, other activities (which might pose conflicts of interest), or anything else they deemed relevant. Such advisory firms might have included the Big Three rating agencies or others with a similar structure and procedures. But the category of advisors might also have expanded to include investment banks (if they could erect credible "Chinese walls" against conflicts of interest); industry analysts; or upstart advisory firms whose precise form and practices cannot be known, since we cannot re-run history to see what entrepreneurs might have created, and which of these creations would have survived. Whether they would have followed the "issuer pays" model in free competition with the Big Three cannot be predicted.

The end result of this market for advice—the safety of an institution's bond portfolio—should have, and surely would have, remained subject to review by an institution's regulator. Nevertheless, it seems highly likely that the bond-information market would have been opened up to new ideas, not only about appropriate business models, but also about rating methodologies and technologies. This has not been possible since 1975—or, arguably, since 1936.

If we are interested, then, in understanding the historical causes of the financial crisis rather than in meting out moral judgments, our attention should be fixed on the incremental regulatory process by which the credit-rating agencies' judgments acquired official status, starting in 1936; and then, thirty-nine years later, by which they acquired legal protection against competition.

Chapter 10

Credit-Default Swaps and the Crisis

PETER J. WALLISON

After the failure of Bear Stearns, Lehman Brothers, and AIG had signaled the global financial meltdown, Securities and Exchange Commission chair Christopher Cox was quoted in the *Washington Post* as telling an SEC roundtable:

> The regulatory black hole for credit-default swaps is one of the most significant issues we are confronting in the current credit crisis . . . and requires immediate legislative action. . . . The over-the-counter credit-default swaps market has drawn the world's major financial institutions and others into a tangled web of interconnections where the failure of any one institution might jeopardize the entire financial system. (O'Harrow and Dennis 2008)
>
> Cox's statement is puzzling for reasons both abstract and concrete.

First, it is in the nature of credit markets to be interconnected. That is the way money moves from where it is less useful to where it is more useful, and why financial institutions are called "intermediaries."

Second, a credit-default swap (CDS) is, loosely speaking, a form of insurance.[1] The seller of a CDS protects against loss the loans the buyer of a CDS holds. Far from being destabilizing, a CDS simply transfers risk.

Third, there is very little evidence that the failed financial institutions were the victims of their participation in credit-default swaps, or that their failure jeopardized their swap counterparties and, thus, the global financial system.

Credit-Default Swaps in the Panic of 2008

Had the Treasury Department and the Federal Reserve really believed that Bear Stearns had to be rescued because the market was interconnected through credit-default swaps, they would never have allowed the failure of Lehman, which was a much bigger player in credit-default swaps than Bear. Moreover, while Lehman was a major dealer in credit-default swaps—and a borrower on which many credit-default swaps had been written—when it failed there was no discernible effect on its swap counterparties.

Within a month after its bankruptcy, the swaps in which Lehman was an intermediary dealer had been settled bilaterally, and the swaps written on Lehman itself ($72 billion, notionally) were settled by the Depository Trust and Clearing Corporation (DTCC). The settlement was completed without incident, with a total cash exchange among all counterparties of $5.2 billion. There is no indication that the Lehman failure caused any systemic risk arising out of its CDS obligations—either as one of the major CDS dealers, or as a failed company on which $72 billion in notional credit-default swaps had been written.

The fact that AIG was rescued almost immediately after Lehman's failure led once again to speculation that AIG had written a lot of CDS protection on Lehman, and had to be bailed out for that reason. When the DTCC Lehman settlement was completed, however, AIG had to pay only $6.2 million on its Lehman exposure—a rounding error for this huge company. AIG's failure was due not to its exposure to Lehman through credit-default swaps, but to its use of a credit model that did not account for all the risks it was taking (O'Harrow and Dennis 2008).

The collapse of AIG, then, had nothing to do with credit-default swaps per se. The cause was the same as with the collapse of the financial system as a whole: the faulty evaluation of the risks of residential mortgage-backed securities (RMBSs) that contained subprime loans. Apparently, AIG's credit-risk model failed adequately to account for the risks of subprime RMBSs; for a sharp decline in the mortgage market; and for a downgrade in AIG's credit rating, as a result of the first two failures. Initially, the counterparties in AIG's credit-default swaps generally agreed that AIG did not have to post collateral, because its debt was rated AAA. When it was downgraded by the rating agencies, it was immediately required by its CDS agreements to post collateral. In addition, since AIG had written a great deal of protection on RMBS portfolios, as these declined in value, AIG was again required by its counterparties to post collateral to cover its increased exposure. When AIG could not do so, it was threatened with bankruptcy, and that is when the Fed stepped in with a rescue.

This narrative highlights a fact that gets too little attention in the discussion of credit-default swaps: that the best analogy for a CDS is an ordinary commercial loan. The seller of a CDS is taking on virtually the same risk exposure as a lender. It is no more mysterious than that.

Successful lending requires expertise in assessing credit—the same skill required for writing CDS protection. AIG, like many banks, misjudged the riskiness of portfolios of securitized subprime mortgages, and therefore sold insurance on them through credit-default swaps. These swaps were no riskier than the loans contained in the portfolios; if AIG, instead of selling protection on the portfolios, had bought the portfolios themselves, commentators would have merely clucked about the company's poor credit judgment. For some reason, the fact that it did substantially the same thing by selling protection on these securities through credit-default swaps has caused hysteria about the swaps that insured the securities. Regardless of how it was insured, however, the real risk was created when banks borrowed the funds necessary to assemble a portfolio of subprime mortgage-backed securities. The fact that AIG was the final counterparty and suffered the loss means that someone else did not. Ultimately, there is only one real risk, represented by the original loan or purchase transaction (in the case of an asset like an RMBS portfolio). Credit-default swaps merely transfer that risk, for a price, to someone else.

Credit was extended unwisely (at least in retrospect)—there is no doubt about that. The question is, Why? The answer is unlikely to relate to the vehicles in which the credit was packaged after it was issued—or the CDSs that were purchased as insurance. Credit-default swaps were that insurance. There is no analytical difference between issuing a residential mortgage (or buying a portfolio of RMBS) and writing protection on any of these assets through a CDS. Faulty credit evaluation will, in either case, result in losses. If we wanted to prevent losses that come from faulty credit analysis, we would have to prohibit lending.

If credit-default swaps did not trigger the rescue of Bear Stearns and AIG, what did? The most plausible explanation is that in March 2008, when Bear was about to fail, the international financial markets were very fragile. There was substantial doubt among investors and counterparties about the liquidity and even the solvency of many of the world's major financial institutions. It is likely that Treasury and Fed officials believed that if a major player like Bear Stearns were allowed to fail, there would be runs on other institutions. As Fed chairman Ben Bernanke said at the time, "Under more robust conditions, we might have come to a different decision about Bear Stearns" (quoted in *Wall Street Journal* 2008).

When the markets are in panic mode, every investor and counterparty is on a hair-trigger alert, because the first one out the door is likely to be repaid in full, while the latecomers will suffer losses. The failure of a large bank like Bear in that frenzied environment can be responsible for a rush to the exits; in a normal market, there would have been a much more muted reaction. For example, when Drexel Burnham Lambert failed in 1990, there was nothing like the worldwide shock that ensued after the Lehman Brothers collapse, although Drexel was as large a factor in the market at that time as Lehman was before its failure.

The Lehman bankruptcy demonstrates what Bernanke feared would happen if he did not rescue Bear Stearns. When Lehman was allowed to fail, the markets froze, overnight interbank-lending spreads went straight north, and banks stopped lending to one another. In these circumstances, the rescue of AIG was inevitable. If the reaction to the Lehman failure had not been so severe, it is likely that AIG would have been allowed to fail. In the Fed's words, "in

A	Bond	B	Premium	C	Premium	D	Premium	E
Reference Entity	$10M Loan	Lender	Protection / Collateral	CDS Dealer	Protection / Collateral	Insurance Company	Protection / Collateral	Bank

Figure 10.1. Credit-default swap.

current circumstances, a disorderly failure of AIG could add to already significant levels of financial market fragility and lead to substantially higher borrowing costs, reduced household wealth, and materially weaker economic performance" (quoted in O'Harrow and Dennis 2008).

How Credit-Default Swaps Work

A CDS is nothing more than a contract in which one party (the protection seller) agrees to reimburse another party (the protection buyer) against default on a financial obligation by a third party (the reference entity).

In Figure 10.1, which shows a series of simple CDS transactions, the reference entity is A, the protection buyer is B, and the protection seller is C. Bank B has bought a $10 million bond from company A, so B now has exposure to A. If B does not want to keep this risk—perhaps B believes that A's prospects are declining, or perhaps it wants to diversify its assets—it has two choices: sell the bond or transfer the credit risk. For a variety of tax and other reasons, B may not want to sell the bond. But it is able to eliminate most or all of the credit risk of keeping the bond and entering into a CDS contract with a counterparty, C.

The CDS market is a dealer market, so transactions take place over the counter rather than on an exchange. Accordingly, in purchasing protection against A's default, B's swap is with C, a dealer—one of many, including the world's leading banks, that operate in this market.

Although Figure 10.1 shows B purchasing protection against its entire $10 million loan to A, it is important to note that B also could have purchased protection for only a portion of the principal amount of the $10 million bond. The amount of protection that B purchases is called the "notional amount."

Thus, C, the dealer, agrees to pay $10 million (or whatever notional amount the parties negotiate) if A defaults, and B agrees to make an ongoing premium payment (usually paid quarterly) to C. The size of this premium will reflect the risk that C believes it is assuming in protecting B against A's default. If A is a good credit risk, the premium will be small.

Under the typical CDS contract, B is entitled to request collateral from C in order to assure C's performance. As a dealer, C generally aims to keep a matched book. For every risk it takes on, C typically acquires an offsetting hedge. So C enters a CDS with D, and D posts collateral. Sixty-three percent of all credit-default swaps—and 65 percent of the dollar exposure—are collateralized, precisely because the parties that are paying for protection want to make sure it is there when they need it (Gibson 2007).

The transfer of B's risk to C and then to D (and occasionally from D to E and so on) is often described by CDS critics as a "daisy chain" of obligations, but this description is misleading. Each transaction between counterparties in Figure 10.1 is separate. B can look only to C if A defaults, and C must look to D. B will not usually deal directly with E. However, there are now services, such as those of a firm called Trioptima, that are engaged in "compressing" this string of transactions so that the intermediate obligations are "torn up." This reduces existing interparty obligations and counterparty risk.

Does this hypothetical string of transactions create any significant new risks—beyond the risk created when B made its loan to A?

In the transaction outlined in Figure 10.1, each of the parties in the chain has two distinct risks in case of a default: that its counterparty will be unable to perform its obligation either *before* or *after* the default.

If C becomes bankrupt *before* A defaults, B will have to find a new protection seller. If C defaults *after* A defaults, B will lose the protection it sought from the swap. The same is true for C and D if their respective counterparties default.

In the CDS market, premiums are negotiated based on current views of the risk of A's default. Accordingly, the premium for new

CDS coverage against A's default could be more costly for B, C, and D than the premium that was initially negotiated. Although this might mean a potential loss to any of these parties, it is likely—if the risk of a default by A has been increasing—that the seller of protection will have posted collateral, so that each buyer will be able to reimburse itself for the additional premium cost for a new CDS.

It is important at this point to understand how the collateral process works. Either the buyer or the seller in a CDS transaction may be "in the money" at any point. That is, the CDS premium—also known as the spread—may be rising or falling, depending on the market's judgment of the reference entity's credit worthiness. At the moment the CDS transaction was entered into, the buyer and seller were even. But if the credit of the reference entity begins to decline, the CDS spread will rise, and at that point the buyer is in the money: it is paying a lower premium than the risk would now seem to warrant. Depending on the terms of the original agreement, the seller then may have to post collateral—or more collateral than originally agreed upon. But if the reference entity's credit improves, then the CDS spread will fall and now the seller is in the money. In this case, the buyer may have to put up collateral to ensure that it will continue to make the premium payments.

What happens if A defaults? Assuming that there are no other defaults among the parties in Figure 10.1, there is a settlement among them in which E is the ultimate obligor. Conceptually, C has paid B, D has paid C, and E has paid D. But if E defaults, D becomes the ultimate payer, and if D defaults, C ends up holding the bag. Of course, D then would have a claim against E, or E's bankrupt estate; and the same holds for C if D defaults.

Do Credit-Default Swaps Pose Systemic Risks?

Critics of credit-default swaps argue that the interconnections they create might lead to systemic risk as each member of the string of transactions defaults because of the new liability it must assume. But this analysis is superficial. If credit-default swaps did not exist, B would suffer the loss associated with A's default, and there is no reason to believe that the loss would stop with B. B is undoubtedly indebted to others, and its loss on the loan to A might cause B to default on these obligations, just as E's default might have caused D to default on its obligations to C.

In other words, the credit markets are already interconnected. That is their very purpose. With or without credit-default swaps, the failure of a large enough participant can—at least theoretically—send a cascade of losses through a highly interconnected structure. Credit-default swaps simply move the risk of that result from B to C, D, or E. They do not, however, materially increase the risk created when B made its loan to A. No matter how many defaults occur in the series of transactions presented in Figure 10.1, there is still only one $10 million loss. The only question is who ultimately pays it.

If anything, credit-default swaps *reduce* systemic risk.

Financial regulators have few tools that will materially reduce risk taking. They can insist on more capital, which provides a cushion against losses. They can clamp down on innovation, which can always be a source of uncertainty and therefore risk. But beyond that, they are limited to ensuring that banks, securities firms, and insurance companies—to the extent that they are regulated for safety and soundness—carefully review the risks they are taking and document the process of review.

We have no reason to think that regulators' second-guessing of these risks will be any more insightful into actual creditworthiness than the judgments of those who are making the loans. The current crisis is testimony to that fact. Despite the most comprehensive regulatory oversight of any industry, the banking sector was riddled with bad investments and the resulting losses.

In fact, by creating moral hazard, it is likely that the regulation of banks has reduced the private-sector scrutiny that banks would have received as part of a fully operating system of market discipline. In light of the consistent failure of traditional regulation, the risk-management innovations that have been fostered by the private sector may have a greater potential to control risk than does government oversight.

An outstanding example is the interest-rate swap, which—like the

CDS—was developed by financial intermediaries looking for ways to manage risk.

Say that a bank has deposits on which it must pay a market or "floating" rate of interest, but it also holds mortgages on which it receives only a fixed monthly interest payment. This is a typical position for a bank—but a risky one. If interest rates rise, it may be forced to pay more interest to its depositors than it is receiving from the mortgages it holds, and thus would suffer losses.

Ideally, this bank would want to trade the fixed rate it receives on its mortgage portfolio for a floating rate that will more closely match what it pays its depositors. That way, it is protected against increases in interest rates. An interest swap, in which the bank pays a fixed rate to a counterparty and receives a floating rate in return, is the answer; it matches the bank's interest rate receipts to its payment obligations.

Who else might want to engage in such a swap?

Consider an insurance company that is obliged to pay out a certain sum monthly on the fixed-rate annuities it has written. Insurance companies try to match this obligation with bonds and notes that are the ultimate source of the funds for meeting their fixed obligations, but these do not necessarily yield a fixed return for periods long enough to fully fund their annuity commitments. They mature well before the annuity obligations expire, and may—if interest rates decline—yield less than is needed for paying annuitants.

The insurance company, then, would be able to avoid risk with a swap that is the mirror image of what the bank needs.

Into this picture steps a swap dealer, who arranges a fixed-for-floating interest-rate swap between the bank and insurance company. The notional amount can be set at any number; its purpose in an interest-rate swap is simply to provide the principal amount on which the interest will be paid. Suppose the parties agree on $100 million. The bank agrees to pay the insurance company a fixed amount—say, 5 percent—on $100 million, and the insurance company agrees to pay the bank a floating rate of interest on the same notional amount. If interest rates rise to 6 percent, the bank is in the money and the insurance company pays the bank the 1 percent difference; if rates fall to 4 percent, the bank pays the insurance company 1 percent.[2]

The important thing to notice is that both the bank and the insurance company have reduced their risks. The bank gets a floating payment that assures it of the funds necessary to pay its depositors, no matter how high interest rates rise. The insurance company is better off because it gets a fixed payment from the bank that allows it to pay its annuitants no matter how far interest rates fall. Overall risk has declined. This is the only feasible way to reduce systemic risk.

The Notion of Notional Amounts

Shortly after Bear Stearns was rescued, George Soros (2008) wrote:

> There is an esoteric financial instrument called credit-default swaps. The notional amount of CDS contracts outstanding is roughly $45 [trillion]. . . . To put it into perspective, this is about equal to half the total U.S. household wealth.

This is not putting credit-default swaps "into perspective." "The notional amount of credit-default swaps outstanding"—although suitable for scaring people, because it is so large—is not in any sense relevant to the size of the risks associated with credit-default swaps.

Returning again to the hypothetical transaction in Figure 10.1, we can calculate the notional amount that comes out of the reporting of the transaction by the various participants. B reports that it is paying a premium for protection on a notional amount of $10 million (the loan to A), C reports that it has sold protection for this amount, as have D, E, and the dealer intermediary between D and E. Thus, the total notional amount arising from this series of transactions is $50 million, or five times the actual potential loss in the event that A defaults. The same risk has been counted five times because, under different scenarios, B, C, D, E, or the intermediary between D and E will cover A's default.

The Depository Trust and Clearing Corporation recently began publishing data on credit-default swaps from its Trade Information Warehouse, which gathers information about 90 percent of all CDS transactions (Rogoff and Anderson 2008). The DTCC data eliminated the multiple counting in each swap transaction and reported that, as of the week ending 12 December 2008, the "gross notional amount" of credit-default swaps outstanding was $25.6 trillion (DTCC 2008)— about half Soros's figure, $45 trillion.

Even $25.6 trillion, however, vastly overstates the real potential loss on all credit-default swaps outstanding, because the protection sold must be reduced by the protection bought. When this fact is taken into account, the result, the "net notional amount," has been estimated at 10 percent of the gross notional amount (Rogoff and Anderson 2008). Accordingly, the net notional amount is actually about 5 percent of the figure Soros used.

That is still a lot of money, of course, but it does not threaten to overwhelm the economy, as Soros would have it.

The most troubling aspect of credit-default swaps is not their financial effects, which are to move and, at best, to reduce risk. It is their political effects. They are sufficiently complex that, like "speculation" in general, they can become political piñatas, and divert scrutiny from the actual causes of problems such as the financial calamity that began in 2008.

PART III

Economists, Economics,
and the Financial Crisis

Chapter 11

The Crisis of 2008: Lessons
for and from Economics

DARON ACEMOGLU

We do not yet know whether the global financial and economic crisis of 2008 will go down in history as a momentous or even a uniquely catastrophic event. Unwritten history is full of events that contemporaries thought were epochal but are today long forgotten. Conversely, much of what we think of as critical was, at the time, considered insignificant; in the early stages of the Great Depression, for instance, many people belittled its import.

Regardless whether the second half of 2008 will be featured in history books, however, it is a critical opportunity for many in the economics profession—unfortunately, myself included—to be disabused of certain notions that we should not have accepted in the first place. It is an opportunity for us to step back and consider which, among the conclusions to our theoretical and empirical investigations led us, remain untarnished by recent events—and to figure out what intellectual errors we have made, and what lessons these errors offer.

Whatever the intellectual currents of the past, however, economic theory still has a lot to teach us as we make our way through the crisis. Several economic principles related to the most important aspect of economic performance—the long-run growth potential of nations— are still valid and hold important lessons in our intellectual and practical deliberations. But, curiously, these principles have played little role in recent academic debates and have been entirely absent in policy debates. Academic economists should not let these principles be forgotten, even as we acknowledge our mistakes.

There remains much uncertainty about what happened in the financial markets and inside many corporations. We will know more in the years to come. From what we know today, many of the roots of our current problems are apparent; but most of us did not recognize them before the crisis. Three inaccurate notions impelled us to ignore these impeding problems and their causes.

The Unconquered Business Cycle

The first notion to be discarded is that the era of aggregate volatility has come to an end. We believed that, through astute policy or new technology (including better methods of communication and inventory control), the business cycle had been conquered. Our belief in a more benign economy made us more optimistic about the stock market and the housing market. If all economic contractions must be soft and short lived, then it becomes easier to believe that financial intermediaries, firms, and consumers should not worry about large drops in asset values.

Even though the data robustly show a negative relationship between an economy's income per capita and its volatility, and many measures did show a marked decline in aggregate volatility since the 1950s and certainly since the prewar era, these empirical patterns neither mean that business cycles have disappeared nor that catastrophic economic events are impossible. The same economic and financial changes that have made our economy more diversified and individuals and firms better insured have also increased the interconnections among them.

The diversification of *idiosyncratic* risks shares them among many companies and individuals, creating a multitude of counterparty relationships. Such interconnections make the economic system more robust against small shocks, but they also make the economy more vulnerable to certain low-probability, "fat tail" events because of potential domino effects among financial institutions, companies, and households. In this light, perhaps we should not find it surprising that years of economic calm can be followed by tumultuous times and notable volatility.

There is another sense in which the myth of the end of the business cycle is at odds with fundamental properties of the capitalist system. As Joseph Schumpeter argued long ago, the market depends on innovation, which involves a heavy dose of creative destruction—where new firms, procedures, and products replace old ones.

Much of the market system's creative destruction takes place at the micro level. But not all of it. Many companies are so large that their replacement by new firms and products will have aggregate effects. Moreover, many general-purpose technologies are shared by diverse companies in different lines of business, so their failure and potential replacement by new processes will also have aggregate effects. Equally important, businesses and individuals make decisions under imperfect information, and they may learn from each other and from past practices. This learning process will introduce additional correlation and co-movement in the behavior of economic agents, which will also extend the realm of creative destruction from the micro to the macro.

The large drops in asset values and simultaneous insolvencies of many companies should alert us that aggregate volatility is part and parcel of the market system. Understanding that such volatility is inherent to any interconnected modern economy should redirect our attention toward models that help us interpret the various sources of volatility, delineating which components are the result of efficiently working markets and which result from avoidable market failures. Deeper studies of aggregate volatility also require conceptual and theoretical investigation of how the increasingly interconnected nature of our economic and financial system affects the allocation of resources and the sharing of risks among both companies and individuals.

The Importance of Institutions

Our second too-quickly-accepted notion was that the capitalist economy lives in an institutionless vacuum, where markets miraculously monitor opportunistic behavior. We mistakenly equated free markets with markets unregulated by institutions, including legal ones. Although we understand that even unfettered competitive markets are based on a set of laws and institutions that secure property rights, ensure the enforcement of contracts, and regulate firms' behavior and product and service quality, our conceptualization of markets increasingly abstracted from the role of the institutions and regulations that support market transactions.

To be sure, institutions have received more attention since the mid-1990s than before, but the thinking was that we had to study the role of institutions to understand why poor nations were poor, as opposed to probing the nature of the institutions that ensured continued prosperity in the advanced nations, and how institutions should change in the face of ever-evolving economic relations.

In our obliviousness to the importance of market-supporting institutions we were in sync with policy makers. They were lured by ideological notions derived from Ayn Rand novels rather than from economic theory. We let these notions set the agenda for our thinking about the world and worse, perhaps, for our policy advice.

In hindsight, we should not be surprised that unregulated profit-seeking individuals have taken risks from which they benefit and others lose. But we now know better. Few among us will argue today that market monitoring is sufficient against opportunistic behavior.

Many may view the need to include more than self-interest in economic models as marking a failure of economic theory. I strongly disagree: the recognition that markets live on foundations laid by institutions—that free markets are not the same as unregulated markets—enriches both economic theory and its practice. We must now start building a theory of market transactions that is more in tune with their institutional and regulatory foundations. We must also turn to the theory of regulation—of both firms and financial institutions—with renewed vigor and with insights gained from current experience.

The discipline of economics has given us the insight that greed is neither good nor bad in the abstract. When channeled into profit-maximizing, competitive, and innovative behavior under the auspices of sound laws and regulations, greed can act as the engine of innovation and economic growth. But when unchecked by the appropriate institutions and regulations, it will degenerate into rent-seeking, corruption, and crime. Economic theory provides guidance in how to create the right incentive structures and reward systems to contain greed and turn it into a force for progress.

The Insufficiency of Reputation

The third notion that has also been destroyed by recent events is at first less obvious. It is also one that I strongly believed in.

Our logic and models suggested that even if we could not trust individuals, particularly when information was imperfect and regulation lackluster, we could trust the long-lived large firms—the Bear Stearnses, the Merrill Lynches, the Lehman Brothers of the world—to monitor themselves, because they had accumulated sufficient "reputation capital" that they would not want to waste it. Our faith in such organizations was shaken but still standing after the accounting scandals in Enron and other giants of the early 2000s. It may now have suffered the death blow.

Our trust in the self-monitoring capabilities of organizations ignored two critical difficulties. The first is that even within firms, monitoring must be done by individuals—the chief executives, the managers, the accountants. And in the same way that we should not have blindly trusted in the incentives of stockbrokers willing to take astronomical risks for which they were not the residual claimants, we should not have put our faith in individuals monitoring others simply because they were part of larger organizations.

All this is troubling for economists' way of thinking about the world. Reputational monitoring requires that failure be punished severely. But the scarcity of specific capital and knowhow means that the prospect of such punishment is often less than credible. The intellectual argument for the financial bailouts in September 2008 was that the organizations clearly responsible for the problems we are in today should nonetheless be saved because they are the only ones that have the "specific capital" to get us out of our current predicament. This is not an invalid argument. Neither is it unique to the financial crisis.

Whenever there are incentives to compromise integrity, to sacrifice quality, and to take unnecessary risks, most companies will do so, in tandem with each other. And since punishing such behavior would lead to a vacuum of specific skills, capital, and knowledge that would be too costly to allow, prospective punishments lose their ability to deter.

The lessons are twofold. First, as we rethink the role that maintaining a firm's reputation may play in its internal governance, we need to highlight the scarcity value of firms' skills and expertise if several of them fail simultaneously. Second, we need to remember that firms' reputations are derived from the behavior—and interactions—of directors, managers, and employees, not (as so much of the literature assumes) the behavior of a hypothetical principal who maximizes the net present discounted value of the firm.

Lessons from the Political Economy of Growth

Those of us who are economists can, with some justification, blame ourselves for missing important economic insights and not being more farsighted than policymakers. We can even blame ourselves for being complicit in the intellectual atmosphere leading up to the current disaster. But on the bright side, the crisis has increased the vitality of economics and highlighted several challenging, relevant, and exciting questions. These range from the ability of the market system to deal with risks, interconnections, and the disruptions brought about by the process of creative destruction to issues of a better framework for regulation and the relationship between underlying institutions and the functioning of markets and organizations. It should be much less likely in the decade to come for bright young economists to worry about finding new and relevant questions to work on. And even now, economics offers lessons that are still worth heeding.

For example, despite the ferocious severity of the global crisis—and barring a complete global meltdown—the possible loss of GDP for most countries is in the range of just a couple of percentage points—and most of this might have been unavoidable anyway, given the overexpansion of the economy in prior years. In contrast, within a decade or two, we may see modest but cumulative economic growth that more than outweighs the current economic contraction. The preoccupation of economic theory with growth therefore offers a cautionary note against overreacting to the crisis.

Moreover, many of the main sources of economic growth are reasonably well understood. There is broad theoretical and empirical agreement on the importance of technology, physical capital, and human capital. Economists also understand the role that innovation and reallocation play in propagating economic growth, and recognize the broad outlines of the institutional framework that makes innovation, reallocation, and long-run growth possible.

Recent events have not cast doubt on the importance of innovation. On the contrary, we have enjoyed prosperity over the past two decades because of rapid innovations—quite independent from financial bubbles and troubles. A breakneck pace of innovations in software, hardware, telecommunications, pharmaceuticals, biotechnology, entertainment, and retail and wholesale trade are responsible for the bulk of the increases in aggregate productivity over the past two decades. Even the financial innovations, which have been somewhat tainted in the recent crisis, are in most cases socially valuable and have contributed to growth. Complex securities were misused to take risks, with the downside being borne by unsuspecting parties. But when properly regulated, these securities, such as derivatives, also enable more sophisticated strategies for risk sharing and diversification. They have enabled, and will eventually again enable, firms to reduce the cost of capital.

Technological ingenuity is the key to the prosperity and success of the capitalist economy. New innovations and their implementation and marketing will play a central role in renewed economic growth in the aftermath of the crisis.

The other pillar of economic growth is reallocation. Because innovation often comes in the form of Schumpeterian creative destruction, new production processes and firms with new technologies will replace old ones. This is only one aspect of capitalist reallocation, however.

Volatility—the incessantly shifting degree to which companies and services are relatively more productive and enjoy greater demand—has perhaps been strengthened now more than ever because of the greater global interconnections. Volatility is not necessarily a curse; for the most part, it can be an opportunity for the market economy by reallocating resources to areas where productivity and demand are greatest. The developments of the last two decades again highlight the importance of reallocation, since economic growth, as usual, coincided with the movement of output, labor, and capital away from many established companies towards their (often foreign) competitors, and away from sectors in which the United States and other advanced countries ceased to have a comparative advantage toward sectors where their advantages became stronger.

The final principle that I would like to emphasize relates to the political economy of growth. Economic growth will only take place if a society creates the institutions and policies that encourage innovation, reallocation, investment, and education. But the creation and adjustment of such institutions should not be taken for granted.

Because of the reallocation and creative destruction brought about by economic growth, there will always be parties—often politically influential parties—that oppose certain aspects of economic growth. In many less-developed economies, therefore, the key prerequisite is to ensure that incumbent producers, elites, and politicians do not hijack the political agenda and create an environment inimical to economic progress and growth. Another threat to the institutional foundations of economic growth, however, comes from its ultimate beneficiaries. Creative destruction and reallocation harm not only established businesses but also their employees and suppliers, sometimes destroying the livelihood of millions of workers and peasants. It is easy for impoverished populations suffering from adverse shocks and economic crises—particularly in societies where the political economy never generated an effective safety net—to turn against the market system and support populist policies that will create barriers to economic growth. In the midst of an economic crisis, these threats may become as important in advanced economies as in less-developed countries.

The importance of political economy has also been underscored by recent events. It is difficult to tell the story of the failure of regulation of investment banks and of the financial industry at large over the past two decades, and of the approval of the bailout plan, without some reference to political economy. The United States is not Indonesia under Suharto or the Philippines under Marcos. But we need not go to such extremes to imagine that when the financial industry contributes millions of dollars to the campaigns of senators and congressmen, it will have an acute influence on financial regulation; or to imagine that the investment bankers who set up—or fail to set up, as the case may be—the regulations for their former partners and colleagues without oversight will likely cause political-economy problems. It is also difficult to envisage a scenario in which current and future policies will not be influenced by the backlash against markets that those who have lost their houses and livelihoods feel at the moment.

Political Economy During the Crisis

It is remarkable, then, that in the politics of the crisis, little attention has been given to the effect of proposed policies on long-run economic growth, innovation, and reallocation.

A large stimulus plan that includes bailouts for banks, the financial sector at large, auto manufacturers, and others will undoubtedly influence innovation and reallocation. Without taking a position on the wisdom of such a plan, reallocation will clearly suffer as a result of many aspects of it. Market signals suggest that labor and capital should have been reallocated away from the Detroit Big Three, and that highly skilled labor should have been reallocated away from the financial industry toward more innovative sectors. The latter reallocation would have been critically important in view of the fact that Wall Street had attracted many of the best (and most ambitious) minds over the past decades; in retrospect, while these bright young minds have contributed to financial innovation, they also used their talents for devising new methods of making money by shifting risks to others. Yet the focus of policy efforts was on propping up and even consolidating the huge financial firms and the Big Three.

Several other areas of potential innovation may directly suffer as a result of the politics and economics of the current crisis. Improvements in retail and wholesale trade and service delivery will undoubtedly slow down as consumer demand contracts. A key area of innovation for the next decade and beyond, energy, may also become a casualty. The demand for alternative energy sources was strong before the crisis and promised a platform for synergies between scientific research and profitability such as have been witnessed in computing, pharmaceuticals, and biotechnology. With the decline in oil prices and the odds turning against higher taxes on gasoline, some of the momentum is undoubtedly lost.

There may also be a risk of an "expectational trap," in which consumers and policy makers become pessimistic about future growth and the promise of markets. We do not understand expectational traps well enough to know exactly how they happen and what economic dynamics they unleash. But if consumers delay purchases of durable goods, it can certainly have major effects, particularly when inventories are already high and credit is tight. An expectational trap of this sort would deepen and lengthen the recession and create extensive business failures and liquidation rather than the necessary creative destruction and reallocation.

In my opinion, however, the greater danger from an expectational trap and a deep recession lies elsewhere. We may see consumers and policy makers start believing that free markets are responsible for the crisis and shift their support away from the market economy. We would then see the pendulum swing too far, taking us to an era of heavy government involvement (as opposed to a reform of the foundational regulation of free markets). I believe that such a swing, and its attendant anti-market policies, would be a real threat to the future growth prospects of the global economy. Restrictions on trade in goods and services would be a first step. Industrial policy that stymies reallocation and innovation would be a second, equally damaging, step. When the talk is of bailing out and protecting selected sectors, more systematic proposals for trade restrictions and industrial policy may be around the corner.

The risk that belief in the capitalist system may collapse should not be dismissed. After all, the past two decades were heralded as the triumph of capitalism. It is then natural for many to conclude that the bitter aftermath of that period must be the failure of the capitalist system. In reality, what we are experiencing is not a failure of capitalism or free markets per se, but the failure of unregulated markets—in particular, of an unregulated financial sector and unregulated risk management. As such, the crisis should not make us less optimistic about the growth potential of market economies—provided that markets are based on solid institutional foundations. But since the rhetoric of the past decades equated capitalism with lack of regulation, this nuance will be lost on many who are suffering from the crisis. It is one thing for the population at large to think that markets do not work as well as the pundits promised. It is an entirely different level of disillusionment for them to think that markets are just an excuse for the rich and powerful to fill their pockets at the expense of the rest. But how could they think otherwise, when the bailouts were designed by bankers to help bankers and to minimize damage to those responsible for the debacle in the first place?

Although the economics profession was partly complicit in the buildup to the current crisis, economists still have important things to say if the crisis and its supposedly "capitalist" origins are not to impede the innovation and reallocation necessary for economic growth.

Chapter 12

The Financial Crisis and the Systemic Failure of the Economics Profession

DAVID COLANDER, MICHAEL GOLDBERG,
ARMIN HAAS, KATARINA JUSELIUS, ALAN KIRMAN,
THOMAS LUX, AND BRIGITTE SLOTH

The global financial crisis has revealed the need to rethink fundamentally how financial systems are regulated. It has also made clear a systemic failure of the economics profession.

Since the 1970s, most economists have developed and come to rely on models that disregard key factors—including heterogeneous decision rules, revisions of forecasting strategies, and changes in the social context—that drive outcomes in asset and other markets. It is obvious, even to the casual observer, that these models fail to account for the actual evolution of the real-world economy. Moreover, the current academic agenda has largely crowded out research on the inherent causes of financial crises. There has also been little exploration of early indicators of systemic crisis and potential ways to prevent this malady from developing. In fact, if one browses through the academic macroeconomics and finance literature, "systemic crisis" seems to be an otherworldly event, absent from economic models. Most models, by design, offer no immediate handle on how to think about or deal with this recurring phenomenon.[1] In our hour of greatest need, societies around the world are left to grope in the dark without a theory. That, to us, is a *systemic failure of the economics profession.*

Economists' Failure to Anticipate
and Understand the Crisis

The implicit view behind standard equilibrium models is that markets and economies are inherently stable and only temporarily get off track. The majority of economists thus failed to warn about the threatening systemic crisis and ignored the work of those who did.

Ironically, as the crisis has unfolded, economists have had no choice but to abandon their standard models and produce hand-waving common-sense remedies. Common-sense advice, although useful, is a poor substitute for an underlying model. It is not enough to put the existing model to one side, observing that one needs "exceptional measures for exceptional times." What we need are models capable of envisaging such "exceptional times."

The confinement of macroeconomics to models of stable states that are perturbed by limited external shocks, but that neglect the intrinsic recurrent boom-and-bust dynamics of our economic system, is remarkable. After all, worldwide financial and economic crises are hardly new, and they have had a tremendous impact beyond the immediate economic consequences of mass unemployment and hyperinflation in various times and places. This is even more surprising given the long academic legacy of earlier economists' study of crises, which can be found in the work of Walter Bagehot (1873), Hyman Minsky (1986), Charles Kindleberger (1989), and Axel Leijonhufvud (2000), to name a few prominent examples. This tradition, however, has been neglected and even suppressed. Much of the motivation for economics as an academic discipline stems from the desire to explain phenomena like unemployment, boom-and-bust cycles, and financial crises, but dominant theoretical models exclude many of the aspects of the economy that lead to such phenomena. Confining theoretical models to "normal" times without consideration of these aspects might seem contradictory to the focus that the average taxpayer would expect of the scientists on his payroll.

The most recent literature provides us with examples of blindness against the approaching storm that seem odd in retrospect. For example, in their analysis of the risk management implications of CDOs (collateralized debt obligations), Krahnen 2005 and Krahnen and

Wilde 2006 mention the possibility of an increase of "systemic risk." But they conclude that such risk should not be the concern of the banks engaged in the CDO market, because it is the governments' responsibility to provide costless insurance against a system-wide crash. On the more theoretical side, a recent and prominent strand of literature essentially argues that consumers and investors are too risk averse because of their memory of the (improbable) event of the Great Depression (e.g., Cogley and Sargent 2008).

The failure of economists to anticipate and model the financial crisis has deep methodological roots. The often-heard definition of economics—that it is concerned with the "allocation of scarce resources"—is short sighted and misleading. It reduces economics to the study of optimal decisions in well-specified choice problems. Such research generally loses track of the complex dynamics of economic systems and the instability that accompanies it. Without an adequate understanding of these processes, one is likely to miss the major factors that influence the economic sphere of our societies. This insufficient definition of economics often leads researchers to disregard questions about the coordination of actors and the possibility of coordination failures. Indeed, analysis of these issues would require a different type of mathematics than that which is generally used in most prominent economic models.

Economists' Role in Fostering the Crisis

Financial economists gave little warning to the public about the fragility of their models,[2] even as they saw individuals and businesses build a financial system based on their work. There are a number of possible explanations for this failure to warn the public. One is a "lack of understanding" explanation. The researchers did not know the models were fragile. We find this explanation highly unlikely; financial engineers are extremely bright, and it is almost inconceivable that such bright individuals did not understand the limitations of their models. A second, more likely explanation for this failure is that they did not consider it their job to warn the public. We believe that this view involves a misunderstanding of the role of the economist—and an ethical breakdown. Economists, like all scientists, have an ethical responsibility to communicate the limitations of their models and the potential misuse of their research. Currently, there is no ethical code for professional economic scientists. There should be one.

Economic textbook models, which focus the analysis on the optimal allocation of scarce resources, are predominantly Robinson Crusoe (representative-agent) models. Financial-market models are obtained by letting Robinson manage his financial affairs as a sideline to his well- considered utility maximization over his (finite or infinite) expected lifespan, taking into account with "correct" probabilities all potential future happenings. This approach is mingled with insights from Walrasian general-equilibrium theory, in particular the finding of the Arrrow-Debreu two-period model that all uncertainty can be eliminated if only there are enough contingent claims (i.e., appropriate derivative instruments). This theoretical result (a theorem in an extremely stylized model) underlies the common belief that the introduction of new classes of derivatives can only be welfare enhancing. It is worth emphasizing that this view is not empirically grounded but is derived from a benchmark model that is much too abstract to be confronted with data.

On the practical side, mathematical portfolio- and risk-management models have been the academic backbone of the tremendous increase of trading volume and diversification of instruments in financial markets. Typically, new derivative products achieve market penetration only if a certain industry standard has been established for the pricing and risk management of these products. Mostly, pricing principles are derived from a set of assumptions about an "appropriate" process for valuing the underlying asset (i.e., the primary assets on which options or forwards are written), together with an equilibrium criterion such as arbitrage-free prices. From these assumptions springs advice for hedging the inherent risk of a derivative position (for example, by balancing it with other assets that neutralize the risk exposure).

The most prominent example is the development of a theory of options pricing by Fischer Black and Myron Scholes that eventually (in the 1980s) was preprogrammed into pocket calculators. Simultaneously with Black-Scholes options pricing, the same principles led to the widespread introduction of new strategies, under the headings of portfolio insurance and dynamic hedging, that tried to achieve a theoretically risk-free portfolio composed of both assets and options, and to keep it risk-free by frequent rebalancing after changes in its input data (e.g., asset prices).

With structured products for credit risk, however, the basic paradigm of derivative pricing—perfect replication—is not applicable, so that one has to rely on a kind of rough-and-ready evaluation of these contracts on the basis of historical data. Unfortunately, historical data were hardly available in most cases, which meant that one had to rely on simulations with relatively arbitrary assumptions about correlations between risks and default probabilities. This made the theoretical foundations of these products highly questionable—the equivalent to erecting a building's foundation without knowing the materials of which the foundation was made.

The dramatic recent rise of the markets for structured products (most prominently collateralized debt obligations and credit-default swaps) was made possible by the development of such simulation-based pricing tools and the adoption of an industry standard for these under the lead of the bond-rating agencies. Barry Eichengreen (2008) rightly points out that the "development of mathematical methods designed to quantify and hedge risk encouraged commercial banks, investment banks and hedge funds to use more leverage," as if the managers of these institutions believed that the very use of the mathematical methods diminished the underlying risk. He also notes that the models were estimated on data from periods of low volatility and thus could not deal with the arrival of major changes. But such major changes are endemic to the economy and cannot simply be ignored.

A somewhat different aspect is the danger of a *control illusion*. The mathematical rigor and numerical precision of risk-management and asset-pricing tools have a tendency to conceal the weaknesses of models and assumptions to those who have not developed them (as Eichengreen emphasizes). Naturally, models are, at best, only approximations to real-world dynamics, and they are built in part on quite heroic assumptions (most notoriously, the normality of asset-price changes, which can be rejected at a confidence level of 99.999 percent). Of course, considerable progress has been made by moving to more refined models with, for instance, "fat-tailed" Levy processes as their driving factors. However, while such models better capture the intrinsic volatility of markets, their improved performance, taken at face value, might again contribute to enhancing the control illusion of the naïve user.

The increased sophistication of extant models, moreover, does not overcome the robustness problem and should not absolve the authors of the models from explaining their limitations to the users in the financial industry. As in nuclear physics, the tools provided by financial engineering can be put to very different uses, so that what is designed as an instrument to hedge risk can become a weapon of "financial mass destruction" (in the words of Warren Buffett) if used for increased leverage. This seems to have been the case with derivative positions that were built up to profit from high returns as long as the downside risk did not materialize.

Researchers who develop such models can claim they are merely neutral academics developing tools that people are free to use or reject. We do not find that view credible. Researchers have an ethical responsibility to point out to the public when the tools that they developed are misused. And it is the responsibility of the researcher to make clear from the outset the limitations and underlying assumptions of his models and to warn of the dangers of their mechanistic application.

Because researchers did not point out the difficulties with their models, the new derivatives markets were flawed in ways that contributed to the financial crisis. One of the most important problems was that while the possibility of systemic risk was not entirely ignored, it was defined as lying outside the responsibility of market participants. In this way, moral hazard concerning systemic risk was a built-in attribute of the system. The neglect of systemic externalities by market participants and policy makers is not only unethical; it is a prudential lapse as well. Market participants' use of these models undermines the stability of the system that the models imply is stable, meaning that participants should not use the models if they want to avoid being the victims of the endogenous boom-and-bust fluctuations so typical of markets.

Blame should not only fall on market participants and policy makers; it should also fall on economists, who insisted on constructing models that ignored the systemic risk factors. In failing even to point out their weaknesses to the public, they were participants in what might be called *academic* moral hazard.

What follows from our diagnosis? Market participants and regulators have to become more sensitive toward the potential weaknesses of risk-management models. Since we do not know the "true" model, robustness should be a key concern. The uncertainty of models should also be taken into account by applying more than a single model. For example, one might use an imperfect knowledge economics (IKE) model (Frydman and Goldberg 2007, 2008) that makes use of probability theory, but also recognizes that no one, including the economist, knows the processes driving market outcomes. One might also rely on probabilistic projections that cover a whole range of specific models (cf. Föllmer 2008). The theory of robust control provides a toolbox of techniques that could be applied for this purpose, and it is an approach that should be considered.

Ignoring Market Participants' Own Models of Markets

A related flaw of asset-pricing and risk-management tools is their individualistic perspective, which takes as given (*ceteris paribus*) the behavior of all other market participants. However, if popular asset-pricing and risk-management models are used by a large number (or even the majority) of market participants, then the individualistic assumption is false and can be expected to produce misleading predictions. By the same token, a market participant (e.g., the notorious Long-Term Capital Management) might become so dominant in certain markets that the *ceteris paribus* assumption becomes unrealistic. The simultaneous pursuit of identical micro strategies leads to synchronous behavior and built-in contagion. This simultaneous application might generate an unexpected macro outcome that jeopardizes the success of the underlying micro strategies.

A perfect illustration was the U.S. stock market crash of October 1987. Triggered by a small decline in prices, automated hedging strategies produced an avalanche of sell orders that, out of the blue, led to a fall in U.S. stock indices of about 20 percent within one day. Engaging in massive sales to rebalance their portfolios (along the lines of Black and Scholes), the relevant actors could not realize their attempted incremental adjustments, but instead suffered major losses from the huge ensuing macro effect. The model was self-reflexive; people's collective use of the model changed the model, and brought about a result not predicted by the original model.

Similarly, many economic models are built on the twin assumptions of "rational expectations" and a representative agent. That is, *all* market participants are homogenized into a single agent with rational expectations, and these are defined to be fully consistent with the structure of the economist's own model. Since the economist's model is, of course, treated as true (which is odd given that even economists are divided in their views about the correct model of the economy), the implication is that the representative individual, hence everyone in the economy, behaves as if he had *a complete understanding of the economic mechanisms governing the world.*

Such models do not attempt to formalize individuals' actual expectations: specifications are not based on empirical observation of how people form expectations. Thus, even when applied economics research and psychology provide insights about how individuals actually form expectations, they cannot be used within rational-expectations models. Leaving no place for real-world individuals' imperfect knowledge and adaptive adjustments, rational-expectations models are typically found to have dynamics that are grossly inconsistent with economic data.

Technically, rational-expectations models are often framed as solving dynamic-programming problems in macroeconomics. But dynamic-programming models as models of the aggregate economy have serious limitations (Colander 2006; Colander et al. 2008). If they are to be analytically tractable, not more than one dynamically maximizing agent can be considered, and consistent expectations have to be imposed on this agent. Therefore, dynamic-programming models are hardly imaginable without the assumptions of a representative agent and rational expectations. This prerequisite has generated a vicious cycle in which technical tools developed on the basis of the chosen assumptions prevent economists from moving beyond these restricted settings to explore more realistic scenarios. While other currents of research do exist, economic policy advice, particularly in financial economics, has far too often been based (consciously or not) on a set of axioms and hypotheses derived ultimately from a highly limited dynamic-control model that couples the Robinson Crusoe approach with "rational" expectations.

The major problem is that despite its many refinements, this is not an approach based on, and confirmed by, empirical research to anywhere near the degree that it should be.[3] In fact, the assumptions underlying models too often stand in stark contrast to a broad set of regularities in human behavior discovered both in psychology and in what is sometimes called behavioral economics, as well as in experimental economics. The cornerstones of many models in finance and macroeconomics are maintained despite all the contradictory evidence discovered by such research. Much of this literature shows that in experiments, human subjects act in ways that bear little resemblance to how they are assumed to act in rational-expectations models. Real-world people do not exhibit ultra-rationality. Rather, agents display various forms of "bounded rationality," using heuristic decision rules and displaying inertia in their reaction to new information. They have also been shown in real financial markets to be strongly influenced by emotional and hormonal reactions (Lo et al. 2005; Coates and Herbert 2008). Incorporating such findings into an economic model may help us better understand dynamics in real-world markets.

What we are arguing is that as a modeling requirement, internal consistency must be complemented with *external consistency*. Economic modeling cannot be inconsistent with insights about real-world human behavior obtained from other branches of science. It is highly problematic to insist on a specific view of humans in economic settings that is irreconcilable with empirical evidence.

Conceptual Reductionism

The representative-agent assumption in many current models in macroeconomics (including macro finance) means that modelers subscribe to the most extreme form of conceptual reductionism (Lux and Westerhoff 2009). By assumption, all concepts applicable to the macro sphere (i.e., the economy or its financial system) are fully reduced to concepts and knowledge in the lower-level domain of the individual agent. This is quite different from the standard reductionist concept that has become widely accepted in the natural sciences, which reduces complex phenomena to the interactions of their parts, allowing the scientist to understand new,

emergent phenomena at the higher hierarchical level (the concept of "more is different"; cf. Anderson 1972).

By contrast, in economics, the representative-agent approach simply *equates* the macro sphere with the micro sphere. One could, indeed, say that this equation negates the existence of a macro sphere and the necessity of investigating macroeconomic phenomena, in that it views the entire economy as an organism governed by a universal will.[4] Any notion of "systemic risk" or "coordination failure" is necessarily absent from, and alien to, such a methodology.

For natural scientists, the distinction between micro-level phenomena and macro, system-wide phenomena that emerge from the interaction of microscopic units is well known. In a dispersed system, the financial crisis would be seen as an involuntary emergent phenomenon of microeconomic activity. The conceptually reductionist paradigm, however, blocks, from the outset, any understanding of the interplay between micro and macro levels. The differences between the overall system and its parts remain simply incomprehensible from the viewpoint of this approach.

In order to develop models that allow us to deduce macro events from microeconomic regularities, economists have to rethink the concept of micro foundations. Economists' micro foundations should allow for the interactions of economic agents, since economic activity is, essentially, interactive. And since interaction depends on differences in information, motives, knowledge, and capabilities, this implies the *heterogeneity*—not the "representativeness"—of agents.

For instance, only a sufficiently rich model of connections between firms, households, and a dispersed banking sector is likely to allow us to get a grasp on "systemic risk," domino effects in the financial sector, and their repercussions on consumption and investment. The dominance of the extreme form of representative-agent conceptual reductionism has prevented economists from even attempting to model these important phenomena. It is this flawed methodology that is the ultimate reason for the lack of applicability of the standard macro framework to current events. It also explains, in part, the growing separation of academic economics from issues relating to the real-world economy. For example, the recent surge of research in network theory has received relatively scarce attention in economics, even though it could provide a window into the interaction of ensembles of heterogeneous actors. "Self-organized criticality" theory may also help to explain boom-and-bust cycles (cf. Scheinkman and Woodford 1994). But instead, given the established curriculum of economic programs, a young economist would find it much more tractable to study adultery as a dynamic-optimization problem of a representative husband, and to derive the optimal time path of marital infidelity (and to publish his exercise) than to investigate financial flows in the banking sector within a network-theory framework. This is more than unfortunate in view of the network aspects of interbank linkages that have become apparent during the current crisis.

In our view, a change of focus is necessary that takes seriously the regularities in expectation formation revealed by observations of actual behavior from applied and behavioral research, and also allows for the independent role of the diverse expectations of heterogeneous economic actors. On the one hand, it would not be appropriate, empirically, to universalize laboratory findings on risk aversion to all agents in all contexts; nor, on the other hand, would it be appropriate to insist that homogeneous herd behavior is never possible. Neither conclusion would be empirically warranted. It would also be fallacious to replace rational-choice theory with an insistence that the "nonrational" actor is representative. Rather, an appropriate micro foundation is needed that considers interaction at a certain level of complexity and extracts macro regularities (where they exist) from microeconomic models with dispersed activity.

Once one acknowledges the importance of empirically based behavioral micro foundations and the heterogeneity of actors, a rich spectrum of new models becomes available. The dynamic coevolution of expectations and economic activity would allow one to study out-of-equilibrium dynamics and adaptive adjustments. Such dynamics could reveal the possibility of multiple and evolving equilibria (e.g., with high or low employment) depending on agents' expecta-tions—or even on the propagation of positive or negative "moods" among the population. This would capture the psychological compo-nent of the business cycle, which—while prominent in many policy-oriented discussions—is never taken into consideration in contempo-rary macroeconomic models. Finally, a focus on the heterogeneity of imperfect knowledge might provide a better framework for the analy-sis of the use and dissemination of information through market oper-ations and more direct forms of communication. If one accepts that the dispersed economic activity of many economic agents could be described by statistical laws, one might even take stock of methods from statistical physics to model dynamic economic systems (e.g., Aoki and Yoshikawa 2007; Lux 2009).

Whatever Happened to Empirical Testing?

Not only do currently popular models (in particular, dynamic gen-eral-equilibrium models) have weak micro foundations, but their empirical performance is far from satisfactory (Juselius and Franchi 2007). Indeed, the relevant strand of empirical economics has more and more avoided testing its models, worrying about calibration with-out explicitly considering goodness-of-fit.[5] This calibration is achieved by using "deep economic parameters," such as the parame-ters of utility functions derived from microeconomic studies. How-ever, at the risk of being repetitive, it should be emphasized that there is no compelling argument as to why micro parameters should be used directly in the parameterization of a macroeconomic model. The aggregation literature is full of examples that point out the varieties of the fallacy of composition. The "deep parameters" seem sensible only if one considers the economy as a universal organism without interactions. But if interactions are important (as we believe they are), the restriction of the parameter space imposed by using micro param-eters is inappropriate. Another concern about aggregation is nonstationarity due to structural shifts in the underlying data. Macro models, unlike many financial models, are often calibrated over long time horizons that include major changes in the regulatory framework of the countries investigated, such as alterations in exchange-rate regimes and the deregulation of financial markets during the 1970s and 1980s.

In much of the macroeconomics and finance literature there is an almost scholastic acceptance of axiomatic "first principles" (basically, the building blocks of an intertemporally optimizing representative agent with completely rational-expectation formation) independent of any empirical evidence.[6] Even dramatic differences between the model's behavior and empirical data are not taken as evidence against the model's underlying axioms. Quite in contrast to what one would expect of an applied science, most contemporary work in macroeconomics and finance is thus characterized by a pre-analytic belief in the validity of certain models that are never meaningfully exposed to empirical tests (Juselius and Franchi 2007). In our view, macroeconomics as an empirical science should not be pursued in an axiomatic fashion, and the goal of macroeconometrics should be to use data to choose among competing models.

David Hendry (1995, 2009) provides a well-established empirical methodology for such exploratory data analysis as well as a general theory for model selection (Hendry and Krolzig 2005). Clustering techniques such as projection pursuit (e.g., Friedman 1987) might provide alternatives for the identification of key relationships and the reduction of complexity on the way from empirical measurement to theoretical models. Cointegrated Vector Auto Regression (VAR) models could provide an avenue towards identifying robust structures within a set of data (Juselius 2006)—for example, the forces that move equilibria (*pushing forces*, which give rise to stochastic trends) and the forces that correct deviations from equilibrium (*pulling forces*, which give rise to long-run relationships). Interpreted in this way, the "general-to-specific" empirical approach has a good chance of nesting a multivariate, path-dependent, data-generating process and relevant dynamic macroeconomic theories. Unlike approaches in which data are silenced by prior restrictions, the cointegrated VAR model gives the data a rich context in which to speak freely (Hoover et al. 2008).

A chain of specification tests and estimated statistical models for simultaneous systems would provide a benchmark for the subsequent development of tests of models based on economic behavior. Significant and robust relations within a simultaneous system would provide empirical regularities that one would attempt to explain, while the quality of fit of the statistical benchmark would offer a confidence band for more ambitious models. Models that do not reproduce (even) approximately the quality of the fit of statistical models would be rejected. (The majority of currently popular macroeconomic and macro finance models would not pass this test.) Again, we see an aspect of the ethical responsibility of researchers: economic policy models should be theoretically and empirically sound. Economists should avoid policy recommendations on the basis of models with a weak empirical grounding and should, to the extent possible, make clear to the public how strongly—or weakly—the data support the models and the conclusions drawn from them.

The Failure of Economic Theory in the Crisis of 2008

The notion of financial fragility implies that a given system might be more or less susceptible to producing crises. For instance, it seems clear that financial innovations prior to 2008 made the system more fragile. Apparently, the existing linkages within the worldwide, highly connected financial markets generated spillovers from the U.S. subprime problem to other layers of the financial system. Many financial innovations had the effect of creating links between formerly unconnected players.

All in all, the degree of connectivity of the system probably increased enormously over the last decades. As is well known from network theory in the natural sciences, a more highly connected system might be more efficient in coping with certain tasks (perhaps by distributing risk components), but will often also be more vulnerable to shocks and systemic failure.

A systematic analysis of network vulnerability has been undertaken in the computer-science and operations-research literature (e.g., Criado et al. 2005). Such research has, however, been largely absent from financial economics. The introduction of new derivatives was rather seen through the lens of general-equilibrium models: more contingent claims help to achieve higher efficiency. Unfortunately, the claimed efficiency gains through derivatives are merely a theoretical implication of a highly stylized model and, therefore, should be seen as a *hypothesis* to be tested, not a fact that is assumed. Since there is hardly any supporting empirical evidence (or even analysis of this question), the claimed real-world efficiency gain from derivatives is unjustified. Meanwhile, the possibility of negative effects was neglected—with real-world consequences. Specifically, the idea that the system was made less risky by the development of more derivatives may have led financial actors to take positions with extreme degrees of leverage. (The leverage of financial institutions rose to unprecedented levels prior to the crisis, partly by evading Basel capital regulations through structured investment vehicles; see Acharya and Schnabl 2009b.) The interplay between leverage, connectivity, and systemic risk needs to be investigated at the aggregate level.

The economics profession also has to re-investigate the informational role of financial prices and financial contracts. While trading in stock and bond markets is usually interpreted as, at least in part, transmitting information, this information transmission seems to have broken down in the case of structured financial products. It seems that securitization rather led to a loss of information by anonymous intermediation (often multiple) between borrowers and lenders. In this way, the informational component was outsourced to rating agencies and typically, the buyer of a tranche in a collateralized debt obligation would not have spent any effort himself on information acquisition concerning his far-off counterparts. This centralized information processing by the rating agencies, in contrast to the dispersed processing in traditional credit relationships, might have led to a severe loss of information. Standard loan-default models of the sort on which rating agencies relied failed dramatically in recent years (Rajan et al. 2008).

It should also be noted that the price system itself can, like trading in securities markets, exacerbate problems rather than just neutrally transmitting information (see Hellwig 2008). One of the reasons for the sharp fall in the asset valuations of major banks was not only the loss in the assets on which their derivatives were based, but also the general reaction of the markets to this decline. As markets became aware of the risk involved, all such assets were written down, and in this way a small sector of the market "contaminated" the rest. Large parts of the asset holdings of major banks abruptly lost much of their value. Thus, the price system itself can be destabilizing as expectations change, and the consequences can be severe.

On the macroeconomic level, it would be desirable to develop early warning schemes that indicate the formation of unsustainable price swings away from historical benchmark levels. Combinations of indicators with time-series techniques could be helpful in detecting deviations of financial or other prices from such levels. Indications of structural change (particularly toward nonstationary trajectories) would be a signature of changes of the behavior of market participants leading to unsustainable fluctuations.

The financial crisis might be characterized as an example of the final stage of the well-known boom-and-bust pattern that has been repeated so often in the course of economic history. There are, nevertheless, some aspects that make this crisis different from its predecessors. First, the preceding boom may have had its origin—at least in large part—in the development of new financial products that opened up new investment possibilities, while most previous crises were the consequence of overinvestment in new physical investment possibilities. Second, the global dimension of the current crisis is presumably due to the increased connectivity of our already highly interconnected financial system. Both aspects have been largely ignored by academic economics. Research on the origin of instabilities, overinvestment, and subsequent slumps has been considered as an exotic side track from the academic research agenda (and the curriculum of most economics programs). This occurred because such research was incompatible with the premise of the rational representative agent, which had come to be thought the only allowable model. That belief made the economics profession blind to the role of interactions and connections between actors (such as the changes in the network structure of the financial industry brought about by deregulation and introduction of new structured products). Indeed, much of the work on contagion and herding behavior (see Banerjee 1992 and Chamley 2002), which is closely connected to the network structure of the economy, has not been incorporated into macroeconomic analysis.

We believe that economics has been trapped in a suboptimal equilibrium in which much of its research efforts are not directed towards the most pressing social needs. Self-reinforcing feedback effects among economists may have led to the dominance of a paradigm that has no solid methodological basis and whose empirical performance is, to say the least, modest. Defining away the most prevalent economic problems of modern economies and failing to communicate the limitations and assumptions of its popular models, the economics profession bears some responsibility for the financial and economic crisis. It has failed in its duty to provide needed insight into the workings of the economy and markets, and it has been reluctant to emphasize the limitations of its analysis. We believe that the failure even to envisage hypothetically the current problems of the worldwide financial system, and the inability of standard macro and finance models to provide any insight into ongoing events, make a strong case for a major reorientation in these areas and a reconsideration of their basic premises.

Afterword

The Causes of the Financial Crisis

RICHARD A. POSNER

I am honored to have been asked by Jeffrey Friedman to write an afterword to this fine collection of essays that he assembled for a special issue of *Critical Review* (which he edits), now being published in book form, with some revisions by the authors. Although written within months of the financial collapse that occurred in September 2008, these essays will, I predict, pass the test of time with flying colors and thus stand as durable contributions to our understanding of the crisis.

There are twelve essays in all, including Friedman's introductory Chapter 1, and I will try to touch on all of them, though some very briefly. But I want to begin with a brief statement of my own view of the causes of the crisis, to frame my discussion of the essays (Posner 2010, especially chaps. 1–2).

Two Key Causes of the Crisis

I believe there were two main causes: unsound monetary policy by the Federal Reserve in the early 2000s; and inadequate (at times inept) regulation of financial intermediation ("banking" in the broad sense, including "shadow banks" such as broker-dealers—Goldman Sachs, Morgan Stanley, Lehman Brothers, Bear Stearns, etc.—as well as commercial banks). As John Taylor (of the "Taylor rule") explains in Chapter 5, beginning in late 2001 the Federal Reserve, under the chairmanship of Alan Greenspan, began pushing the federal funds rate way down, eventually to a level at which it was actually negative; and when the Fed finally began pushing rates back up in 2004, it did so very gradually, even while Greenspan promised, in effect, that if high rates had a negative impact on the economy he would lower them. This was taken as a commitment that if housing prices began to tumble, the Fed would cushion the fall by pushing interest rates back down again.

The result was that for several years the federal funds rate was far below the optimal level prescribed by the Taylor rule, which calculates that level on the basis of inflation and output. Low interest rates increase the demand for housing, because a house is a product typically bought mainly with debt—a mortgage is conventionally equal to 80 percent of the purchase price of the house, and often close to 100 percent. Very low interest rates can cause an extremely steep increase in demand for houses and therefore (because of the durability of the housing stock) in house prices. At some point rising prices can, and in the housing market of the early 2000s did, become self-sustaining. That was the housing bubble.[1] Because the housing market is vast, and, as I said, houses are bought mainly with debt, the banking industry (broadly but also narrowly defined) was deeply invested in the bubble. When it burst, it carried the banking industry down with it (Posner 2010, chap. 2). Greenspan's promise to use monetary policy to cushion any steep drop in housing promises encouraged continued mortgage lending even after the bubble began to deflate—with disastrous consequences.

I am painting with a broad brush. There are issues concerning the relation of short-run interest rates, the traditional focus of Fed monetary policy, and long-run rates, such as mortgage interest rates. Greenspan has argued that he had no control over the latter. That isn't true (Posner 2010, chap. 1). Long-term rates are strongly influenced by short-term rates, and even if they weren't, when lenders can borrow their capital at a very low short-term rate, competition among them will compel them to lend the capital, long-term or short-term, at low rates. But these are details, and I wish only to indicate my views of the causes of the crisis, not defend them in detail here (Posner 2009).

The financial crisis would have been averted, or at least would have much less grave, despite the very low interest rates, had it not been for the second cause—inadequate banking regulation: a compound of deregulation, lax regulation, regulatory inattention, and regulatory ineptitude (the regulatory history is well discussed in Chapter 2). The movement to deregulate finance, part of the larger deregulation movement that began in the 1970s, culminated in 1999 in the repeal of the Glass-Steagall Act, and was succeeded during the Bush administration by notably lax enforcement of the remaining regulations. At the same, the regulators, notably Greenspan and his successor Ben Bernanke, took their eye off the ball. Fooled by the fact that, despite the very low interest rates, the consumer price index rose only moderately, they thought they had squared the circle. The low interest rates stimulated economic activity, driving down the unemployment rate, yet without causing excessive inflation. What they missed (partly because of the way in which housing costs are reflected in the Consumer Price Index) was that the low interest rates were causing inflation in asset prices (houses and common stocks) rather than the more conventional goods-and-services inflation that is tracked well by the CPI.

The Fed not only failed to notice the housing bubble, despite warnings, but, partly because of what appears to have been the government's ignorance about the rise and risks of the shadow-banking industry, the Fed and the Treasury were caught completely unaware by the financial crisis of September 2008, even though it had been building for more than a year. Surprised and unprepared, the regulators refused to save Lehman Brothers from bankruptcy in mid-September. I do not agree with Professor Taylor and others that the collapse of Lehman was inconsequential, or with Bernanke that the Fed lacked legal authority to bail out Lehman with a loan. Had Lehman's collapse been isolated it would not have been catastrophic. But all the broker-dealers, constituting in the aggregate a very major part of the entire banking industry, had business models like Lehman's; that is, like Lehman, they were financed mainly by short-term capital, with of course no federal deposit insurance to discourage runs. So when Lehman was allowed to fail, the suppliers of short-term capital to the other broker-dealers began pulling their capital out of them, starting a run that would have brought down the entire banking industry had the Fed not quickly realized its mistake regarding Lehman and saved the other broker-dealers (and other imperiled financial intermediaries). As it was, the run damaged the banking industry grievously, causing a tightening of credit that more than a year later was still constricting activity in the nonfinancial as well as financial sectors of the economy.

Why the Economists Failed

A full analysis of the causes of the financial crisis would not stop with the two causes that I have just summarized. Those causes themselves had causes, one of which—emphasized by Daron Acemoglu in Chapter 11—was a series of mistaken ideas held by the economics profession, ideas that were highly influential with Greenspan, Bernanke, and other regulators, many of whom (including both Greenspan and Bernanke) were professional economists themselves.

Acemoglu identifies three mistaken ideas. One is the belief that increased diversification of risk made banking safe; as he points out, diversification increases risk at the same time that it reduces it, because by definition diversification is a means not of eliminating risk but of shifting it to someone else, who then bears a risk that he did not bear before. The second mistaken idea was that institutional detail is unimportant in analyzing the economies of developed nations; their institutional structure is assumed to be adequate. In fact, the structure and practice of banking and of financial regulation had to be understood in order for the risk of a financial crisis to be appreciated. And third, economists exaggerated the degree to which concern with reputation disciplines market participants, such as the credit-rating agencies, often referred to in economic analysis as "reputational intermediaries" between the sellers and buyers of financial products.

Acemoglu is right about all three ideas, but I would emphasize in addition the surprising neglect, notably by Greenspan and Bernanke but also by some economic commentators on the causes of the crisis, including Joseph Stiglitz (Chapter 4), of the externalities of banking. That neglect is the other side of my declining to assign causal responsibility for the financial crisis to the bankers themselves. The decision of bankers to engage in risky financial practices was, it is true, a sine qua non of the crisis: no risky banking, no financial crisis. But no risk, no banking.

Blame the Regulators, not the Bankers

Banking is inherently risky, as the more precise term "financial intermediation" brings out. Banks lend mainly borrowed capital. To cover their costs and provide a return to their stockholders, they have to borrow the capital at a lower interest rate than they lend it. They do this typically by borrowing short and lending long. Short-term interest rates are lower than long-run rates because a short-term loan creates less credit risk and interest risk for the lender; it also is more liquid, and other things being equal, more liquidity is preferred to less. The more competitive banking is, the more compressed the spread between the rate at which banks borrow and the rate at which they lend, which puts pressure on banks to take more risks in their lending. One way to jack up the spread is to increase the amount of debt in the bank's capital structure. This strategy compounds risk, but it also increases profits, because risk and return are positively correlated. And it is a particularly attractive strategy when short-term interest rates are very low, which makes debt a much more attractive form of capital than equity.

The combination of very low interest rates and very little regulation created a competitive free-for-all in which profit maximization pushed banks to take greater risks than they would have under a different regime of monetary and banking regulation. The risky practices that they adopted are well analyzed by the authors of Chapter 7 (and Chapter 8),[2] who rightly stress the banks' ingenuity in circumventing regulations designed to limit risk. In a competitive market, which is a pretty good imitation of the Darwinian jungle, such behavior by some firms exerts competitive pressure on other firms: firms that do not maximize their profits shrink and die.

A bank will increase its risk of bankruptcy above the existing level only if the increment in expected profit exceeds the increment in expected bankruptcy cost (roughly, the cost of bankruptcy to the shareholders and managers multiplied by the probability of bankruptcy, and all discounted to present value). What it will not do is include in the cost of bankruptcy the costs borne by people and firms with which the bank has no actual or potential contractual relationship. The cost to those strangers is an external cost, and for a bank to include it in its cost-of-risk calculations would be inconsistent with profit maximization. And so it will do what it can, usually within the bounds of the law, to get around regulations designed to prevent it from taking on an amount of risk that endangers the entire economy.

Think of this in expected-cost terms. Suppose the cost of bankruptcy to a bank is x and the probability of bankruptcy is .01. Then the expected cost of bankruptcy is $.01x$, which may be much less than the expected profit, y, from taking the level of risk that creates that expected cost. (Suppose for simplicity that $y = x$.) Further suppose, however, that there is a .002 probability of a bankruptcy that because of correlated risk across banks will impose a cost on society of $1000x$, while the cost to the bank of not taking the bankruptcy risk is, as we know, only $y - .01x = .99x$. Then, because $y = x$, the expected macroeconomic cost of the bank's risk-taking, net of the benefit to the bank, is $.002 \times 990x = 1.98x$. The social cost is larger than the private cost. That is an argument for financial risk regulation, but not an argument for blaming the crisis on the banks' proclivity for taking all the risk that regulation allows them to take.

The responsibility for preventing external costs—which, in the case of the banking crisis, were the horrendous costs that the financial and then general economic collapse imposed on people and businesses that had nothing to do with the banking industry—is the government's. That is why there is, for example, government regulation of pollution: pollution is an externality imposed by rational private actors on their fellow human beings. The government failed to fulfill its responsibility to prevent costly externalities by failing to prevent the banks from taking risks that, while they were prudent ex ante from the limited perspective of profit maximization (albeit mistaken ex post), created an unacceptably large expected cost to the American (and world) economy as a whole. Greenspan ignored the external costs of banking in thinking that the banks' own incentives would suffice to minimize macroeconomic risk.

Causes Versus Preconditions

I must pause here to consider what should count as a "cause" of the financial crisis. Acemoglu's analysis shows that there are causes of causes. But it would be more precise to borrow from philosophy and distinguish "necessary conditions" from causes. A necessary condition is a condition without which some event would not have happened. Were there no oxygen in the atmosphere, there would be few fires. But it would be odd to call oxygen a cause of arson. Usually we just pick from among the vast array of the necessary conditions of an event the one or ones that we might want to change. We don't call oxygen a cause of arson because we don't think that removing the oxygen from the atmosphere would be a sensible way of reducing the amount of arson. Similarly, we don't think that abandoning money and banking and restoring a prehistoric barter economy would be a sensible response to the risk of another financial crisis, painful as this one has been. Risky banking, was, in other words, a necessary condition of the crisis. But it was neither a sufficient condition nor a cause we want to change; we want banks like other firms to seek to maximize profits, within lawful bounds.

We can identify other necessary conditions that are not good candidates to be causes of the financial crisis because while they may deserve to be changed, the political will is lacking. In that category are the tax deductions for mortgage interest payments and interest payments on home-equity loans (see Chapter 6); the exemption from capital-gains tax on the sale of a house (see Chapter 3); and the tax deduction for corporate debt. These tax preferences, in conjunction with the nondeductibility of most other kinds of interest, and of corporate earnings (that is, the cost of equity) as distinct from the cost of debt (interest), create an incentive for banks to take on more debt, and for homeowners and homebuyers to borrow more using a house as collateral, than is good for the economy. But these elements of tax

law are deeply entrenched and very unlikely to be changed, so we
would do better to treat them not as causes of the crisis but as
enabling factors that must be accepted as constraints on any reform
that might be seriously proposed, just as the importance of preserving
profit maximization as a goal of businesses must be accepted as a
constraint. But bad monetary policy and inadequate financial regulation are properly deemed causes of the financial crisis, because they
can and should be changed, and indeed are undergoing change at this
moment.

Yet what about the failures of understanding of the economics
profession? Weren't they a sufficiently important, and corrigible, factor in the crisis to warrant their being denominated as a cause? Acemoglu is not alone among economists in thinking so. Chapter 12 (an
expansion of a paper by David Colander and seven other economists
known as the "Dahlem Report") excoriates the economics profession
for its failure to have foreseen the financial crisis. They conclude per-
tinently that the profession

> failed in its duty to provide needed insight into the workings
> of the economy and markets, and it has been reluctant to
> emphasize the limitations of its analysis. We believe that the
> failure even to envisage hypothetically the current problems of
> the worldwide financial system, and the inability of standard
> macro and finance models to provide any insight into ongoing
> events, make a strong case for a major reorientation in these
> areas and a reconsideration of their basic premises.

But it is difficult to see what kind of intervention would improve
economists' understanding of the business cycle. Economists are who
they are; determining the why of it would require a deep exploration
of the sociology of the profession. We would find, I think, that the
aspiration of economics to be a genuine science—the first social science worthy of the name—has driven economists to an ever-greater
insistence on formal rigor in both theory and empirical inquiry, and
hence an ever-greater reliance on mathematical and statistical techniques; and that these techniques have not proved adequate for
understanding financial crises and the business cycle. But whether the

emphases of the modern economics profession can or even should be changed (for there would be losses as well as gains) is a question that will be answered only from deep within the profession.

I don't want to leave Acemoglu's chapter without noting a passage in it, unrelated to the question of economists' responsibility, that suggests a certain insensitivity to the costs of a depression or severe recession. He writes that "despite the ferocious severity of the global crisis—and barring a complete global meltdown—the possible loss of GDP for most countries is in the range of just a couple of percentage points—and most of this might have been unavoidable anyway, given the overexpansion of the economy in prior years. In contrast, within a decade or two, we may see modest but cumulative economic growth that more than outweighs the current economic contraction" (Chapter 11).

I don't agree that the only cost of a depression (or recession) is a temporary, and relatively minor, decline in the Gross Domestic Product. This ignores negative effects on economic growth (Barlevy 2004) resulting from (in our current depression, at least) reductions in research and development, worker training, and product design (Mandel 2009). It also ignores the profound psychological costs of a depression,[3] including the anxieties of those who lose their jobs or their homes or their retirement incomes, or who fear losing them. It ignores as well the long-term economic consequences of the immense costs that governments incur to halt a severe economic decline and speed recovery, and the political effects that bring economic consequences in their train—consequences such as a permanent increase in the size and intrusiveness of government.

That "most of [the loss of GDP] might have been unavoidable anyway, given the overexpansion of the economy in prior years" does not mitigate the severity of the downturn. The idea seems to be that people were living high on the hog because of excessive borrowing and the day of reckoning has now arrived. But most of the people hurt were not living high on the hog during the boom years; of the millions of people involuntarily unemployed as a result of the depression, how many acquired enough wealth during the boom years of the early 2000s to compensate them for the loss of their jobs?

In the passage I quoted from Acemoglu's chapter I sense a trace of the economics profession's complacency about the self-regulating character of our economic system, a trace that is in some tension with Acemoglu's cogent criticisms of economists' exaggerated faith in self-regulation.

Jeffrey Friedman, in Chapter 1, nominates six (actually I think five) causes of the financial crisis:

1. Government encouragement of mortgage lending to people who are not good credit risks.
2. & 3. Government regulation of credit-rating agencies.
4. Unsound monetary policy.
5. "Nonrecourse" laws.
6. The Basel accords, which established standards to govern capital requirements of banks, especially as these were amended by U.S. financial authorities in 2001.

I agree of course with the fourth point. I agree with the sixth as well. Basel I (adopted in 1988) established risk-weighted capital requirements, which allowed banks to increase their leverage if they increased their "safe" assets. But the American amendment to Basel I adopted in 2001, and Basel II, adopted in 2004, underestimated the riskiness of mortgage-backed securities by assigning them a minimal risk weight, and so gave banks a green light to buy more of these assets than turned out to be safe for the economy as a whole.

Friedman's first point is one explored at greater length by Peter Wallison in Chapter 6 (and in much other writing by Wallison—he is the scourge of the Community Reinvestment Act of 1977, Fannie Mae, and Freddie Mac), and I'll defer discussion of it for the moment. The fifth point I consider relatively minor, but it requires some discussion.

A mortgage is a security interest in a property. It secures a debt—the mortgage loan—and the borrower owes the amount of the debt regardless of the value of the security. Suppose the unpaid principle of the mortgage is $100,000; the borrower defaults; the lender forecloses; and the foreclosure sale fetches $70,000. The borrower still owes the lender $100,000, and therefore the lender can sue him for the difference between what the foreclosure sale yielded and the amount of the debt: $30,000—in some states. But in other states, including California and Arizona, both Ground Zero of the subprime crisis, the law makes mortgage loans "nonrecourse." This means that the lender cannot sue the borrower for a deficiency, that is, for the difference between the amount of the debt and the value of the house; he has no "recourse" against the personal assets or income of the borrower. As a result, when housing prices plummet and the owner of a house finds himself owing more on his mortgage than the house is worth, he may be tempted to abandon the house. If he does, the bank can seize and sell the house but cannot sue the owner for the deficiency. The more houses that are abandoned, the farther housing prices will fall, the less mortgages will be worth, and the lower the proportion of the unpaid principal of a mortgage that a bank can hope to recover in the event of an abandonment or other default.

I doubt that this has been a significant factor in the economic crisis. For one thing, reducing indebtedness is actually an objective of economic policy in a depression, because the greater the debt load on consumers the less they spend; the less they spend, the less is produced; and the less is produced, the fewer people are employed. For another thing, a suit for a deficiency is rarely worth bringing even when permitted by law, because people who abandon their house, or otherwise default on their mortgage, rarely have enough assets to justify the costs of the suit. In general, given the cost of legal services, the only people worth suing are wealthy ones, and if they're wealthy they're unlikely to abandon their home or otherwise default on their debts. Of course there are exceptions, but not enough to have macroeconomic significance.

Friedman assigns a particularly large role in causing the financial crisis to the credit-rating agencies, whose function in the financial system has, he argues, been distorted by the government. I think that he is right about the distortion, but I rate the causal significance of the agencies' ratings lower than he does. It is true that the agencies gave triple-A ratings to the senior tranches of mortgage-backed securities and other debt securities that later plunged in value, to the great harm of the banks invested in them. Had they not done so, fewer such securities would have been originated and purchased. The banking industry might still have collapsed, however, because it would have been heavily invested in home mortgages even if mortgages had not been securitized.

But set that question to one side. The limitations of the credit-rating agencies were well known to professional investors (and securitized debt is sold only to such investors, not to hapless individuals). The agencies are paid by the issuers of the securities that they rate; they are under pressure to rate securities triple-A, because these are preferred by many institutional investors; they do not pay high salaries by Wall Street standards, and as a result do not hire the cream of the financial-analyst crop; they are reluctant to downgrade a debt issue because of changed circumstances, as that places a cloud over the issuer's creditworthiness—and the issuer, to repeat, is the credit-rating agency's customer.[4] Professional investors who failed to treat their ratings of complex securities with a degree of skepticism despite knowing all this had only themselves to blame.

It is also unclear whether the agencies' ratings were actually inaccurate. That depends on how likely it seemed that the securities they rated triple-A were likely to tank. To most observers, including regulators, financial journalists, economists, and the professional investment community, the probability seemed remote. We must be wary of hindsight bias, a potent source of unjust blame.

Friedman is rightly concerned with the quasi-official status of the "Nationally Recognized Statistical Rating Organizations." Ten credit-rating agencies have been given this designation by the Securities and Exchange Commission, though there were only three at the height of the mortgage-backed securities boom; the three were the traditionally leading, and still leading, agencies—Moody's, Standard and Poor, and Fitch. The SEC allows issuers of debt rated by an NRSRO to provide prospective investors with a less elaborate offering document. And insurance companies, pension funds, and other investment entities that are permitted to invest only in "investment-grade" securities cannot be sued for investing in securities rated triple-A by an NRSRO. This puts the NRSROs under pressure to give the issuers of securities a high rating, and thus weakens market discipline. It also, and more seriously, reduces the incentive to the investor to use care in making investment decisions rather than relying blindly on an NRSRO's credit rating.

There is no reason for giving a federal stamp of approval to any credit-rating agencies or for granting them any other privileges denied competitors, just as there is no good reason to have the government sponsor mortgage companies (Fannie Mae and Freddie Mac). Elimination of NRSRO certification would be a worthwhile reform, and has in fact been proposed by Barney Frank. But even if the NRSRO program were disbanded, credit-rating agencies would still have the characteristics that resulted in the positive ratings of the debt securities that imploded.

Against this Friedman argues that the NRSRO program limited entry into the credit-rating market, and some of the entrants that were discouraged might have had rating methods superior to those of the NRSROs. He means by this methods that might have detected the riskiness of the securities that the leading credit-rating agencies were rating triple-A. But what would have been the market for such wet-blanket raters?

There was nothing to prevent an investment adviser from advising a prospective purchaser of a triple-A-rated security not to do so, and from charging for his advice. The fact that, so far as appears, few advisers did that reflected the strength of the belief throughout the financial community that these securities were safe. No reform of credit-rating agencies would have been likely to shake that belief. Thus I am skeptical of Friedman's claim that "bankers . . . were ignorant of the fact that triple-A rated securities might be much riskier than advertised." The banks had more sophisticated financial analysts than the rating agencies had, and they knew it. They sought and welcomed triple-A ratings, but they were not fooled by them. As Acharya and Richardson point out (Chapter 7), the banks themselves, which knew all about the risks of securitized debt, as they were creators of such debt, were also major purchasers of it.

The remaining cause, which comes first on Friedman's list, but is emphasized by Wallison rather than Friedman, is the government's long-standing policy of encouraging home ownership. Were there no such policy, and no governmental or government-sponsored institutions to implement it, such as the Federal Housing Administration and the two government-sponsored (at present government-owned) mortgage banks, Fannie Mae and Freddie Mac, there would be less home ownership and fewer mortgages, and so less risk of a financial collapse triggered by the collapse of a housing bubble financed by the banking industry. But again I doubt that this was a big factor in the financial crisis.

I have no truck with these "government-sponsored enterprises." They are compelling illustrations of the folly of hybridizing business and government. Because of their government sponsorship, lenders assumed correctly that they would not be permitted to default, and so the GSEs could borrow at very low interest rates (almost as low as the interest rates at which the U.S. government borrows) to finance their activities, enabling them to earn huge profits. The quid pro quo was their cooperation with the government's policy—irresistible because bipartisan—of promoting a nation of homeowners. I disapprove not only of GSEs but also of encouraging homeownership— and I note that an economic advantage of a nation of renters is that relocation to a different city or state to pursue new job opportunities is easier when one rents rather than owns one's home, and job mobility is one of the great strengths of the American economy. But I think that Wallison exaggerates the effect of the Community Reinvestment Act, the GSEs, and the Clinton and Bush administrations' "ownership society" propaganda in fostering the risky mortgage lending that got the banking industry into such deep trouble.

The argument is that the GSEs and the government's encouragement of risky mortgage lending caused loose lending practices to spread to the prime loan market, vastly increasing the availability of credit for mortgages and thereby leading to speculation in houses and ultimately to the housing bubble. It is true that at the height of the housing bubble the GSEs, which formerly had bought only securitizations of prime mortgages, were providing a large market for mortgage-backed securities backed by subprime mortgages, and thus encouraging the creation of such securities. But when the default rate on the mortgages that the GSEs had bought skyrocketed, the loss fell on the GSEs rather than on the banking industry as a whole, and the government quickly took over the GSEs, assuming their debts. The problem of the GSEs' irresponsible lending, fostered by its implicit federal guaranty, was thus contained.

The other banks got into trouble because so much risky mortgage lending occurred outside the chain of distribution that led to the GSEs. Broker-dealers and other entirely private banks created mortgage-backed bonds by securitizing mortgages sold to them by mortgage specialists—just as the GSEs did. Then these nongovernmental creators of mortgage-backed bonds (called "private label" bonds in the trade) sold them to other banks, hedge funds, and other investors—just as the GSEs did. But the private issuers of mortgage-backed securities didn't do any of this because the GSEs did it. The GSEs provided a market for substandard mortgage loans and mortgage-backed securities, but that was irrelevant to the decision of private bankers to do the same thing, and irrelevant to the decision of private investors (including banks themselves) to buy these securities. Had the banks and (other) investors thought subprime mortgage loans excessively risky, they would have ceded this part of the market entirely to the GSEs. There was no governmental pressure on anyone to create or invest in mortgage-backed securities.

The Community Reinvestment Act doesn't even apply to financial intermediaries other than commercial banks and thrifts. And while the commercial banks and the thrifts were major originators of mortgages, including subprime mortgages, that were securitized, they did not do so because of the Act. These were lucrative transactions.

And finally, it is not even clear that the loans the GSEs bought and packaged into mortgage-backed securities were of lower average quality than the ones issued privately. There was government pressure, but it was pressure exerted against an open door. There were profit opportunities in subprime loans, and the opportunities were eagerly grasped by profit-making institutions—including the GSEs.

Which brings me back to the basic point that banks engaged in highly risky lending—with their eyes more or less wide open—because such lending was vastly profitable: too profitable for the good of the economy as a whole, but too profitable only because interest rates were too low and banking regulation too lax. Everything else, I believe, was secondary.

Friedman (Chapter 1) states that "Clearly this was a crisis of regulated capitalism, but the pressing question is whether it was the capitalism or the regulations that were primarily responsible." I don't think capitalism can be separated from regulation. Capitalism doesn't mean unregulated markets. It is a system of regulated markets; a central bank, courts to enforce property rights, regulators to prevent banks from engaging in practices that create macroeconomic risk and thus to control externalities—without these and other forms of government regulation a capitalist economy would fall to pieces. So the financial crisis was a failure of capitalism (the title of my first book on the crisis), but it was a failure of the regulatory arm of capitalism. Or as Acemoglu (Chapter 11) puts it, "what we are experiencing is not a failure of capitalism or free markets per se, but the failure of unregulated markets—in particular, of an unregulated financial sector and unregulated risk management."

Abbreviations and Acronyms

ABCP	asset-backed commercial paper (short-term funding issued by OBSEs)
ABS	asset-backed security (such as an MBS)
ABX	a source of price indices for MBSs and CDSs
ARM	adjustable-rate mortgage
BIS	Bank for International Settlements (located in Basel, Switzerland)
CDO	collateralized debt obligation (derivative that tranches pools of ABSs)
CDS	credit-default swap (insurance against default)
CFTC	Commodities Futures Trading Commission
CLO	collateralized loan obligation
CMBS	commercial MBS (as opposed to residential)
CRA	Community Reinvestment Act
DTCC	Depository Trust and Clearing Corporation
Fannie Mae	Federal National Mortgage Association
FDIC	Federal Deposit Insurance Corporation
FASB	Federal Accounting Standards Board
FHA	Federal Housing Administration
FOMC	Federal Open Market Committee
Freddie Mac	Federal Home Loan Mortgage Corporation
Ginnie Mae	Government National Mortgage Association
GSE	government-sponsored enterprise (e.g., Fannie Mae, Freddie Mac)
HELOC	home equity line of credit
HUD	Department of Housing and Urban Development
IMF	International Monetary Fund
LCFI	large, complex financial institutions
LIBOR	London Interbank Offered Rate

LMI	low and moderate income
LTV	loan-to-value ratio (of a mortgage)
MBS	mortgage-backed security (usually used interchangeably with RMBS)
NRSRO	Nationally Recognized Statistical Rating Organization
OBSE	off-balance-sheet entity (includes SIVs)
OECD	Organization for Economic Cooperation and Development
OTC	over the counter
OTTI	other than temporarily impaired
PLMBS	private-label MBS
RMBS	residential MBS (as opposed to commercial MBS)
SEC	Securities and Exchange Commission
SIV	structured investment vehicle (a type of OBSE)
TARP	Troubled Asset Relief Program
VaR	Value at Risk (mathematical model of financial risk probability)

Notes

Chapter 1. Capitalism and the Crisis:
Bankers, Bonuses, Ideology, and Ignorance

1. Richard Gugliada, who was in charge of S&P's CDO ratings until 2005, told a reporter that "the mortgage market had never, ever, had any problems, and nobody thought it ever would" (quoted in Jones 2008). First Pacific Advisors was one skeptic, and sold its investment of $1.85 billion in mortgage-backed bonds in September 2005. Later, discussing a conference call with Fitch in March 2007, First Pacific CEO Robert L. Rodriguez (2007) described the Fitch representative as "highly confident regarding their models and their ratings," even though the representative admitted that the model "would start to break down" if "home price appreciation was flat for an extended period of time" or declined. Not to leave out Moody's, it often "piggybacked" off of S&P's ratings, and vice versa (Smith 2008a).

2. Chapter 3, however, suggests that the bubble actually began in the late 1990s, after capital gains on the rising value of a house were exempted from taxation. This would explain why the flood of credit released by central banks in 2001 went into the housing market (and into mortgage- rather than other asset-backed securities): a boom in the housing market was already under way. As suggested in the text, however, another contributory factor may have been the even more affordable mortgages that were (at first) made possible by the GSEs, which could borrow money even more cheaply than the banks that took advantage of the extraordinarily low interest rates in the first half of the decade.

3. A home-equity loan is cash lent to the mortgagor at interest. The loan amount and interest are added to the mortgage. A home equity line of credit (HELOC) is like a credit card where the purchases and interest are added to the mortgage. Cash-out refinancings allowed the borrower to take out "a larger mortgage, pa[y] off the previous one, and pocke[t] the difference. With mortgage rates low and falling, homeowners could increase the size of a loan without increasing the monthly payment" (Zandi 2009, 59).

4. The IMF (2008, 62) also notes that "the risk assumptions for low- and no-documentation housing loans were too low," and that "the likelihood of early delinquencies going into foreclosure seems to have been underestimated."

The primary reason for requesting a low- or no-documentation loan seems to have changed during the boom: prior to the boom the reason was self-employment or cash-economy employment; soon the reason became house flipping—something else that would be missed by pre-boom models. A house flipper would be more likely to allow foreclosure if prices went down, since he or she had never intended to live in the house.

5. Some experts have been credited with prescience about the bubble. The most-often cited seer has been Robert Shiller, the author of *Irrational Exuberance* (2000). In fact, however, Shiller said in 2003 that "he'd only predict a nationwide housing slump if a worldwide economic slump 'kills' consumer confidence. Only some 'high-flying' cities like San Francisco, Denver and Boston are at risk of price depreciations, and the chances of declines in those regions are less than a third, he said" ("Fannie Mae's Raines Sees No Housing Bubble, Low Interest Rates." Bloomberg.com, 6 June 2003). Although Shiller predicted that housing prices would rise "everywhere," he denied that this would result in a bubble. "'It would be quite daring to predict' a nationwide housing bubble, he said." This was the same year in which Alan Greenspan, then the Chairman of the Fed, "said that any comparison between the housing market and a stock market bubble was 'rather a large stretch'" (Bartlett 2009).

In July 2004, an economist at Northern Trust predicted a housing-related financial crisis, noting that "60 percent of banks' earning assets were mortgage-related—twice as much as was the case in 1986." Simultaneously, however, a Bear Stearns analyst noted solid fundamentals underlying the housing boom: "declining unemployment, low interest rates, a decline in the inventory of unsold homes and the 1997 cut in capital gains taxes on owner-occupied homes" (Bartlett 2009). Only in 2005, the year that housing sales began to fall, did Shiller begin sounding alarms about a nationwide housing bubble and the possibility that its bursting could lead to a recession, although he did not see the connection between housing and the banks via mortgage-backed securities (Leonhardt 2009, 36). In the same year, conflicting studies of the matter were published by the IMF and the Federal Reserve (Bartlett 2009).

Nouriel Roubini, another analyst credited with prescience, did warn about exactly what would happen in 2007–8—a housing bust followed by a financial crisis and a worldwide recession, due to the declining value of mortgage-backed securities. His warning came in the autumn of 2006, after the Case-Shiller index of house prices had already fallen by 4.5 percent (Wesbury 2010, 59). Roubini was laughed at when he made his prediction at an IMF conference. But Chapter 3 shows that Goldman Sachs escaped disaster by beginning to use CDSs to bet against housing in December, 2006, when the "experts" were still laughing.

6. Some did. A BIS study (2005, 39) of the rating of structured securities included interviews with institutional investors, from which the researchers

concluded that "few respondents said that they rely solely on external ratings, but instead use them as independent second (or third) opinions." There is no mention, however, of reluctance to rely solely on rating agencies because of investors' awareness that the agencies were being protected from competition. Instead, large institutional investors often had their own risk-assessment techniques; sometimes they used the rating agencies' own models but plugged in more conservative assumptions, "for example on default correlations"; and sometimes they would perform their own due diligence on the underlying collateral. Consequently, many stayed away from CDOs and CDOs squared. However, "smaller AAA investors, which do not have the capacity to develop their own models," said they relied on the ratings. In contrast to Chapter 7, the BIS report also maintains that the spreads between triple-A corporate bonds and triple-A tranches of MBSs were negligible, which often meant that larger institutions' own modeling and due diligence were restricted to their investments in the higher-yielding subordinate tranches (BIS 2005, 45), which were purchased for income purposes, not regulatory-capital relief, and where defaults were more likely.

7. No news about this crucial aspect of the rating agencies can be found even in the best journalistic reports, such as Dizard 2009a, b; Jones 2008, 2009; and Plender 2009 in the *Financial Times*; Norris 2008 in the *New York Times* business section (or Morgenson 2008 on the front page of the *Times*); and Smith 2008a, b at Bloomberg.com. The sole exceptions I can find are Lowenstein 2008, which buries the information about the 1975 SEC decision, without comment, deep inside an excellent article in the *New York Times Magazine*; and Lewis and Einhorn 2009, which mentions obscurely that the SEC "sanctioned" the oligopoly of the rating agencies, implying that the SEC permitted the oligopoly—rather than creating it.

8. Alan Greenspan (2009) publicly disputed Taylor's argument in the pages of the *Wall Street Journal*, as did Ben Bernanke (2010) in a speech to the American Economic Association. Taylor responds in Taylor 2010.

9. For a full treatment of the details of both Glass-Steagall and Gramm-Leach-Bliley, see Wallison 2009.

10. On March 9, 2009, the disastrous unintended consequences of this policy led the Comptroller of the Currency, John Dugan, to take an implicit swipe at a sister regulatory agency (the SEC) for helping to exacerbate the financial crisis:

> "We would be considerably better off today if there had not been so many impediments to building larger reserves," he told a conference hosted by the Institute of International Bankers. "Had banks built stronger reserves during the boom years, they would not need to

reserve as much now; and they would be in a stronger position to support economic growth." (quoted, Hopkins 2009)

11. Table 7.1, row 1, column 3 ($852 billion of GSE MBSs) + column 4 ($383 billion of AAA PLMBS tranches) + column 5 ($90 billion of CDOs) = $1.325 billion of total MBS/CDO holdings of U.S. banks and thrifts. $1.325 billion − $90 billion = $1.235 billion of GSE plus AAA holdings. 1.235 divided by 1.325 = 93.2 percent.

12. The original source for Table 7.1 is an April 2008 Lehman Brothers study (Lehman Brothers 2008, Fig.4), where column 6 is labeled "CDOs (res[i-dentical] sub[ordinate]s). There were two types of CDOs: "high-grade" and "mezzanine." A high-grade CDO would, through the tranching of several A, AA, and AAA tranches of PLMBSs, produce an AAA tranche typically constituting 93 percent of the bond (IMF 2008, 60). In contrast, "mezzanine CDO" is a synonym for "subordinate residential CDO." This is the type of PLMBS in which U.S. commercial banks' holdings had a face value of $90 billion (Table 7.1, row 1, col. 5). Mezzanine CDOs "effectively leverage BBB-[rated] to AA-rated subprime MBS tranches" (IMF 2008, 60, Box 2.2). Thus, where the IMF estimates that 80 percent of all PLMBSs' original tranches were rated AAA, 11 percent AA, 4 percent A, 3 percent BBB, and 2 percent equity (unrated), mezzanine tranching turned the BBB and equity tranches into CDOs averaging 76 percent AAA tranches and 8 percent AA tranches (with the remaining 16 percent unrated or rated BBB or A). Even though 100 percent of U.S. commercial banks' PLMBS holdings were rated AAA, 19 percent were CDOs constructed from lower-rated PLMBS tranches.

It is worth noting that while Basel II assigned a 50 percent risk weight to A-rated ABSs and a 100 percent risk weight to BBB-rated ABSs, it also assigned a 350 percent risk weight to BB-rated assets, versus a 200 percent risk weight assigned by the Recourse Rule to BB-rated ABSs. European banks' on-balance-sheet demand under Basel II might therefore account for the structuring of mezzanine CDOs not only to maximize AAA and AA tranches, but to minimize BB- and B-rated tranches.

13. For example, before a single study of the matter had appeared, the finance ministers of France, Germany, Italy, Luxembourg, the Netherlands, and Sweden issued a public appeal to the G-20 to resolve to put an end to "the bonus culture" to which the writers, without any evidence, attributed the crisis (Lagarde et al. 2009). At its annual meeting in Pittsburgh in September 2009, the G-20 did just that.

14. "Bear Stearns Chairman Sells Stake." BBC online, 28 March 2008.

15. Table 7.1, row 1: column 4 ($383 billion) added to column 5 ($90 billion) provides the total holdings of commercial banks' PLMBSs as of April

2008: $473 billion. $383 billion (the AAA-rated tranches) divided by $473 billion equals 80.9 percent, leaving 19.1 percent invested in CDOs rated AAA but built from subordinate tranches (see n12 above).

16. Unfortunately, some of this insurance was bought from AIG—which, having a triple-A rating of its own, was released by many of its counterparties from posting the collateral that was customary with most credit-default swaps. As James Keller (2009) put it:

> In the world of derivatives trading, Lehman, not AIG, was the norm. What this means is that in general, banks have adequate collateral against counterparty claims. Those who traded derivatives with Lehman seem to have had sufficient collateral to cover the unwinding of their trades following Lehman's bankruptcy filing. . . .
>
> [But] AIG would often not have to post collateral . . . provided it maintained its AAA rating. In retrospect, the decision to buy protection from AIG without adequate collateral mechanics was just another foolish credit decision by the banks.

However, see n18 below.

17. Economists do not make this claim explicitly, but their models rest on it implicitly. Thus, when they do try to explain ignorance, economists fall back, naturally, on incentives. For instance, in a different context Richard A. Posner, the leader of the law and economics movement and a prominent advocate of the corporate-compensation theory of the crisis (Posner 2009, 93–99), writes: "To the extent that the ignorance of home buyers played a role in the housing bubble, as undoubtedly it did, this just means that information is costly" (Posner 2009, 101). But "costly information" explains only ignorance of things that people know that they don't know, and that they know would not be valuable to learn, and thus that they choose not to expend time and money to learn. The costliness of information therefore cannot explain ignorance of "unknown unknowns." Only to an omniscient agent are there no unknown unknowns. Thus, the economists' treatment of ignorance, in the form of "the economics of information," preserves the omniscient agent in that it assumes agents know not only of the existence, the location, and the cost, but also the *value* of all information relevant to their decisions. Only in this way can they make a rational decision to remain "ignorant" of the irrelevant information. But only if they already know what they don't know could they assess the value of knowing it.

The bank executives who lost billions of dollars—and who, in the cases of Ralph Cioffi and Matthew Tannin, risked jail sentences—had the highest conceivable incentives to be right, short of a death sentence for being wrong.

But being wrong—mistaken—is not a matter of lacking the incentives to be right. It is a matter of lacking the knowledge to be right. Incentives affect the will to do what one knows how to do, not the mind that does not know how to do it—and does not know that it does not know.

18. Market prices—such as the market prices of the senior tranches of sub-prime securities at the height of the panic over their value—are not necessarily "correct" (see n39 below). The real value of those tranches, as of September 2008, depended on something that could not be known then: whether the stream of mortgage principal and interest payments promised to investors in the AAA tranches would, in fact, be diminished—and if so, by how much—by future defaults and delinquencies on the part of the mortgagors. Since the securities were overcollateralized, and since income to all of the subordinate tranches would have had to stop before investors in the senior tranches experienced any losses, the severity of those losses, hence the true value of the securities, depended on such *ex ante* unknowables as how many "underwater" mortgagors would choose to walk away from their mortgages, which in turn would depend on such factors as the depth to which home prices would drop once the bubble had fully popped—and the depth of the recession, and thus the unemployment and the fear that would be experienced by the mortgagors. Even a year and a half later, as I write, these matters are not decided.

Were the rating agencies actually wrong, then, to assign those AAA ratings, however questionable their procedures in predicting the proper width of the tranches? We still don't know. But there is anecdotal evidence that they might have been at least partly right. For instance, a banker in Wichita, Kansas told the *Wall Street Journal* in January 2010 that his bank's portfolio of $100 million in PLMBSs was generating lower returns than anticipated, but that the return was still positive (Scism and Tamman 2010). Much more impressive is the story of PLMBSs that passed into the hands of the Federal Reserve during AIG's bailout. On September 16, 2008, Moody's and S&P downgraded AIG's triple-A credit rating to double-A because it had acted as CDS counterparty to Merrill Lynch, Goldman Sachs, and Société Générale on CDOs with a face value of $62.1 billion (Sender 2010). Without the triple-A credit rating, AIG had to post $16 billion in collateral on these CDSs, which it did not have. This bankrupted AIG, which was bailed out by the U.S. Treasury. In October 2008, the Fed "decided to take those CDOs onto its own books and pay the banks to extinguish the contracts" (Story and Morgenson 2010), even though Goldman Sachs and Société Générale "were willing to tear up the contracts with AIG if they were allowed to keep the underlying CDO's, indicating that both banks thought they could increase in value" (ibid.).

The Federal Reserve, Goldman Sachs, and Société Générale were, in effect, fighting over the right to hang onto those CDOs. In the case of the Fed, this was because "there was a 'discrepancy' between 'what [its] advisers [were] saying these CDOs [were] worth and where the firms [had] them marked." The "marks" in question were the market prices of the securities as of October 2008 (see n39 below): $29.6 billion (Sender 2010). The Fed, Goldman, and Société Générale all believed that those marks were too low.

This may explain the Fed's controversial decision to pay AIG's counterparties the full value of the CDS contracts, even though "many analysts say they believe the government could have negotiated a price for a fraction of that amount, reducing taxpayer funds used in the rescue" (Story and Morgenson 2010). In January 2010, a Treasury spokesman told the *New York Times* that "'those investments have turned out to be very sensible, and the fund at the center of the controversy,'" dubbed Maiden Lane III, "may well yield a profit." By then, the value of the CDOs, based on their performance to date, had risen to $45 billion (Sender 2010).

19. According to the report, "UBS's Market Risk framework relies on VaR and Stress Loss to set and monitor market risks at a portfolio level. . . . VaR methodologies relied on the AAA rating of the Super Senior positions. . . . With the benefit of hindsight, granularity of data regarding particular investments beyond looking at ratings etc. might have been appropriate (UBS 2008, 19, 20, 21). It is true that, as Chapter 7 emphasizes, the report (42) confirms that UBS employees had incentives to do what they did—which was to buy "mezzanine" CDOs that, despite their overall triple-A rating (through tranching), had been built from non-AAA or AA tranches of MBSs (see n12 above), and which therefore brought in higher income streams. However, there is no evidence that the employees knew the risks involved and suppressed the information so as to increase their compensation. Rather, the responsibility for evaluating risk was assigned to a different group of employees, and they "relied on the AAA rating of certain Subprime positions, although the CDOs were built from lower rated tranches of RMBS. This appears to have been common across the industry" (39).

20. UBS reports that its "value-at-risk" or VaR measurements were "calculated using a historical time series for other triple-A rated positions" (BIS 2009, sec. 4.1). (In short, it effectively attributed to triple-A-rated PLMBS tranches the historical 0.0005 default rate of AAA-rated corporate bonds.)

21. See n18 above.

22. Jeffrey Rogers Hummel has suggested to me that the government was trying to create the appearance of homogeneity among the banks by forcing Wells Fargo to go along with its bailout, and by refusing at first to allow banks to return their TARP subsidies. This would prevent a costly panic among counterparties to the large American commercial banks that really did, apparently, "blow up," such as Citigroup and Bank of America. An inadvertent side effect

of treating all the banks as if they were equally in trouble, however, was to create the impression that this was indeed a systemic crisis of capitalism—a homogeneous error on the part of all bankers that could be explained only by some psychological trait in which they all shared, such as greediness, hubris, or the nonexplanatory "irrationality."

That said, with the exception of CapitalOne the big banks did all seem to make the widespread error of assuming that there was no nationwide housing bubble: even JPMorgan and Wells Fargo originated nonprime and subprime mortgages. They did, however, apparently identify the danger in trusting the ratings of PLMBSs—in contrast to the regulators.

23. Hence the foolishness of psychologizing what turns out to be mistaken behavior as "irrational." With the luxury of hindsight, we can look back on the participants in the subprime boom and call them "irrationally exuberant." But they showed no signs of psychological disorder at the time; indeed, at the time, they thought it was Beal who was being "irrational." Had Beal turned out to be mistaken, they would still think so. The diagnosis of irrationality is, in this context, just a radically misleading synonym for error.

24. Yet JPMorgan did pay performance bonuses. An executive-compensation regulation imposed on all firms to rectify this "problem" would probably have the effect of destroying the balance between personal incentives and teamwork that may have contributed to JPMorgan's success for so long.

25. The evolutionary filter that "runs" this process is the ultimate need to sell consumers products they like at prices they will pay. Fallible consumer like/dislike decisions constitute the final selection mechanism that leads to the extinction of maladapted businesses—not individuals (Friedman 2006, 477–81). For this reason, Alchian's comparison of economics with evolution has nothing to do with Social Darwinism, as a careless journalist has recently suggested (Fox 2009, 93). Human individuals enter the theory (as consumers) in the form only of the "environment" that determines the competing businesses' adaptive fitness. Nor does Alchian attach normative weight to adaptivity per se, as Social Darwinists did. Only if one inserts the normative premise that consumers' felt needs should be attended to can the competitive economic process qualify (arguably) as "good." One would insert this premise only if one believed that consumers, as human beings, were entitled to something like happiness, satisfaction, or relief from discomfort. But such a premise is inherently egalitarian (see Sen 1979), contradicting the Social Darwinist notion that "unfit" human beings should be left to perish.

26. Fallible though consumers are, however, Joseph Schumpeter (1950, 263) pointed out the transience of many consumer errors, relative to political ones:

The picture of the prettiest girl that ever lived will in the long run prove powerless to maintain the sales of a bad cigarette. There is no equally effective safeguard in the case of political decisions. Many decisions of fateful importance are of a nature that makes it impossible for the public to experiment with them at its leisure and at moderate cost. Even if that is possible, however, judgment is as a rule not so easy to arrive at as it is in the case of the cigarette, because effects are less easy to interpret.

For more on experimentation in the private versus the public sphere, including the obvious problems raised by Schumpeter's example, see Friedman 2005.

27. See n24 above. However, "the last time Congress took action in response to outrage at executive pay, it changed tax laws to bar salaries of more than $1 million from being deducted as corporate expenses. Payments based on performance could still be deducted" (Norris 2009)—and bonuses are payments based on performance (see also Macey 2009).

28. The BIS report notes that "CDO rating methodologies used by the three major rating agencies Fitch, Moody's and Standard and Poor's are broadly similar" (2005, 19).

29. The three agencies might at least have competed with each other, although in reality, they seem to have found it more profitable to allow clients to "ratings shop" so as to find the most lenient rater of a particular security; if there was any competition, it was competition to lower standards. The lowering of standards may have been encouraged by the fact that various regulations required that most bonds have two AAA ratings (Jones 2008), which would have left a dissident agency bereft of any business if it did not play along with the other two (which could then have monopolized the two-ratings business between them). Given these two-ratings regulations, three happened to be the ideal number to keep the agencies' methods fairly homogeneous and to keep any doubts about each other's methods quiet. And it may explain why their standards began an apparent decline after Fitch, long a minor agency (albeit one of the three NRSROs), became a serious player in the 1990s.

But all this is to assume that the only problems created by barriers to entry are the incentives they foster among the extant firms. Even if there had been four or five firms, however, the real problem with barriers to entry is harder to grasp, but no less real for that. We can only guess at the methods and insights of the firms that never came into being because of the regulatory protection of a small number of them.

30. James Surowiecki 2009 has pointed out that one of these experts, through his gigantic exposure to bank stocks, was Warren Buffett.

31. I leave aside asset sales caused by the seller's liquidity needs, or other

differences between buyer and seller over the utility of the asset to them personally—as with consumption goods—rather than asset sales caused by different
views of the income potential or eventual resale value of the asset.

32. See n23 above.

33. But see DeCanio 2000, 2006, emphasizing the autonomy that regulators
and other state officials enjoy, due to the public's ignorance of their actions.

34. I use "communism" in the sense of central planning, even though that
is not what Marx had in mind. This is because, while Marx did not write recipes
for the cookshops of the future, a communist society would be faced with the
same question confronting capitalist regulatory states. How should people's
problems be solved?

This is not the place to demonstrate it, but both Marxism and the Progressive movement that spawned the modern regulatory state failed to ask this question because both took the people's self-interest to be self-evident. For this
reason the Progressives favored democracy-increasing measures such as initiative, referendum, and recall elections, and a reintepretation of the Constitution
to get around its barriers to popular action. All of these measures were supposed
to give the people the power to assert their obvious interest in curbing industrial
capitalism. Since this interest was self-evident to the Progressives, their only
explanation for why, in a putative democracy, this interest was being blocked
was the machinations of special (as opposed to general) interests—lobbyists in
"smoke-filled rooms" (Friedman 2007). The conceptual parallel to these
behind-the-scenes machinations in Marxism is the very system of capitalism
itself. Once that is overthrown, the proletariat would (Marx appears to have
thought) know what to do in order to serve its class interests (which were
general interests because of the unique place of the proletariat in world history).

Thus, the only real problem that Marxist revolutionaries and Progressive
reformers thought they faced was mobilizing the proletariat and the public,
respectively; once mobilization had overwhelmed the narrow class interests/
special interests that had gained precedence over the general interest, the newly
empowered class or public would know how best to pursue its (self-evident)
interest. This proved to be a naïve view in the case of Marxists in power, such
as Lenin, who had little choice but to turn to a central planning board once
capitalism, hence money, had been abolished. There immediately arose a debate
over the feasibility of central planning that, in retrospect, revolved around the
complexity of the economy being planned and, thus, the almost logically inescapable ignorance of the planners about precisely what needed to be done to
serve general social interests (Lavoie 1985). My argument in this section and
the next is, in effect, that the same problem faces the regulatory state created by
the Progressives, who willy-nilly found themselves turning to expert bureaucrats
who, given the complexity of the economy they are trying to regulate—and the

complexity of the skein of rules their predecessors have now erected to regulate it—face problems of ignorance comparable to those that faced Lenin's planners.

35. For a brief explanation of the clearinghouse mechanism, see Gorton 2008, 64.

36. Conceivably, the monotonous repetition of the bankers-gone-wild trope after each financial crisis is due to the fact that all mistaken loans look "wild and speculative" in retrospect; so when bankers err, the reaction is to assume that they ignored risk rather than being ignorant of it.

37. What she is not aware of is the historical scholarship cited above, which suggests that capital minima are unnecessary because deposit insurance is unnecessary to prevent bank runs, which were caused by obscure nineteenth-century currency regulations. By the same token, of course, the historians cited are not aware of any information that contradicts their claims, or they would not make those claims.

38. The phrase takes inspiration from Jerry Z. Muller's use of "dialectical failure" (Muller 2009) to describe the creative-destruction process of capitalism. However, Muller's point is that business failures lead to future successes, while we have no reason to think that political failures have the same progressive aspect—lacking a selection mechanism such as consumer satisfaction or dissatisfaction to substitute for cognitive processes such as voters' or regulators' deliberation (Friedman 2005).

39. Mark-to-market or "fair-value" accounting is mandatory for all investment-bank holdings, and for all commercial-bank assets that are "available for sale." Assets that, in contrast, are being "held to maturity" by a commercial bank need not be marked to market—unless "the collection of all contractual cash flows are [sic] not deemed probable." In that case, the asset is deemed to be "other than temporarily impaired" (OTTI). Thus, "if the company determines that it does not expect to collect all of the contractual amounts due on an investment over the life of that security, the company must mark the investment security down from its carrying value to its current fair value, even if it intends to hold the investment security until recovery" (Bailey 2009, 2). Banks themselves are required to analyze whether or not an asset is OTTI; but if it is, then the current market price, or some proxy for it (when markets have dried up)—not the value derived from the analysis that led to the OTTI determination—must be recorded on the bank's balance sheet. Indeed, "some auditors have insisted on OTTI writedowns simply because current market values were very depressed, even if the institution did not reasonably expect to lose any principal or interest" (2, emphasis added). "Fair-value" accounting also applies to assets placed by banks in off-balance-sheet entities (OBSEs), such as SIVs, because "a sufficiently large reduction in the fair value of an OBSE's assets—as occurred in many cases during the second half of 2007—might find a sponsoring bank now

absorbing more than half of the loss, thus triggering a requirement to bring the OBSE onto the balance sheet" (IMF 2009, 72).

The problem with fair-value accounting per se is with the underlying notion that market prices are anything but a fluctuating barometer of how many people are taking which side of the bull/bear disagreement over the future value of a particular asset (Frydman and Goldberg 2009)—a barometer that does not necessarily predict the "true" future value of the asset. The true future value is either the price at the time the asset actually gets sold, or the income it actually produces if held to maturity. In contrast,

> fair value reflects a single, point-in-time exit value for the sum of all the risks the market assigns to the asset, including credit and liquidity risks. If the market overreacts in its assessment of any risk component, then fair value will reflect this. Hence, the heavy discounting during the [financial] crisis of any asset containing securitized instruments produced fair values much lower than their underlying expected future cash flows would imply, even allowing for possible impairment of sub-prime elements. (IMF 2008, 65)

For an example, see n18 above.

However short-sighted they may be, legally required fair-value markdowns "that are realized by a bank, either by sale of the debt security or determination that the decline in the fair value of the debt security is other-than-temporary, are reflected in regulatory capital" by reducing retained earnings (SEC 2009, 115, 116). A panicked market-price write-down of bank assets, therefore, may spark a gigantic contraction in bank lending, because a bank can lend only in proportion to its regulatory capital; and because banks fearing such write-downs will hoard funds that otherwise could be lent, in order to avoid transgressing the regulatory capital mimimum.

According to the IMF (2008, Table 1.1), of the roughly $225 billion of mark-to-market write-downs on all asset-backed securities taken by the world's banks as of March 2008, 34–58 percent were taken by U.S. banks, yielding $77–131 billion in losses to their regulatory bank capital. At the 10 percent regulatory capital level of "well-capitalized" U.S. banks, that would have meant a reduction in American banks' lending capacity of between $770 billion and $1.31 trillion as of March 2008—and Figure 8.13 shows that most of the decline in market prices for these securities took place later, during the last three months of 2008. The decline in regulatory capital caused by mark-to-market accounting may thus have caused the decline in lending illustrated by Figure 1.1, and thus the recession.

Even if the panic-driven marks at the end of 2008 proved to be accurate in the long run, only the interaction of FAS 115 with the Basel rules required that the losses on banks' PLMBS holdings had to be translated into reduced lending so *suddenly*. Without FAS 115, commercial banks could have marked down their assets as they were sold or revalued during the long period until the housing market had bottomed out and stabilized, defaults had peaked and begun to fall, and, thus, the full effects of the popping of the bubble on the AA- and AAA-rated tranches could have been determined. The banks also could have simply held the assets to maturity, recording the income and the losses from them ex post.

Worse still, there is no reason to believe that the low marks during the 2008 panic *were* accurate. For instance, a Lehman Brothers study put marked-to-market losses as of March 2008 at twice the level of losses based on PLMBS cash-flow projections (Lehman Brothers 2008, 3). Lehman Brothers (2008, 5) projected a mark-to-market loss of $872 billion in the future, but the current (actual) losses at that point were only $321 billion, and the projected cash-flow loss was only $393 billion. Given Lehman's own precarious position, one may have reason to doubt its projections. But the ultimate fate of the AIG-insured CDOs, recounted in note 18 above, tends to confirm Lehman's projections.

Chapter 2. An Accident Waiting to Happen: Securities Regulation and Financial Deregulation

1. Kay 2009 and personal communication.

2. Indeed the assumption is so farfetched that its existence is virtually never acknowledged when MBAs are taught CAPM. Yet many empirical tests of market "efficiency" rely on CAPM, a circularity suggesting that many researchers are unaware that their research tool presupposes the absence of the phenomena they are testing for.

3. I critiqued the Samuelson prescription in the same journal twenty years later (Bhidé 1994b).

4. *The Economist*, 19 May 1990: 91.

5. These were the Depository Institutions Deregulation and Monetary Control Act of 1980 (DIDMCA); the Garn-St. Germain Depository Institutions Act of 1982 (Garn-St. Germain); the Competitive Equality Banking Act of 1987 (CEBA); the Financial Institutions Reform, Recovery, and Enforcement Act of 1989 (FIRREA); and the Federal Deposit Insurance Corporation Improvement Act of 1991 (FDICIA). Source: FDIC 1997.

6. Importantly, passage of the Commodity Futures Modernization Act of 2000 specifically barred the CFTC from regulating credit-default swaps.

7. http://www.bloomberg.com/apps/news?pid = newsarchive&sid = aqPE txa1cSag

8. Very likely, the knock-on effects of the rapid but uneven advances of

the Chinese economy provided an important catalyst. After Deng's reforms (as Edmund Phelps and I wrote in 2005), China's capacity to produce modern goods increased faster than its capacity to consume them. Nike could make fancy sneakers in China more quickly than it could create and satisfy local demand. Hence a "savings glut." But if the Chinese saved, someone had to borrow. And the borrowing had to be channeled through a financial system that could screen for creditworthiness and guarantee repayment. The U.S. financial system offered the illusion of such a capacity but in fact, for reasons discussed in the main text, buckled under the amounts that passed through it.

9. Mark Granovetter's 1985 paper is the seminal work on embedded transactions.

Chapter 3. Monetary Policy, Credit Extension, and Housing Bubbles, 2008 and 1929

1. Price/rent ratios calculated from data compiled and analyzed in Davis, Lehnert, and Martin 2008.

2. Data from 2003 and 2004 monthly CPI news releases, https://www.bls.-gov/schedule/archives/cpi_nr.htm.

3. Karl Case and Robert Shiller initiated their twenty-city index in January 2000, so we use it rather than their ten-city index beginning then. It covers metropolitan areas that are home to over 90 million Americans, and includes many cities that had a severe bubble, as well as many that had a moderate one. Since the mortgage defaults that cascaded into the financial system originated in cities with severe bubbles, it is useful to examine price paths there, rather than broader national indices such as the Median Sales Price of Existing Homes (from National Association of Realtors) or the Conventional Mortgage Home Price Index (from Freddie Mac: http://www.freddiemac.com/finance/cmhpi/). Case-Shiller data are available at http://www2.standardandpoors.com/spf/pdf/index/CSHomePrice_History_022445.xls. Case-Shiller tiered price indices are at http://www2.standardandpoors.com/spf/pdf/index/cs_tieredprices ...022445.xls.

4. Even in 2005, the average federal funds rate was lower than in every year between 1964 and 2001, with the single exception of 1993. The rate was increased so slowly starting in May 2004 that monetary policy remained lax (until late 2005) by the standards of the past half century.

5. These figures on serious delinquency (defined as mortgage payments over 90 days past due plus foreclosures in process) are taken from the third and fourth quarter 2006 National Delinquency Survey, published by the National Association of Realtors.

6. Goldman was not the only firm that made extensive bets against the subprime market. Pittman 2007 recounts the steps taken by J. Kyle Bass of

Hayman Capital Partners to track down the source of some of the worst sub-prime loans and bet against them with synthetic collateralized debt obligations. Lewis 2008 tells a similar story about FrontPoint Partners. Weiss 2009 describes the bets made by John Paulson against both subprime mortgages and the firms that wrote them.

7. Figures from Inside Mortgage Finance Publications 2008, 2: 149–50.

8. By 2006, the characteristics and performance of many of these securities were extremely poor. For example, on 17 August 2006, Goldman Sachs issued a security, GSAMP Trust 2006-S5, which consisted of 5,321 second-lien mortgages totaling $330,816,621. The loan-to-value ratio in the pool was 98.7 percent, the average FICO score of the borrowers was 666, and the average loan term remaining on these second-lien mortgages at the time the security was issued was 25.25 years. The two top tranches of the bond, A1 and A2, were rated AAA by Moody's and S&P. These tranches amounted to $231,571,000. Thirty-nine days later, in the 25 September 2006 Distribution Report filed with the SEC, $26,129,089 of the loan pool was delinquent. By the end of 2006, over $40 million was delinquent. On 12 September 2008, Standard and Poor's "Revised Projected Losses for 2005–2007 Vintage U.S. Closed-End Second Lien RMBS Transactions" estimated that total losses on GSAMP Trust 2006-S5 would reach 68 percent.

9. By betting against the market, Goldman Sachs, Hayman Capital Partners, FrontPoint Partners, and Paulson & Co. made tens of billions of dollars, but their bets drove the cost of insurance on new mortgage-backed securities up to a level that deterred the flow of capital into these securities. These firms have been criticized for making money from the economic collapse, but their actions arguably stanched the hemorrhaging of capital into this destructive housing-market bubble.

10. AIG Financial Products stopped writing credit-default swaps on RMBSs "in late 2005 based on fundamental analysis and based on concerns that the model was not going to be able to handle declining underwriting standards," according to AIGFP risk management consultant Gary Gorton (quoted in O'Harrow and Dennis 2008). Curiously, AIG saw the problems more than a year before Goldman Sachs, but did nothing during an eighteen-month period when it could have taken steps to reduce its exposure.

11. Lehman went into bankruptcy. Bear Stearns, Merrill, and Wachovia were all taken over by other firms in the face of imminent collapse. Washington Mutual was seized by the Office of Thrift Supervision and placed into receivership with the FDIC in late September, filed for bankruptcy, and had major assets taken over by JPMorganChase. Citigroup and AIG became wards of the state.

12. The data in Figure 3 come from the Federal Reserve Flow of Funds

historical data table F.218 (Home Mortgages). The data are available at http://www.federalreserve.gov/releases/z1/Current/data.htm in the file utabs.zip. Table F.218 is in the file utab218d.prn. The net flow of mortgage funds is in the third column.

13. Negative equity figures from First American CoreLogic Negative Equity Report, fourth quarter of 2008:http://www.loanperformance.com/loanper formance_hpi.aspx#NegEqReport.

14. We follow the convention of calling even the weakest borrowers "homeowners," even though "high-margin speculators" more accurately describes their activities.

15. The equity value figure for first quarter 2000 from fourth quarter 2000 Federal Reserve Flow of Funds document, Table L.213, line 1; the equity figure for the third quarter of 2002 is taken from the fourth quarter 2003 Flow of Funds document, 67, Table L 213.

16. In nominal terms, the BKX index rose slightly during a period when the stock market lost 49 percent of its value.

17. Residential real estate values, third quarter 2008 Flow of Funds document, Table B100, line 4.

18. The International Swaps and Derivatives Association publishes summary data on outstanding derivatives contracts; http://www.isda.org/statistics/pdf/ISDA-Market-Survey-historical-data.pdf.

19. Concept Release press statement, http://www.cftc.gov/opa/press98/opa4142–98.htm; the release itself http://www.cftc.gov/foia/fedreg98/foi980512 a.htm

20. See http://www.treas.gov/press/releases/rr2426.htm for joint statement from Treasury Secretary Rubin, Federal Reserve Board Chairman Greenspan, and SEC Chairman Levitt.

21. Summers—who spearheaded opposition to the regulatory review of the derivatives markets proposed by the CFTC and was the apparent architect of derivatives-market deregulation—nonetheless said, in an interview with George Stephanopoulos on March 15, 2009, that "there are a lot of terrible things that have happened in the last eighteen months, but what's happened at AIG . . . the way it was not regulated, the way no one was watching . . . is outrageous."

22. The decline after 1929 was severe, but occurred after Persons's paper was published in 1930. Grebler, Blank, and Winnick (1956, Table B-3) show that residential construction expenditures in 1930 were 53 percent of their 1929 level; by 1932 they were 12.5 percent of their 1929 level and a mere 7.5 percent of their 1925 level.

23. Automobile production figures are from NBER Macrohistory production data, series m01107a, http://www.nber.org/databases/macrohistory/rect data/01/m01107a.da t 24.

24. According to the Motor Vehicle Manufacturers Association, 1932 auto sales were only 25 percent of 1929 sales. See MMVA, Facts and Figures, various years.

25. See http://www.federalreserve.gov/newsevents/press/monetary/200708 17b.htm

26. Cecchetti (2009, 55) discusses reasons banks may be reluctant to borrow at the discount window.

Chapter 4. The Anatomy of a Murder: Who Killed America's Economy?

1. Greenspan supported the 2001 tax cut even though he should have known it would lead to the deficits he had previously treated as such an anathema. His argument that, unless we acted now, the surpluses accumulating as a result of Clinton's prudent fiscal policies would drain the economy of all its T-bills, which would make the conduct of monetary policy difficult, was one of the worst arguments from a respected government official I have ever heard; presumably, if the contingency he imagined—wiping out the national debt—was imminent, Congress had the tools and incentives with which to correct the situation in short order.

Chapter 5. Monetary Policy, Economic Policy and the Financial Crisis: An Empirical Analysis of What Went Wrong

1. Taylor 2007, delivered at a policy panel at the annual conference held in Jackson Hole, Wyoming, August 30–September 1, 2007, reports on research completed in the summer of 2007, before the August flare-up in the financial markets. It focuses on the relationship between monetary policy and the housing boom. All papers mentioned in this chapter are available on the Working Group on Global Markets website, http://www.hoover.org/research/globalmar kets.

2. When he was president of the Federal Reserve Bank of St. Louis, William Poole (2007) presented a similar figure covering a longer period and without the smoothing.

3. Ahrend, Cournède, and Price 2008 provide a fascinating analysis of the experiences in Organisation for Economic Co-operation and Development (OECD) countries during this period. They show that the deviations from the Taylor rule explain a large fraction of the cross-country variation in housing booms in OECD countries.

4. Taylor 2009b, which was prepared for a talk at an NBER conference in Girona, Spain, on 11 June 2007, summarizes research on globalization and monetary policy, pointing to the potential problem caused by central banks following each other either directly or indirectly. It provides an explanation for why several central banks held interest rates too low in the 2002–2004 period.

5. Taylor and Williams 2009 is the final revision of research we began in autumn 2007 on whether the unusual jump in interbank lending rates in August 2007 was caused by liquidity problems or counterparty risk. A working paper (2008-04) of the same title was issued by the Federal Reserve Bank of San Francisco in April and another working paper, "Further Results on a Black Swan in the Money Market," was issued in May by the Stanford Institute for Economic Policy Research.

6. Taylor 2008c reports on a project to estimate the impact on the economy of the 2008 tax rebates, with more formal econometric evidence in a paper prepared for the American Economic Association meeting, San Francisco, January 2009.

7. Taylor 2008d laid out the case for developing a more systematic approach to the Federal Reserve's interventions and bailouts of financial institutions or their creditors. It followed the Bear Stearns intervention but preceded the Lehman bankruptcy.

Chapter 6. Cause and Effect: Government Policies and the Financial Crisis

1. See the extensive discussion of the Community Reinvestment Act development in Hossain 2004.

2. Quoted in Mason 2007. The National Homeownership Strategy was removed from the Department of Housing and Urban Development website in 2007.

3. Economagic.com, "Economic Time Series Page: U.S.: Average Price of Houses Actually Sold," www.economagic.com/em-cgi/data.exe/cenc25/c25q07. The average price of homes sold increased from $153,500 in the fourth quarter of 1995 to $322,100 in the first quarter of 2007.

Chapter 7. How Securitization Concentrated Risk in the Financial Sector

1. Coval, Jurek, and Stafford 2009b calls these kinds of tranche products "economic catastrophe bonds."

2. See Rajan et al. 2008 for an early hint of this problem with bankers' pay. Acharya and Volpin 2010 and Acharya, Pagano, and Volpin 2010 provide a model explaining why pay may have risen in the banking industry, and why at the same time risk-management (governance) quality deteriorated, due to greater mobility of risk-takers across financial institutions. Acharya and Richardson 2009 provides a detailed account of such governance failures (see, especially, chaps. 7 and 8).

3. The following account is taken from UBS 2008, prepared for the Swiss Federal Banking Commission.

Chapter 8. A Regulated Meltdown: The Basel Rules and Banks' Leverage

The views expressed in this chapter are those of the authors and not necessarily those of the National Bank of Poland.

1. Another form of systemic risk encouraged by deposit insurance was a "bias toward illiquidity": a tendency to hold illiquid but higher-yielding securities. Tim Congdon (2007) has pointed out that in the 1950s, British banks' liquid assets (mostly short-term government securities) stood at roughly 30 percent of total assets. Now such liquid holdings have come down to just 1 percent.

2. Specifically, tier 1 consisted of issued and fully paid common stock, disclosed reserves, and retained earnings. Tier 2 was defined as undisclosed reserves, revaluation reserves, loan-loss reserves, hybrid-debt instruments (e.g., convertible bonds, cumulative preference shares), and subordinated debt. For the technicalities of the regulations see BCBS 1988.

3. Should a bank fail to satisfy the conditions for being "well capitalized," there are four other categories it might fit into: "adequately capitalized," "undercapitalized," "significantly undercapitalized," and "critically undercapitalized." Once it stops being "adequately capitalized," a bank would typically have to face restrictions on the rates it can pay on deposits, as well as supervisory actions and—perhaps most important—reputational costs and adverse market reactions.

4. Asset-backed securities might consist not only of mortgages, but also of car loans, student loans, credit-card loans, and so forth

5. Proceeds from the sale of loans could be used to repay the bank's obligations to creditors (on the interbank market or otherwise), thus reducing its liabilities.

6. For the sake of simplicity, tax deductions and possible servicing fees, which do not substantially change the overall picture, are omitted.

7. A similar point is made by one of the rating agencies: "ABCP programs (essentially SIVs) also offer advantages to their bank sponsors. The programs are typically structured and accounted for by the banks as an off-balance-sheet activity. If the bank were to provide a direct corporate loan, even one secured by the same assets, it would appear on the bank's balance sheet as an asset and the bank would be obligated to maintain regulatory capital for it. An ABCP program permits the sponsor to offer receivable financing services to its customers without using the Sponsor's balance sheet or holding incremental regulatory capital" (Moody's 2003, 15).

8. This simple balance-sheet analytics framework was developed in Adrian and Shin's (2007, 2008) pathbreaking analyses.

9. Quarterly Report Submitted to Securities and Exchange Commission, Form 10-Q, March 2008, Citigroup. http://www.citigroup.com/citi/fin/data/q0801c.pdf?ieNocache = 340

10. Ibid., 54.

11. Citigroup news release, December 13, 2007; http://www.citigroup.com/citi/press/2007/071213c.htm

12. The measurements of capital and of risk-weighted assets are themselves ambiguous. Capital can be boosted or manipulated just as risk weights might be (since in economics there is no objective and apodictically certain risk probability calculus).

Chapter 9. The Credit-Rating Agencies and the Subprime Debacle

1. This rule did not apply to savings institutions until 1989. Its application to them in that year forced them to sell substantial holdings of "junk bonds" (i.e., below investment grade), causing the crash of the junk-bond market.

2. In the early 1990s, the SEC again made use of NRSRO ratings when it established safety requirements for the short-term bonds (e.g., commercial paper) held by money market mutual funds.

3. The SEC bestowed the NRSRO designation on Duff & Phelps in 1982, on McCarthy, Crisanti & Maffei in 1983, on IBCA in 1991, and on Thomson Bank-Watch in 1992.

4. Other examples of "two-sided" information markets include newspapers and magazines, where business models range from subscription revenues only (e.g., *Consumer Reports*) to a mix of subscription revenues and advertising revenues (most newspapers and magazines) to advertising revenues only (e.g., the *Village Voice*, some metropolitan "giveaway" newspapers, and some suburban weekly "shoppers").

5. See note 2 above.

6. This seems a reasonable assumption, since the bond market is, for the most part, one where financial institutions are the major buyers and sellers. It is not a market where "widows and orphans" are likely to be major participants.

Chapter 10. Credit-Default Swaps and the Crisis

1. The term "insurance" is used here in its broadest sense, protection against loss. Credit-default swaps are not insurance in the strict sense—the service provided by insurers of life and property. Insurance of that kind is an actuarial, not a credit activity, and depends on an understanding of the likelihood that losses will occur to similar pooled risks, not to a specific insured party.

2. An excellent discussion of the role of credit-default swaps appears in Mengle 2007.

Chapter 12. The Financial Crisis and the Systemic
Failure of the Economics Profession

1. Carmen Reinhart and Kenneth Rogoff (2008) argue that the current financial crisis differs little from a long chain of similar crises in developed and developing countries. We certainly share their view. The problem is that the received body of models in macro finance, to which these authors have prominently contributed, provides no room whatsoever for such recurrent boom and bust cycles. The literature has, therefore, been a major source of the illusory "this time it is different" view that the authors themselves criticize.

2. Indeed, few researchers explored the consequences of a breakdown of their assumptions, even though this was rather likely.

3. The historical emergence of the representative-agent paradigm is a mystery. Ironically, it appeared during the 1970s, after a period of intense discussion of the problem of aggregation in economics (which basically yielded negative results). The representative agent, however, appeared without similar methodological discussion. In the words of Deirdre McCloskey, "It became a rule in the conversation of some economists because Tom and Bob said so" (personal communication). Today, this convention has become so strong that many young economists wouldn't know of an alternative way to approach macroeconomic issues.

4. The reductionist conceptual approach of the representative-agent model is also remarkably different from the narrative of the "invisible hand," which also has the flavor of "more is different."

5. It is pretty obvious how the currently popular class of dynamic general-equilibrium models would have to "cope" with the financial crisis. It would be covered either by a dummy variable or interpreted as a very large negative stochastic shock to the economy, i.e., as an event equivalent to a large asteroid strike.

6. Robert Solow (2008, 235) has called it a "rhetorical swindle" that the "macro community has perpetrated on itself, and its students."

Afterword: The Causes of the Financial Crisis

1. Chapter 3 by Gjerstad and Smith is excellent on the economics of bubbles in general and the housing bubble in particular.

2. Chapter 8 contains a particularly good narrative of the events culminating in the financial collapse of September 2008.

3. See the classic study by Truman E. Bewley 1999; cf. Chatterjee and Corbae 2007. For evidence regarding the current depression from an opinion poll conducted by Rutgers University, see Marsh 2009. For other evidence, see Luo 2009. Alonso and Prado 2008 show that, because of people's aversion to

uncertainty, the welfare loss caused by the business cycle is much greater than other economists have believed. (I discuss uncertainty aversion in Posner 2010, chap. 9.)

4. The problems of the rating agencies are well discussed by Lawrence White in Chapter 9.

References

Acharya, Viral V., Douglas Gale, and Tanju Yorulmazer. 2008. "Rollover Risk and Market Freezes." Working Paper, New York University Stern School of Business.

Acharya, Viral V., Marco Pagano, and Paolo Volpin. 2010. "Seeking Alpha: Excess Risk Taking and Competition for Managerial Talent." Working paper, NYU-Stern School of Business.

Acharya, Viral V., and Matthew Richardson, eds. 2009. *Restoring Financial Stability: How to Repair a Failed System.* New York University Stern School of Business/John Wiley.

Acharya, Viral V., and Philipp Schnabl. 2009a. "Securitization Without Risk Transfer: The Anatomy of Hidden Bank Debt." Working Paper, New York University Stern School of Business.

———. 2009b. "How Banks Played the Leverage 'Game.'" In Acharya and Richardson, eds. 2009.

Acharya, Viral V., and Paolo Volpin. 2010. "Corporate Governance Externalities." *Review of Finance* 14 (1): 1–33.

Adrian, Tobias, and Hyun Song Shin. 2007. "Liquidity and Leverage." Working paper, Federal Reserve Bank of New York.

———. 2008. "Financial Intermediary Leverage and Value at Risk." Working paper, Federal Reserve Bank of New York.

Ahrend, Rudiger, Boris Cournède, and Robert Price. 2008. "Monetary Policy, Market Excesses and Financial Turmoil." OECD Economics Department Working Paper 597 (March).

Akerlof, George A., and Robert J. Shiller. 2009. *Animal Spirits: How Human Psychology Drives the Economy, and Why It Matters for Global Capitalism.* Princeton, N.J.: Princeton University Press.

Alchian, Armen A. 1950. "Uncertainty, Evolution, and Economic Theory." *Journal of Political Economy* 58 (3): 211–21.

Alonso, Irasema, and Jose Mauricio Prado. 2008. "Ambiguity Aversion, Asset Prices, and the Welfare Costs of Aggregate Fluctuations." *Social Science Research Network*, 27 January. http://ssrn.com/abstract = 986559.

Anderson, P. W. 1972. "More Is Different." *Science* 177: 393–96.

Aoki, Masanao, and Hiroshi Yoshikawa. *Reconstructing Macroeconomics: A Perspective from Statistical Physics and Combinatorial Stochastic Processes*. Cambridge: Cambridge University Press.

Ashcraft, Adam B., and Til Schuermann. 2008. "Understanding the Securitization of Subprime Mortgage Credit." Wharton Financial Institutions Center, Working Paper 07-43. www.newyorkfed.org/research/staff_reports/sr318.pdf

Avery, Robert B., Raphael W. Bostic, and Glenn B. Canner. 2000. "The Performance and Profitability of CRA-Related Lending." Economic Commentary, Federal Reserve Bank of Cleveland (November). www.clevelandfed.org/research/Commentary/2000/1100.htm

Bagehot, Walter. 1873. *Lombard Street: A Description of the Money Market*. London: Henry S. King.

Bailey, Thomas. 2009. "Statement of Thomas Bailey, President and CEO, Brentwood Bank, on Behalf of the Pennsylvania Association of Community Bankers and the Independent Community Bankers of America, before the Subcommittee on Capital Markets, Insurance, and Government Sponsored Enterprises of the Committee on Financial Services of the United States House of Representatives." 21 March.

Bair, Sheila C. 2010. "Statement of Sheila C. Bair, Chairman, Federal Deposit Insurance Corporation, on the Causes and Current State of the Financial Crisis, before the Financial Crisis Inquiry Commission." 14 January.

Bajaj, Vikas, and David Leonhardt. 2008. "Tax Break May Have Helped Cause Housing Bubble." *New York Times*, 19 December.

Banerjee, Abhijit V. 1992. "A Simple Model of Herd Behaviour." *Quarterly Journal of Economics* 108: 797–817.

Bank for International Settlements (BIS). 2005. "The Role of Ratings in Structured Finance: Issues and Implications." Report submitted by a Working Group Established by the Committee on the Global Financial System, BIS. January.

———. 2009. "The Role of Valuation and Leverage in Procyclicality." CFGS Paper 34. Report prepared by a joint Working Group of the Financial Stability Forum and the Committee on the Global Financial System, BIS. April.

Barlevy, Gadi. 2004. "The Cost of Business Cycles Under Endogenous Growth." *American Economic Review* 94(4): 964–99.

Barnett-Hart, Anna Katherine. 2009. "The Story of the CDO Market Meltdown: An Empirical Analysis." Bachelor's thesis, Department of Economics, Harvard University.

Bartlett, Bruce. 2009. "Who Saw the Housing Bubble Coming?" *Forbes.com*, 2 January.

Basel Committee on Banking Supervision (BCBS). 1988. "International Convergence of Capital Measurement and Capital Standards." Basel: Bank for International Settlements, July.

———. 1998. "International Convergence of Capital Measurement and Capital Standards" (text of "Basel I, updated to reflect several textual changes made since Basel accords of July 1988). Basel: Bank for International Settlements, April.

Baskin, Jonathan B. 1988. "The Development of Corporate Financial Markets in Britain and the United States, 1600–1914: Overcoming Asymmetric Information." *Business History Review* 62: 199.

Bebchuk, Lucian A., Alma Cohen, and Holger Spamann. 2009. "The Wages of Failure: Executive Compensation at Bear Stearns and Lehman Brothers 2000–2008." Harvard Law and Economics Discussion Paper 657. December.

Benston, George J. 1999. "The Community Reinvestment Act: Looking for Discrimination that Isn't There." Policy Analysis 354. Cato Institute, Washington, D.C., 6 October. www.cato.org/pub_display.php?pub_id = 1213.

Berger, Allen N., Anil K. Kashyap, and Joseph M. Scalise. 1995. "The Transformation of the U.S. Banking Industry: What a Long, Strange Trip It's Been." Brookings Papers on Economic Activity 2: 55–218.

Bergsman, Steve. 2004. "Closing the Gap." *Mortgage Banking* (February): 52–59.

Bernanke, Ben S. 1983. "Nonmonetary Effects of the Financial Crisis in the Propagation of the Great Depression." *American Economic Review* 73: 257–76.

———. 2010. "Monetary Policy and the Housing Bubble." Address at annual meetings of the American Economic Association, Atlanta, 3 January. http://www.federalreserve.gov/newsevents/speech/bernanke20100103a.htm

Berndt, Antje, and Anurag Gupta. 2008. "Moral Hazard and Adverse Selection in the Originate-to-Distribute Model of Bank Credit." Working paper, Tepper School of Business, Carnegie Mellon University.

Bertoneche, Marc. 1984. "Institutional Aspects of European Equity Markets." In *European Equity Markets,* ed. Gabriel Hawawini and Michael Pierre. New York: Garland.

Bewley, Truman E. 199. *Why Wages Don't Fall During a Recession.* Cambridge, Mass.: Harvard University Press.

Bhattacharya, Sudipto, Arnoud W. A. Boot, and Anjan V. Thakor. 1998. "The Economics of Bank Regulation." *Journal of Money, Credit and Banking* 30 (4): 745–70.

Bhidé, Amar. 1993. "The Hidden Costs of Stock Market Liquidity." *Journal of Financial Economics* 34: 31–51.

————. 1994a. "Efficient Markets, Deficient Governance." *Harvard Business Review* 72 (6): 129–39.

————. 1994b. "Return to Judgment." *Journal of Portfolio Management* 20 (1): 19–25.

————. 2008. "Insiders and Outsiders." *Forbes.com*, 25 September.

Bhidé, Amar, and Edmund Phelps. 2005. "A Dynamic Theory of China-U.S. Trade: Making Sense of the Imbalances." *World Economics* 8 (3): 7–25.

Bordo, Michael. 1985. "Financial Crises, Banking Crises, Stock Market Crashes and the Money Supply: Some International Evidence, 1870–1933." *Revista di Storia Economica* 2: 41–78.

Bryan, Lowell L. 1987. "The Credit Bomb in Our Financial System." *Harvard Business Review* (January–February): 45–51.

Buffett, Warren. 1987. Berkshire Hathaway Inc. Letters to Shareholders, 1979–1985.

Caginalp, Gunduz, David Porter, and Vernon L. Smith. 2000. "Momentum and Overreaction in Experimental Asset Markets." *International Journal of Industrial Organization* 18: 187–204.

Carlson, Mark, and Kris James Mitchener. 2006. "Branch Banking, Bank Competition, and Financial Stability." *Journal of Money, Credit, and Banking* 38 (5): 1293–328.

Cassidy, John. 2008. "Subprime Suspect." *New Yorker*, 31 March.

Cecchetti, Stephen G. 2009. "Crisis and Responses: The Federal Reserve in the Early Stages of the Financial Crisis." *Journal of Economic Perspectives* 23: 51–75.

Chamley, Christophe P. 2002. *Rational Herds: Economic Models of Social Learning.* Cambridge: Cambridge University Press.

Chandler, Alfred D. 1990. "The Enduring Logic of Industrial Success." *Harvard Business Review* (March–April): 130–40.

Chandler, Alfred D., and Stephen Salisbury. 1971. *Pierre S. Du Pont and the Making of the Modern Corporation.* New York: Harper and Row.

Chatterjee, Satyajit, and Dean Corbae. 2007. "On the Aggregate Welfare Cost of Great Depression Unemployment." *Journal of Monetary Economics* 54, no. 6: 1529–44.

Cheng, Ing-Haw, Harrison Hong, and Jose Scheinkman. 2009. "Yesterday's Heroes: Compensation and Creative Risk-Taking" (second draft). Manuscript, Princeton University, October.

Coates, John M., and Joe Herbert. 2008. "Endogenous Steroids and Financial Risk Taking on a London Trading Floor." *Proceedings of the National Academy of Sciences* 105 (16): 6167–72.

Cogley, Timothy W., and Thomas Sargent. 2008. "The Market Price of Risk and the Equity Premium: A Legacy of the Great Depression?" *Journal of Monetary Economics* 55: 454–76.

Cohan, William D. 2009a. *House of Cards: A Tale of Hubris and Wretched Excess on Wall Street*. New York: Doubleday.

———. 2009b. "A Tsunami of Excuses." *The New York Times*, 12 March: A23.

Cohen, Richard. 2009. "How Is Cramer to Know What Insiders Don't?" *Investor's Business Daily*, 17 March.

Colander, David. 2006. *Post Walrasian Macroeconomics: Beyond the DSGE Model*. Cambridge: Cambridge University Press.

Colander, David, Peter Howitt, Alan Kirman, Axel Leijonhufvud, and Perry Mehrling. 2008. "Beyond DSGE Models: Toward an Empirically Based Macroeconomics." *American Economic Review* 98 (May): 2.

Condon, Bernard, and Nathan Vardi. 2009. "The Banker Who Said No." *Forbes.com*, 3 April.

Congdon, Tim. 2007. "Pursuit of Profit Has Led to Risky Lack of Liquidity." *Financial Times*, 10 September.

Converse, Philip E. [1964] 2006. "The Nature of Belief Systems in Mass Publics." *Critical Review* 18 (1–3): 1–74.

Coval, Joshua, Jakub Jurek, and Erik Stafford. 2009a. "Economic Catastrophe Bonds." *American Economic Review* 99 (3) (June): 628–66.

———. 2009b. "The Economics of Structured Finance." *Journal of Economic Perspectives* 23 (Winter): 3–25.

Cox, Rob, and Dwight Cass. 2009. "Tests May Spur Bank Mergers." *New York Times*, 8 May.

Criado, Regino, Julio Flores, Benito Hernández-Bermejo, Javier Pello, and Miguel Romance. 2005. "Effective Measurement of Network Vulnerability Under Random and Intentional Attacks." *Journal of Mathematical Modelling and Algorithms* 4: 307–16.

Dash, Eric. 2009. "Banks Holding Up in Tests, But May Still Need Aid." *New York Times*, 9 April.

Davis, Morris A., Andreas Lehnert, and Robert F. Martin. 2008. "The Rent-Price Ratio for the Aggregate Stock of Owner-Occupied Housing." *Review of Income and Wealth* 54: 279–84.

DeCanio, Samuel. 2000. "Bringing the State Back In . . . Again." *Critical Review* 14 (2–3): 139–46.

———. 2006. "Mass Opinion and American Political Development." *Critical Review* 18 (1–3): 143–56.

Dell'Ariccia, Giovanni, Deniz Igan, and Luc Laeven. 2008. "Credit Booms and Lending Standards: Evidence from the Subprime Mortgage Market." Working paper, International Monetary Fund.

Demyanyk, Yuliya S., and Otto van Hemert. 2007. "Understanding the Subprime Mortgage Crisis." Federal Reserve Bank of St. Louis Supervisory Policy Analysis Working Papers. www.stlouisfed.org/news/fiyc/assets/Dec6_DvH_subprime.pdf.

————. 2008. "Understanding the Subprime Mortgage Crisis." *Social Science Research Network*, 19 August. http://ssrn.com/abstract = 1020396.

Depository Trust and Clearing Corporation (DTCC). 2008. "Trade Information Warehouse Data." Week ending 12 December. www.dtcc.com/products/derivserv/data_table_i.php

Diamond, Douglas W. 1984. "Financial Intermediation and Delegated Monitoring." *Review of Economic Studies* 51: 393–414.

Diamond, Douglas W., and Philip H. Dybvig. 1983. "Bank Runs, Deposit Insurance, and Liquidity." *Journal of Political Economy* 91(3): 401–19.

Dimon, Jaime. 2009. "Letter to Shareholders." JPMorgan Chase Annual Report 2008.

Dizard, John. 2009a. "The Inside Story on Reforms Is that There Is No Story." *Financial Times*, 17 February: 10.

————. 2009b. "The Real Reasons Why Banks Are Remaining Reticent on Lending." *Financial Times*, 24–25 October.

Dowd, Kevin, ed. 1992a. *The Experience of Free Banking*. London: Routledge.

————. 1992b. "U.S. Banking in the 'Free Banking' Period." In Dowd 1992a.

Duy, Tim. 2009. "Hawkishness Dominates." *Tim Duy's Fed Watch*, 1 October. http://economistsview.typepad.com/timduy/2009/10/hawkishness-dominates.html

Eichengreen, Barry. 2008. *Origins and Responses to the Crisis*. Manuscript, University of California, Berkeley.

Elster, Jon. 2007. Explaining Social Behavior: *More Nuts and Bolts for the Social Sciences*. Cambridge: Cambridge University Press.

————. 2009. "Excessive Ambitions." *Capitalism and Society* 4(1). http://www.bepress.com/cas/vol4/iss2/art1

England, Robert Stowe. 2002. "Giving It 100 Percent." *Mortgage Banking* (February): 68–76.

Ewing, Jack. 2010. "Risk to European Bank Seen in Austerity Programs." *New York Times*, 8 May.

Fahlenbrach, Rüdiger, and René M. Stulz. 2009. "Bank CEO Incentives and the Credit Crisis." Manuscript, Ohio State University.

Federal Deposit Insurance Corporation. 1984. *The First Fifty Years: A History of the FDIC, 1933–1983*. Washington. D.C.: FDIC.

————. 1997. *History of the Eighties—Lessons for the Future*. Washington, D.C.: FDIC.

Federal Home Loan Mortgage Corporation. 2008. "Freddie Mac Update." 30 August. www.freddiemac.com/investors/pdffiles/investor-presentation.pdf

Federal National Mortgage Association. 2008a. *Fannie Mae 2007 Annual Housing Activities Report.* 17 March. Washington, D.C.: Department of Housing and Urban Development. http://170.97.167.13/offices/hsg/gse/reports/2007 aharfnmanarrative.pdf.

———. 2008b. "2008 Q2 10-Q Investor Summary." 8 August. www.fannie mae.com/media/pdf/newsreleases2008_Q2_10Q_Investor_Summary.pdf.

Fisher, Ernest M. 1950. "Changing Institutional Patterns of Mortgage Lending." *Journal of Finance* 5: 307–15.

Föllmer, Hans. 2008. "Financial Uncertainty, Risk Measures, and Robust Preferences." In *Aspects of Mathematical Finance*, ed. Marc Yor. Berlin: Springer.

Fox, Justin. 2009. *The Myth of the Rational Market: A History of Risk, Reward, and Delusion on Wall Street.* New York: HarperCollins.

Friedman, Jeffrey. 2005. "Popper, Weber, and Hayek: The Epistemology and Politics of Ignorance." *Critical Review* 17 (1–2): i–lviii.

———. 2006. "Taking Ignorance Seriously: Rejoinder to Critics." *Critical Review* 18 (4): 469–532.

———. 2007. "'A Weapon in the Hands of the People': The Rhetorical Presidency in Historical and Contextual Context." *Critical Review* 19 (2–3): 197–240.

Friedman, Jerome H. 1987. "Exploratory Projection Pursuit." *Journal of the American Statistical Association* 82: 249–66.

Friedman, Milton, and Anna Jacobson Schwartz. 1963. *A Monetary History of the United States.* Princeton, N.J.: Princeton University Press.

Frydman, Roman, and Michael D. Goldberg. 2007. *Imperfect Knowledge Economics: Exchange Rates and Risk.* Princeton, N.J.: Princeton University Press.

———. 2008. "Macroeconomic Theory for a World of Imperfect Knowledge." *Capitalism and Society* 3 (1).

———. 2009. "Financial Markets and the State: Price Swings, Risk, and the Scope of Regulation." Working Paper 29, Center on Capitalism and Society at Columbia University. February.

Galbraith, John Kenneth. 1972. *The Great Crash, 1929.* Boston: Houghton Mifflin.

Gibson, Michael S. 2007. "Credit Derivatives and Risk Management." Finance and Economics Discussion Series 2007–47, Divisions of Research & Statistics and Monetary Affairs, Federal Reserve Board of Governors, 22 May. www.federalreserve.gov/pubs/feds/2007/200747/200747pap.pdf

Gjerstad, Steven. 2007a. "Price Dynamics in an Exchange Economy." Krannert School of Management Working Paper, Purdue University. http://ideas.rep ec.org/p/pur/prukra/1205.html

———. 2007b. "The Competitive Market Paradox." *Journal of Economic Dynamics and Control* 31: 1753–80.

Gjerstad, Steven, and John Dickhaut. 1998. "Price Formation in Double Auctions." *Games and Economic Behavior* 22: 1–29.

González-Páramo, José Manuel. 2008. "Financial Turmoil, Securitisation and Liquidity." Speech at Global ABS Conference, Cannes. http://www.bis.org/review/r080603e.pdf?noframes = 1

Gordon, Robert. 2008. "Did Liberals Cause the Sub-Prime Crisis? Conservatives Blame the Housing Crisis on a 1977 Law That Helps Low-Income People Get Mortgages. It's a Useful Story for Them, But It Isn't True." *American Prospect Online,* 7 April.

Gorman, Michael, and William A. Sahlman. 1989. "What Do Venture Capitalists Do?" *Journal of Business Venturing* 4: 231–48.

Gorton, Gary. 2008. "The Panic of 2007." Prepared for Federal Reserve Bank of Kansas City Jackson Hole Conference, August.

———. 2009. "Slapped in the Face by the Invisible Hand: Banking and the Panic of 2007." Prepared for Federal Reserve Bank of Atlanta 2009 Financial Markets Conference, "Financial Innovation and Crisis," 11–13 May.

Graham, Jed. 2009. "Geithner Calls for Systemic Regulator and More Capital." *Investor's Business Daily,* 27 March.

Granovetter, Mark, 1985. "Economic Action and Social Structure: The Problem of Embeddedness." *American Journal of Sociology* 91 (3): 481–510.

Gras, N. S. B. 1938. "Capitalism—Concepts and History." *Bulletin of the Business Historical Society* 16: 21–42.

Grebler, Leo, David M. Blank, and Louis Winnick. 1956. *Capital Formation in Residential Real Estate.* Princeton, N.J.: Princeton University Press.

Greenlaw, David, Jan Hatzius, Anil K. Kashyap, and Hyun Song Shin. 2008. "Leveraged Losses: Lessons from the Mortgage Market Meltdown." Report of the U.S. Monetary Forum.

Greenspan, Alan. 2009. "The Fed Didn't Cause the Housing Bubble." *Wall Street Journal,* 11 March: A15.

"Greenspan Says Didn't See Subprime Storm Brewing." 2007. Reuters, 13 September.

Hagerty, James R., and Dan Fitzpatrick. 2009. "BofA Feels Bite of Move into Mortgage-Backed Securities." *Wall Street Journal,* 25 February.

Hayek, Friedrich A. 1945. "The Use of Knowledge in Society." In Hayek, *Individualism and Economic Order.* Chicago: University of Chicago Press.

———. 1967. "Rules, Perception and Intelligibility." In Hayek, *Studies in Philosophy, Politics, and Economics.* Chicago: University of Chicago Press.

Heffernan, Shelagh. 2005. *Modern Banking.* London: Wiley.

Hellwig, Martin. 2008. "Systemic Risk in the Financial Sector: An Analysis of the Subprime-Mortgage Financial Crisis." MPI Collective Goods Preprint 2008/43.

Hendry, David F. 1995. *Dynamic Econometrics*. Oxford: Oxford University Press.

———. 2009. "The Methodology of Empirical Econometric Modeling: Applied Econometrics Through the Looking-Glass." In *The Handbook of Econometrics*, vol. 2, *Applied Econometrics*, ed. Terence C. Mills and Kerry Patterson. London: Palgrave Macmillan.

Hendry, David F., and Hans-Martin Krolzig. 2005. "The Properties of Automatic Gets Modeling." *Economic Journal* 115 (502): C32–61.

Hoover, Kevin D., Søren Johansen, and Katarina Juselius. 2008. "Allowing the Data to Speak Freely: The Macroeconometrics of the Cointegrated Vector Autoregression." *American Economic Review* 98: 251–55.

Hopkins, Cheyenne. 2009. "Dugan: Turmoil Shows Need for Reserve Leeway." *American Banker*, 3 March.

Hossain, A. K. M. Rezaul. 2004. "The Past, Present and Future of the Community Reinvestment Act (CRA): A Historical Perspective." Working paper 2004–30, Department of Economics, University of Connecticut. www.econ.uconn.edu/working/2004-30.pdf.

Ikeda, Sanford. 1997. *Dynamics of the Mixed Economy: Toward a Theory of Interventionism*. London: Routledge.

Inside Mortgage Finance Publications. 2008. *Mortgage Market Statistical Annual*, vols. 1, 2. www.imfpubs.com

International Monetary Fund. 2005. *World Economic Outlook*, September.

———. 2008. "Global Financial Stability Report: Containing Systemic Risks and Restoring Financial Soundness." April.

———. 2009. "Global Financial Stability Report: Navigating the Challenges Ahead." October.

Isaac, William M. 2009. "Testimony Before the Subcommittee on Capital Markets, Insurance, and Government Sponsored Enterprises of the Committee on Financial Services of the United States House of Representatives." 12 March.

Ivashina, Victoria, and David Scharfstein. 2010. "Bank Lending During the Financial Crisis of 2008." *Journal of Financial Economics*.

Jackson, Patricia, Craig Furfine, Hans Groeneveld, Diana Hancock, David Jones, William Perraudin, Lawrence Radecki, and Masao Yoneyama. 1999. "Capital Requirements and Bank Behaviour: The Impact of the Basle Accord." Basel Committee on Banking Supervision Working Papers 1, April.

Jensen, Michael. 1993. "The Modern Industrial Revolution, Exit, and the Failure of Internal Control Systems." *Journal of Finance* 48 (3): 831–80.

Johnson, Simon, and James Kwak. 2010. *13 Bankers: The Wall Street Takeover and the Next Financial Meltdown.* New York: Pantheon.

Joint Center for Housing Studies, Harvard University. 2008. *The State of the Nation's Housing,* 2008. www.jchs.harvard.edu/publications/markets/son2008/index.htm

Jones, Sam. 2008. "How Moody's Faltered." FT.com, 17 October.

———. 2009. "Of Couples and Copulas." *Financial Times,* 25–26 April.

Juselius, Katarina. 2006. The *Cointegrated VAR Model: Econometric Methodology and Empirical Applications.* Oxford: Oxford University Press.

Juselius, Katarina, and Massimo Franchi. 2007. "Taking a DSGE Model to the Data Meaningfully." *Economics: The Open-Access, Open-Assessment E-Journal* 4.

Kaplan, Steven N. 2009. "Should Banker Pay Be Regulated?" *Economists' Voice,* December.

Kaufman, George, and Larry Mote. 1990. "Glass-Steagall: Repeal by Regulatory and Judicial Reinterpretation." *Banking Law Journal* (September/October): 388–421.

Kay, John. 2009. *The Long and the Short of It: A Guide to Finance and Investment for Normally Intelligent People Who Aren't in the Industry.* London: Erasmus Press.

Keller, James. 2009. "The Myth of Systemic Collapse." *RealClearMarkets,* 4 March.

Kelly, Kate. 2007. "How Goldman Won Big on Mortgage Meltdown." *Wall Street Journal,* 14 December.

Keys, Benjamin, Tanmoy Mukherjee, Amit Seru, and Vikrant Vig. 2008. "Did Securitization Lead to Lax Screening? Evidence from Subprime Loans." *Quarterly Journal of Economics* 125.

Kindleberger, Charles P. 1989. *Manias, Panics, and Crashes: A History of Financial Crises.* London: Macmillan.

Krahnen, Jan Pieter. 2005. "Der Handel von Kreditrisiken: Eine neue Dimension des Kapitalmarktes." *Perspektiven der Wirtschaftspolitik* 6: 499–519.

Krahnen, Jan Pieter, and Christian Wilde. 2006. *Risk Transfer with CDOs and Systemic Risk in Banking.* Frankfurt Center for Financial Studies, Working Paper 2006–04.

Krishnamurthy, Arvind. 2008. "The Financial Meltdown: Data and Diagnoses." Working paper, Northwestern University.

Kroszner, Randall S. 2008. "The Community Reinvestment Act and the Recent Mortgage Crisis." Speech to Confronting Concentrated Poverty Policy Forum, Board of Governors of Federal Reserve System, Washington, D.C., 3 December.

Kuritzkes, Andrew, and Hal Scott. 2009. "Markets Are the Best Judge of Bank Capital." *Financial Times*, 23 September.

Lagarde, Christine et al. 2009. "G20 Must Act to Bring the Banks' Bonus Culture to an End." *Financial Times*, 4 September.

Lavoie, Don C. *Rivalry and Central Planning: The Socialist Calculation Debate Reconsidered.* Cambridge: Cambridge University Press.

Lehman Brothers. 2008. "Residential Credit Losses—Going into Extra Innings?" *U.S. Securitized Products Fixed Income Research*, 14 April.

Leijonhufvud, Axel. 2000. *Macroeconomic Instability and Coordination: Selected Essays.* Cheltenham: Edward Elgar.

Leonhardt, David. 2009. "They Called Him 'Mr. Bubble.'" *Yale Alumni Magazine*, September/ October.

Levy, Ari. 2009. "Wells Fargo Assails TARP, Calls Stress Test 'Asinine.'" *Bloomberg.com*, 16 March.

Lewis, Michael. 2008. "The End." *Portfolio.com* (December). www.portfolio.com/news-markets/national-news/portfolio/2008/11/11/The-End-of-Wall-Streets-Boom.

Lewis, Michael, and David Einhorn. 2009. "The End of the Financial World as We Know It." *New York Times*, 4 January: 9.

Lindbeck, Assar. 1990. "Presentation Speech by Professor Assar Lindbeck of the Royal Swedish Academy of Sciences." 10 December. http://nobelprize.org/nobel_prizes/economics/laureates/1990/presentation-speech.html

Lipsky, John P. 2008. "Commodity Prices and Global Inflation." Speech to Council on Foreign Relations, New York, 8 May.

Lo, Andrew W., Dmitry V. Repin, and Brett N. Steenbarger. 2005. "Fear and Greed in Financial Markets: A Clinical Study of Day-Traders." *American Economic Review* 95 (2): 352–59.

Lowenstein, Roger. 2000. *When Genius Failed: The Rise and Fall of Long-Term Capital Management.* New York: Random House.

Lowenstein, Roger. 2008. "Triple-A Failure." *New York Times Magazine*, 27 April.

Luce, Edward. 2009. "Subprime Explosion: Who Isn't Guilty?" Graphic: "Top Underwriters in Peak Years 2005–06." *Financial Times*, 6 May.

Luo, Michael. 2009. "Recession Exacts an Emotional Toll on Children." *New York Times*, 12 November: A1.

Lux, Thomas. 2009. "Stochastic Behavioral Asset Pricing Models and the Stylized Facts." In *Handbook of Financial Markets: Dynamics and Evolution*, ed. Thorsten Hens and Klaus Schenk-Hoppé. Amsterdam: North-Holland.

Lux, Thomas, and Frank Westerhoff. 2009. "Economics Crisis." *Nature Physics* 5: 2–3.

Macey, Jonathan. 2009. "Washington's Plans May Result in Even Higher Executive Pay." *Wall Street Journal*, 24–25 October.

Mandel, Michael. 2009. "The GDP Mirage: By Overlooking Cuts in Research and Development, Product Design, and Worker Training, GDP Is Greatly Overstating the Economy's Strength." *BusinessWeek*, 29 October. www.businessweek.com/magazine/content/09_45/b4154034724383.htm

Marsh, Bill. 2009. "Jobless, Sleepless, Hopeless." *New York Times Week in Review*, 6 September: 4.

Mason, Joseph R. 2007. "A National Homeownership Strategy for the New Millennium." *Market Commentary*, 26 February.

Mayer, Christopher, Karen Pence, and Shane M. Sherlund. 2009. "The Rise in Mortgage Defaults." *Journal of Economic Perspectives* 23 (Winter): 27–50.

McKinley, Vern. 1994. "Community Reinvestment Act: Ensuring Credit Adequacy for Enforcing Credit Allocation?" *Regulation* 17 (4): 25–37. www.cato.org/pubs/regulation/ regv17n4/vmck4–94.pdf

Mengle, David. 2007. "Credit Derivatives: An Overview." Paper presented at Financial Markets Conference, Federal Reserve Bank of Atlanta, 15 May. www.frbatlanta.org/news/conferen/07fmc/07FMC_mengle.pdf

Merton, Robert C. 1995. "Financial Innovation and the Management and Regulation of Financial Institutions." *Journal of Banking and Finance* 19: 461–81.

Mian, Atif, and Amir Sufi. 2009. "The Consequences of Mortgage Credit Expansion: Evidence from the 2007 Mortgage Default Crisis." *Quarterly Journal of Economics* 124 (4) (November).

Michaud, Francois-Louis, and Christian Upper. 2008. "What Drives Interbank Rates? Evidence from the LIBOR panel." *BIS Quarterly Review* (March).

Minsky, Hyman P. 1986. *Stabilizing an Unstable Economy*. New Haven, Conn.: Yale University Press.

Moody's. 2003. "The Fundamentals of Asset-Backed Commercial Paper." *Structured Finance Special Report*, 3 February.

Morgenson, Gretchen. 2008. "Debt Watchdogs, Caught Napping." *New York Times*, 7 December.

Muller, Jerry Z. 2009. "Our Epistemological Depression." *The American*, 29 January.

Munnell, Alicia H., Lynn E. Browne, James McEneaney, and Geoffrey M. B. Tootell. 1992. "Mortgage Lending in Boston: Interpreting HMDA Data." Working paper 92–7, Federal Reserve Bank of Boston. www.bos.frb.org/economic/wp/wp1992/wp92_7.pdf

Myers, Stewart C. 1977. "Determinants of Corporate Borrowing." *Journal of Financial Economics* 5 (2): 147–75.

Myers, Stewart C., and Nicholas S. Majluf. 1984. "Corporate Financing and

Investment Decisions When Firms Have Information Investors Do Not Have." *Journal of Financial Economics* 13: 187–221.

Neiman, Richard H. 2009. "Don't Blame the CRA for Causing the Housing Bubble." Letter to the editor, *Wall Street Journal*, 5–6 December.

Norris, Floyd. 2008. "Another Crisis, Another Guarantee." *New York Times*, 25 November.

———. 2009. "It May Be Outrageous, But Wall Street Pay Didn't Cause the Crisis." *New York Times*, 31 July.

Oakley, David. 2010. "Default Insurance Costs Soar for Banks." *New York Times*, 8–9 May.

Office of the Comptroller of the Currency. 2009. "Testimony of Kevin J. Bailey, Deputy Comptroller, Office of the Comptroller of the Currency, before the Subcommittee on Capital Markets, Insurance, and Government Sponsored Enterprises of the Committee on Financial Services of the United States House of Representatives." 21 March.

O'Harrow, Robert, and Brady Dennis. 2008. "Downgrades and Downfall." *Washington Post*, 31 December.

Persons, Charles E. 1930. "Credit Expansion, 1920 to 1929, and Its Lessons." *Quarterly Journal of Economics* 45: 94–130.

Pittman, Mark. 2007. "Betting on a Crash: The Gamble of J. Kyle Bass." *Bloomberg News*, 19 December. www.nzherald.co.nz/business/news/article.cfm?c_id=3&objected; eq10484879

Plender, John. 2009. "Error-Laden Machine." *Financial Times*, 3 March: 8.

Poole, William. 2007. "Understanding the Fed." *Federal Reserve Bank of St. Louis Review* 89 (1): 3–14.

Posner, Richard A. 2009. *A Failure of Capitalism: The Crisis of '08 and the Descent into Depression*. Cambridge, Mass.: Harvard University Press.

———. 2010. *The Crisis of Capitalist Democracy*. Cambridge, Mass: Harvard University Press.

Postrel, Virginia. 2008. "Why Asset Bubbles Are Part of the Human Condition that Regulation Can't Cure." *Atlantic* (December).

Rajan, Raghuram. 2006. "Has Financial Development Made the World Riskier?" *European Financial Management* 12: 313–64.

———. 2008. "Bankers' Pay Is Deeply Flawed." *Financial Times*, 9 January.

Rajan, Uday, Amit Seru, and Vikrant Vig. 2008. "The Failure of Models That Predict Failure: Distance, Incentives and Defaults." University of Chicago Graduate School of Business, Research Paper 08-19.

Rappaport, Alfred. 1990. "The Staying Power of the Public Corporation." *Harvard Business Review* (January–Februrary): 96–104.

Reinhart, Carmen M., and Kenneth S. Rogoff. 2008. *This Time Is Different: A*

Panoramic View of Eight Centuries of Financial Crises. Cambridge, Mass.: Harvard University and National Bureau of Economic Research.

Rieker, Matthias. 2009. "Revamp Would Aid Banks in Building Bigger Reserves." *Wall Street Journal,* 23 June: C3.

———. 2010. "At J. P. Morgan, Eye on Consumer Banking." *Wall Street Journal,* 15 January.

Rodriguez, Robert L. 2007. "Absence of Fear." Speech, CFA Society of Chicago, 28 June.

Rogoff, Bradley, and Michael Anderson. 2008. "DTCC Data Show Corporate CDS Fears Overblown." *Barclays Capital Credit Strategy,* 6 November.

Samuelson, Paul. 1974. "Challenge to Judgment." *Journal of Portfolio Management* 1 (1): 17–19.

Samuelson, Robert J. 2008. *The Great Inflation and Its Aftermath.* New York: Random House.

Samolyk, Katherine. 2004. "The Evolving Role of Commercial Banks in U.S. Credit Markets." *FDIC Banking Review* 16 (2): 31–65.

Scheinkman, Jose A., and Michael Woodford. 1994. "Self-Organized Criticality and Economic Fluctuations." *American Economic Review* 84: 417–21.

Schuler, Kurt. 1992. "The World History of Free Banking: An Overview." In Dowd 1992a.

Schumpeter, Joseph A. 1950. *Capitalism, Socialism, and Democracy.* 3rd ed. New York: Harper and Row.

Schwartz, Anna J. 1981. "Understanding 1929–1933." In *The Great Depression Revisited,* ed. Karl Brunner. Boston: Kluwer-Nijhoff.

Schwartz, William, and Roger Lister. 2009. "Catching Up Is Hard." *DBRS North American FT Weekly* 4, 12: April 8.

Scism, Leslie, and Maurice Tamman. 2010. "Small Banks Say a Cure Hurts: Regulators Want Extra Capital Set Aside After Mortgage-Bond Purchases." *Wall Street Journal,* 7 January.

Securities and Exchange Commission. 1984. ". . . Good People, Important Problems, and Workable Laws." Washington, D.C.: SEC.

———. 2009. "Report and Recommendations Pursuant to Section 133 of the Emergency Economic Stabilization Act of 2008: Study on Mark-to-Market Accounting." Washington, D.C.: Office of the Chief Accountant, Division of Corporate Finance, SEC.

Selgin, George A. 1988. *The Theory of Free Banking.* Totowa, N.J.: Rowman and Littlefield.

———. 1994. "Are Banking Crises Free-Market Phenomena?" *Critical Review* 8 (4): 591–608.

Sen, Amartya. 1979. "Equality of What?" Tanner Lecture on Human Values, Stanford University, 22 May.

Sender, Henny. 2010. "Fed Makes 'a Killing' on AIG Contracts." *Financial Times*, 20 January.

Shiller, Robert J. 2000. *Irrational Exuberance*. Princeton, N.J.: Princeton University Press.

Skreta, Vasiliki, and Laura Veldkamp. 2008. "Ratings Shopping and Asset Complexity: A Theory of Ratings Inflation." New York University Stern School of Business, Working Paper EC-08–28. October.

Slater, John. 2009. "How Much Risk Is the Treasury Really Assuming from Financial Institutions?" *Seeking Alpha*, 8 April. http://mergers.com/tough times/2009/how-much-risk-is-the-treasury-really-assuming-from-the-financial-institutions/

Smick, David M. 2010. "A Never-Ending Economic Crisis?" *Commentary*, January.

Smith, Elliot Blair. 2008a. "Bringing Down Wall Street as Ratings Let Loose Subprime Scourge." *Bloomberg.com*, 24 September.

———. 2008b. " 'Race to Bottom' at Moody's, S&P Secured Subprime's Boom, Bust." *Bloomberg.com*, 25 September.

Smith, Vernon L. 1962. "An Experimental Study of Competitive Market Behavior." *Journal of Political Economy* 70: 111–37.

———. 2007. "We Have Met the Enemy, and He Is Us." AEI-Brookings Joint Center Policy Matters, Paper 07–32, 20 December.

Smith, Vernon L., Gerry L. Suchanek, and Arlington W. Williams. 1988. "Bubbles, Crashes, and Endogenous Expectations in Experimental Spot Asset Markets." *Econometrica* 56: 1119–51.

Solow, Robert. 2008. "Reflections on the Survey." In David Colander, *The Making of an Economist, Redux*. Princeton, N.J.: Princeton University Press.

Soros, George. 2008. "The False Belief at the Heart of the Financial Turmoil." *Financial Times*, 3 April.

Stanton, Richard, and Nancy E. Wallace. 2008. "ABX.HE Indexed Credit Default Swaps and the Valuation of Subprime MBS." University of California, Fisher Center for Real Estate and Urban Economics, working paper 312. 15 February.

Stem, Gary H., and Ron J. Feldman. 2004. *Too Big to Fail: The Hazards of Bank Bailouts*. Washington, D.C.: Brookings Institution Press.

Stiglitz, Joseph E. 2003. *The Roaring Nineties*. New York: Norton.

Stiglitz, Joseph E., and Linda Bilmes. 2008. *The Three Trillion Dollar War: The True Costs of the Iraq Conflict*. New York: Norton.

Story, Louise, and Gretchen Morgenson. 2010. "A Rift at the Fed over the Bailout of AIG." *New York Times*, 23 January.

Summers, Lawrence. 1998. "Treasury Deputy Secretary Lawrence H. Summers Testimony before the Senate Committee on Agriculture, Nutrition, and

Forestry on the CFTC Concept Release." http://www.ustreas.gov/press/releases/rr2616.htm.

Surowiecki, James. 2009. "What Would Buffett Do?" *New Yorker*, 24 March.

Taleb, Nassim. 2005. *Fooled by Randomness*. 2nd ed. New York: Random House.

———. 2007. *The Black Swan: The Impact of the Highly Improbable*. New York: Random House.

Taylor, John B. 2007. "Housing and Monetary Policy." Presented at conference, Woods Hole, Wyoming, 30 August–1 September, 2007. In *Housing, Housing Finance, and Monetary Policy: A Symposium*. Kansas City: Federal Reserve Bank of Kansas City.

———. 2008a. "The Costs and Benefits of Deviating from the Systematic Component of Monetary Policy." Keynote address, Federal Reserve Bank of San Francisco conference on "Monetary Policy and Asset Markets," 22 February.

———. 2008b. "Monetary Policy and the State of the Economy." Testimony before Committee on Financial Services, U.S. House of Representatives, 26 February.

———. 2008c. "The State of the Economy and Principles for Fiscal Stimulus." Testimony before the Committee on the Budget, U.S. Senate, 19 November.

———. 2008d. "Toward a New Framework for Exceptional Access." Presentation at Policy Workshop on "The Future Role of Central Banking Policy: Urgent and Precedent-Setting Next Steps," Stanford University, 22 July 2008.

———. 2008e. "The Way Back to Stability and Growth in the Global Economy." Institute for Monetary and Economic Studies Discussion Paper 2008-E-14.

———. 2009a. *Getting off Track: How Government Actions and Interventions Caused, Prolonged, and Worsened the Financial Crisis*. Stanford, Calif.: Hoover Institution Press.

———. 2009b. "Globalization and Monetary Policy: Missions Impossible." In *The International Dimensions of Monetary Policy*, ed. Jordi Galí and Mark Gertler. Chicago: University of Chicago Press.

———. 2010. "The Fed and the Crisis: A Reply to Ben Bernanke." *Wall Street Journal*, 11 January: A19.

Taylor, John B., and John C. Williams. 2009. "A Black Swan in the Money Market." *American Economic Journal: Macroeconomics* 1: 58–83.

Temkin, Kenneth, George Galster, Roberto Quercia, and Sheila O'Leary. 1999. "A Study of the GSEs Single-Family Underwriting Guidelines." Executive summary, Urban Institute, Washington, D.C., 9 April. www.urban.org/url.cfm?ID = 1000205&renderforprint = 1

Tett, Gillian. 2009a. *Fool's Gold: How the Bold Dream of a Small Tribe at J.P.*

Morgan Was Corrupted by Wall Street Greed and Unleashed a Catastrophe. New York: Free Press.

———. 2009b. "Genesis of the Debt Disaster." *Financial Times*, 1 May.

———. 2009c. "Lost Through Creative Destruction." *Financial Times*, 10 March.

Timiraos, Nick. 2010. "Fannie, Freddie Losses May Hit U.S." *Wall Street Journal*, 22 January.

UBS. 2008. "Shareholder Report on UBS's Write-Downs." 18 April.

Vlasenko, Polina. 2008. "Home Ownership in the United States." Great Barrington, Mass.: American Institute for Economic Research.

Wall Street Journal. 2008. "Bear's Market." Editorial, 4 April.

Wallison, Peter J. 2009. "Deregulation and the Financial Crisis: Another Urban Myth." *Financial Services Outlook*, October.

Weiss, Gary. 2009. "The Man Who Made Too Much." *Portfolio.com* (February). www.portfolio.com/executives/features/2009/01/07/John-Paulson-Profits-in-Downturn.

Wesbury, Brian S. 2010. *It's Not as Bad as You Think: Why Capitalism Trumps Fear and the Economy Will Thrive.* Hoboken, N.J.: John Wiley.

Wigmore, Barrie A. 1985. *The Crash and Its Aftermath: A History of Securities Markets in the United States, 1929–1933.* Westport, Conn.: Greenwood.

Williams, Arlington W., Vernon L. Smith, John O. Ledyard, and Steven Gjerstad. 2000. "Concurrent Trading in Two Experimental Markets with Demand Interdependence." *Economic Theory* 16: 511–28.

Wolters Kluwer. 2009. "Comptroller Dugan Views Accounting for Loan Loss Reserves as Procyclical." *Law & Business CCH Financial Crisis News Center*, 5 March.

Zandi, Mark. 2009. *Financial Shock: A 360-Degree Look at the Subprime Mortgage Implosion, and How to Avoid the Next Financial Crisis.* Upper Saddle River, N.J.: FT Press.

———. 2010. "The Causes and Current State of the Financial Crisis." Testimony before Financial Crisis Inquiry Commission. 13 January.

Contributors

Daron Acemoglu, Charles P. Kindleberger Professor of Applied Economics at Massachusetts Institute of Technology, received his M.Sc. and Ph.D. in economics from the London School of Economics. He is the author, inter alia, of *Introduction to Modern Economic Growth.*

Viral V. Acharya, Professor of Finance at New York University Stern School of Business and the London Business School, received his Ph.D. in finance from the Stern School of Business, New York University. He is Academic Director of the Coller Institute of Private Equity, a Research Affiliate of the Center for Economic Policy Research (CEPR), and a Research Associate in Corporate Finance at the National Bureau of Economic Research (NBER). He is coeditor, with Matthew Richardson, of *Restoring Financial Stability: How to Repair a Failed System.*

Amar Bhidé, Thomas Schmidheiny Professor of Fletcher School of Law and Diplomacy, Tufts University, received his M.BA and D.BA from Harvard Business School. Coeditor of *Capitalism and Society* and author of *The Venturesome Economy, The Origin and Evolution of New Businesses, Of Politics and Economic Reality,* and *A Call for Judgment: Sensible Finance for a Dynamic Economy,* he has also taught at Harvard's Kennedy School of Government.

David Colander, Christian A. Johnson Distinguished Professor of Economics at Middlebury College since 1982, received his Ph.D. in economics from Columbia University. In 2001 and 2002, he was Kelly Professor of Distinguished Teaching at Princeton University. He has authored, coauthored, or edited more than 40 books and 100 articles on a wide range of topics, including *The Making of an Economist,*

Redux. He has been president of the Eastern Economic Association and the History of Economic Thought Society and has been on the editorial boards of numerous journals, including *Journal of Economic Perspectives* and *Journal of Economic Education.*

Jeffrey Friedman, a visiting scholar in the Department of Government, University of Texas at Austin, received his M.A. in history from the University of California, Berkeley, and his Ph.D. in political science from Yale University. He is the Max Weber Fellow of the Institute for the Advancement of the Social Sciences, Boston University, editor of *The Rational-Choice Controversy: Economic Models of Politics Reconsidered*, coauthor with Wladimir Kraus of *Engineering the Perfect Storm: How Reasonable Regulations Caused the Financial Crisis* (forthcoming), and editor of *Critical Review: A Journal of Politics and Society*, in which the essays in this volume were originally published.

Michael Goldberg, Roland H. O'Neal Professor of Economics at the Whittemore School of Business and Economics, University of New Hampshire, received his Ph.D. in economics from New York University. He is coauthor with Roman Frydman of *Imperfect Knowledge Economics: Exchange Rates and Risk*. He has written extensively in international finance and macroeconomics, and his columns on asset-price fluctuations and policy reform have been published by leading newspapers in more than 50 countries.

Steven Gjerstad, a visiting professor at Chapman University, received his Ph.D. in economics from the University of Minnesota.

Armin Haas, a senior researcher at the Potsdam Institute for Climate Impact Research (PIK), received his Ph.D. in economics from the University of Karlsruhe in 1999. He is speaker of the research activity Integrated Risk Governance of the European Climate Forum (ECF). He also heads the research group Bayesian Risk Management, a joint initiative of PIK, the University of Potsdam, the German Institute for Economic Research (DIW Berlin), and the ECF.

Juliusz Jabłecki, an economist at the Bureau of Monetary Policy Strategy at the National Bank of Poland, received his M.A. from the Faculty of Economic Sciences at Warsaw University, where he is currently pursuing his Ph.D.

Katarina Juselius holds a chair in time-series econometrics and empirical economics at the Department of Economics, University of Copenhagen. She has published widely in econometric and empirical economics journals and been on the editorial board of *Journal of Forecasting*, *Journal of Business and Economics Statistics*, and *Journal of Economic Methodology*.

Alan Kirman received his Ph.D. in economics from Princeton University. He is a professor emeritus at the Université Paul Cézanne and at the École des Hautes Études en Sciences Sociales and a member of the Institut Universitaire de France. He has held posts at Johns Hopkins University, the Free University of Brussels, the University of Warwick, and the European University Institute in Florence. He is a fellow of the Econometric Society and was awarded the Humboldt Prize in Germany. He has published more than 150 articles in international economics journals, is author and editor of some 12 books, including *Complex Economics: Individuals and Collective Rationality*.

Thomas Lux received a Ph.D. in economics from the University of Würzburg in 1990. He was a professor of economics at the University of Bonn before moving to Christian-Albrechts University at Kiel in 2000. Since 2008, he has also been affiliated with the Kiel Institute for the World Economy. He is associate editor of *Quantitative Finance* and *Journal of Economic Behavior and Organization* and a founding editor of the *Journal of Economic Interaction and Coordination*. He has published widely in such journals as *Economic Journal*, *Journal of Economic Dynamics and Control*, *Journal of Money, Credit and Banking*, *Journal of Mathematical Economics*, *Macroeconomic Dynamics*, and *Journal of Business and Economic Statistics*, as well as in *Nature, Physica A*, and *Reports on Progress in Physics*.

Mateusz Machaj, teaches in the Department of Economics and Management, Wrocław University of Enviromental and Life Science. He received his M.A. from the University of Wrocław and his Ph.D. from Wrocław University of Economics.

Richard A. Posner, who received his LL.B. from Harvard Law School, clerked for Justice William J. Brennan before teaching at Stanford Law School and the University of Chicago Law School, where he remains a Senior Lecturer. Among his many books are *Economic Analysis of the Law* (seventh edition Aspen, 2007), *How Judges Think*, *A Failure of Capitalism: The Crisis of '08 and the Descent into Depression*, and *The Crisis of Capitalist Democracy*. He serves on the U.S. Court of Appeals for the Seventh Circuit.

Matthew Richardson, Charles Simon Professor of Applied Financial Economics at New York University Stern School of Business and Sidney Homer Director of the Salomon Center for Research in Financial Institutions and Markets, received his M.S. in economics at the University of California at Los Angeles, and his Ph.D. in finance from the Graduate School of Business at Stanford University. He is coeditor, with Viral V. Acharya, of *Restoring Financial Stability: How to Repair a Failed System*.

Brigitte Sloth, a professor at the Department of Business and Economics at the University of Southern Denmark, Odense, received her Ph.D. in economics from the University of Copenhagen. She has contributed research papers to several economic theory journals, mainly in the fields of decision and game theory.

Vernon L. Smith, George L. Argyros Chair in Finance and Economics, Economic Science Institute, Chapman University, is a 2002 Nobel laureate in economics. He received his Ph.D. in economics from Harvard and is the author, inter alia, of *Papers in Experimental Economics* and *Bargaining and Market Behavior*.

Joseph E. Stiglitz, University Professor and Professor of Economics at Columbia University, is a 2001 Nobel laureate in economics. He received his Ph.D. in economics from MIT, and is the author, inter alia, of *The Roaring Nineties*.

John B. Taylor, Mary and Robert Raymond Professor of Economics at Stanford University and Bowen H. and Janice Arthur McCoy Senior Fellow at the Hoover Institution, received his Ph.D. in economics from Stanford University. He formerly served as the director of the Stanford Institute for Economic Policy Research, where he is now a senior fellow, and was founding director of Stanford's Introductory Economics Center. He is the author of *Getting Off Track: How Government Actions and Interventions Caused, Prolonged, and Worsened the Financial Crisis.*

Peter J. Wallison, Arthur F. Burns Fellow in Financial Policy Studies at the American Enterprise Institute, received his LL.B. from Harvard Law School and has served as Special Assistant to Governor Nelson A. Rockefeller, General Counsel to the U.S. Treasury Department, Counsel to President Ronald Reagan, Member of the Advisory Committee on Improvements to Financial Reporting, U.S. Securities and Exchange Commission, and Member, Financial Crisis Inquiry Commission, 2009. He is the author, inter alia, of *Competitive Equity: A Better Way to Organize Mutual Funds*; *Privatizing Fannie Mae, Freddie Mac, and the Federal Home Loan Banks*; *The GAAP Gap: Corporate Disclosure in the Internet Age*; and *Optional Federal Chartering and Regulation of Insurance Companies.*

Lawrence J. White, Arthur E. Imperatore Professor of Economics at New York University Stern School of Business, received his M.Sc. from the London School of Economics and his Ph.D. from Harvard University. He is the author, inter alia, of *Reforming Regulation: Processes and Problems* and *The S&L Debacle: Public Policy Lessons for Bank and Thrift Regulation,* and is the editor of *Deregulation of the Banking and Securities Industries*; *Technology and the Regulation of Financial Markets*; *Bank Management and Regulation*; *Structural Change in Banking*; and *The Antitrust Revolution: Economics, Competition, and Policy.* He is also the editor of the *Review of Industrial Organization,* was North American Editor of the *Journal of Industrial Economics,* and served on the Senior Staff of the President's Council of Economic Advisers.

Index

Acknowledgments

The essays in this book (with the exception of the Afterword) originated in a special issue on the causes of the financial crisis published in 2009 in *Critical Review: A Journal of Politics and Society* (vol. 21, nos. 2–3), published by Routledge for the Critical Review Foundation. I thank the authors who appeared in that volume (and this one) for having contributed such a spectacular group of papers, unlike any other that has yet been published, and Routledge for permission to reprint them. I thank Erin Graham at the University of Pennsylvania Press for seeing the potential in that volume for a book that would fill a void in scholarly and public understanding of the financial crisis. Her encouragement and the cooperation of the Press have been invaluable, as has been advice in the revision of my Introduction from Less Antman, Howard Baetjer, Amar Bhidé, William M. Isaac, Ira Kay, Hal Scott, and Bill Woolsey. My warm thanks to Juliusz Jabłecki and Wladimir Kraus, without whose tutorials on the nature of bank capital and the mysteries of capital regulations I would have been quite lost. The usual disclaimer applies with extra force to what I managed to take away from these lessons. Viral V. Acharya, David Bernstein, Peter J. Boettke, Richard A. Brown, Tyler Cowen, Samuel DeCanio, Shterna Friedman, Steven Gjerstad, Juliusz Jabłecki, Garett Jones, Jeffrey Rogers Hummel, William M. Isaac, Arnold Kling, Marisa Maleck, Matthias Rieker, Bill Woolsey, and Todd Zywicki made much-appreciated comments on previous drafts and, in other cases, provided welcome research leads. I am grateful as well to Victoria Ivashina and David Scharfstein for releasing to me the data on which Figure 1.1 is based.

Richard A. Posner deserves special thanks for agreeing to write an Afterword to the book, despite the fact that in my Introduction and elsewhere I have disagreed with his analysis of the causes of the crisis.

Most of all, however, I thank Shterna Friedman, *Critical Review*'s managing editor, for overseeing the production of the special issue of the journal, preparing the revised manuscript for publication in book form, and for being my intellectual soulmate, sounding board, and critic, which meant, in this case, becoming as familiar with the intricacies of the financial crisis as I had to become.

John B. Taylor thanks John Cogan, Angelo Melino, John Murray, George Shultz, and participants in the Global Markets Working Group for helpful comments and suggestions on Chapter 5. It is adapted, with the kind permission of the Bank of Canada, from "The Financial Crisis and the Policy Responses: An Empirical Analysis of What Went Wrong," which appeared in *A Festschrift in Honour of David Dodge's Contributions to Canadian Public Policy* (Ottawa: Bank of Canada, 2009), and was originally a lecture delivered at a conference honoring Dodge sponsored by the Bank of Canada in November, 2008.

Peter J. Wallison thanks Edward Pinto for research in preparing the original version of Chapter 6.

Daron Acemoglu thanks David Autor, Ricardo Caballero, Simon Johnson, Bengt Holmstrom, and James Poterba for comments on Chapter 11, a different version of which appeared as Policy Insight No. 28, published online by the Centre for Economic Policy Research.

David Colander, Michael Goldberg, Armin Haas, Katarina Juselius, Alan Kirman, Thomas Lux, and Brigitte Sloth produced (with Hans Föllmer) a different version of Chapter 12 as the report of the working group on the "Modeling of Financial Markets" at the 98th Dahlem Workshop, "Is There a Mathematics of Social Entities?" in 2008. Colander served as moderator of this group and Lux served as rapporteur. The workshop was organized by Carlo Jaeger and Rupert Klein. An expanded version of the initial conference report can be found at http://ideas.repec.org/p/kie/kieliw/1489.html. The web version of the report, entitled "The Financial Crisis and the Systemic Failure of Academic Economics," has generated much discussion, and the authors are thankful to the many people who sent in suggestions, especially Peter N. Sørensen, who kindly pointed out several imprecise formulations in an earlier version.